PRAISE FOR *UNDAUNTED*

"While reading *Undaunted*, I felt as though I was back on that horrible day. Ed Zier does a remarkable job of personalizing an event that shook the world. A small group of innocent, decent, hardworking Americans now have their story told along with so many others."

—**Thomas Von Essen,** Former FDNY Commissioner for the City of New York and Author of *Strong of Heart*

"*Undaunted* weaves powerful imagery of the unforgettable terrorist attack and tragedy of 9/11 with heartfelt human emotions that involve fear, capitulation, unbelievable resolve, resilience. It is a gripping account and must-read. After reading about what the Baseline family and thousands of others went through, I feel even more proud of the work we did at TSA to better protect the skies above our great nation post 9/11. I highly recommend *Undaunted*."

—**Carol DiBattiste,** Former TSA Deputy Administrator, Former Air Force Under Secretary, and Air Force Retired Officer

"Ed Zier shares this very uplifting personal story about how one of the deadliest moments in American history forever impacted him and his surviving colleagues' lives. He lost four of them in those moments. They almost lost their company too—Baseline. Ed sensitively recounts the absolute pain of those losses. He also describes his co-workers' dogged resolve to ensure Baseline's survival, which became the company's tribute to its fallen colleagues. *Undaunted*—a must read."

—**Phillip B. J. Reid,** Retired Senior FBI Executive and a lead agent in the December 1988, Pan Am 103 Bombing Investigation in Lockerbie, Scotland, and Author of *Three Sisters Ponds*

"Over twenty years ago, my leadership team and I at Wells Fargo decided to make Baseline a foundational toolset for our national buy-side portfolio managers. It was clear from the positive energy of its employees and their zeal to focus on our needs that Baseline was a very special company. *Undaunted* is an insider's story, but really it is an intimate homage to the special culture that Baseline's founder created—leading not only to tremendous business success but fortifying its employees to withstand the destruction of the south tower during 9/11, and do whatever it took to deliver to its customers without a hitch . . . remarkable!"

—**Tim Leach**, Director, Goldman Sachs BDC, Inc (GSDB), Chairman of the Board, Goldman Sachs Middle Market Lending Corp. II, Inc., and former Chief Investment Officer of Wells Fargo Wealth Management

"In *Undaunted*, Ed Zier brings to life a compelling story of corporate survival after the tragic events of 9/11. Ed captures the real-life feelings and emotions of his colleagues at Baseline who emerged as victors because of their dedication, determination, and grit. After reading this book, I am even more resolved to celebrate the victories of success than to sulk in the aftermath when big-business strategy turns corporate survival into collateral damage."

—**Dr. Troy Hall,** Global Speaker, Radio Host, Talent Retention Strategist and bestselling author of *Cohesion Culture: Proven Principles to Retain Your Top Talent* and *FANNY RULES: A Mother's Leadership Lessons That Never Grow Old*

Undaunted: Leadership Amid Growth and Adversity

by Ed Zier

ISBN 978-1-64663-538-2

Published by

◀ köehlerbooks™

3705 Shore Drive
Virginia Beach, VA 23455
800-435-4811
www.koehlerbooks.com

UNDAUNTED

LEADERSHIP AMID
GROWTH AND ADVERSITY

The true story of an entrepreneurial success
and its fortitude through the tragedy of 9/11

ED ZIER

VIRGINIA BEACH
CAPE CHARLES

DEDICATED TO

ROBERT G. PATTERSON

(1937–2017)

TABLE OF CONTENTS

INTRODUCTION

THERE ARE MOMENTS in our lives that are so profound, so world-changing, that we easily remember exactly where we were at that very instant. The phrase "vivid recall" is often used to describe our ability to re-live such moments. As a kindergartner on November 22, 1963, I vividly recall being sent home due to the news of President Kennedy being assassinated. In a manner that would be unheard of today, this five-year-old was sent walking from school, on his own, through a mini-forest of birch trees to the home of his grandparents, who were unaware of his approach. I can still picture with great clarity my grandmother in her front yard as I rounded the corner of her small colonial home. Similarly, my father shared his recollection of December 7, 1941. With visual precision, he could share details of the interruption of a radio broadcast of a football game early that afternoon between the New York Giants and the old Brooklyn Dodgers. He easily recalled sitting with his father and brother around the kitchen table as the announcer informed them of the Japanese attack on Pearl Harbor. The events of September 11, 2001 occupy a similar place in infamy. Most of us know exactly where we were when we heard the news.

Early in the morning on that infamous day, on the 77th and 78th floors of Two World Trade Center (aka the "South Tower"), employees of a small firm readied themselves for another productive day. This financial software firm, called Baseline, was an entrepreneurial success. In less than ten years it had obtained a new lease on life with a customer-inspired vision and sufficient funding to enable execution. Phase Two of the founder's journey would see revenues grow from $1 million annually in 1991 to over $47 million in 2001. Baseline's employees relished the company's growth, corporate culture, and the various amenities bestowed upon them. The firm was well respected in the financial technology industry, and it was poised for continued strong growth. However, that would suddenly, and horribly, be challenged in the coming hours.

As a member of the management team at Baseline, I would argue that the phrase "vivid recall" actually falls short of what my colleagues and I still feel today—nearly twenty years removed from the day known simply as "9/11." So many images are indeed burned into our memories, but in our case the recollections are not just mental pictures. They include raw and tangible emotions, as well as actual physical experiences. Many of my colleagues escaped the burning edifice in a 77-floor descent just moments before the building collapsed. Overall, nearly 3,000 innocent people lost their lives that day in four separate acts of evil. Within our firm, four wonderful people were murdered in the terrorist attack. They were more than co-workers. They were individuals with families that loved them. They were people who had accomplished much, and they were looking forward to additional adventures ahead. They were also our good friends.

While infamous events easily grab our attention, it can also be said that we similarly recall the best times in our lives. Prior to 9/11, Baseline's rise as an entrepreneurial success was magical. It didn't just sport a handsome growth rate and a healthy profit margin, it was also highly regarded as having a tremendous corporate culture and a fine-tuned product vision. The product was a best-in-class resource for the asset management community. It was an interactive software application that enabled institutional investors to better evaluate the equities they maintained in their portfolios. Baseline's revenue growth was made possible by near-flawless execution that included a recruitment regimen, a well-oiled product development process, healthy respect between departments, and a commitment to outstanding customer service. Working at Baseline was a lot of fun, and fond memories are plentiful. Therein lies the incredible dichotomy of Baseline Financial Services. Throughout our corporate journey, my colleagues and I experienced both ends of that recall spectrum.

The brains behind the Baseline enterprise were those of its founder, Rob Patterson. For someone who held degrees from both Harvard and Stanford, Rob was incredibly unpretentious. Brilliant, but kind, steadfast, but fair, he was a classic entrepreneur who possessed a creative, inventive flair. He cared little about personal wealth and less about his own public persona. While Rob was patient, his pursuit of perfection was undeterred. After spending several years in the proverbial start-up wilderness, he finally discovered the right recipe for success. He honed his vision and created a special corporate culture. His constant involvement helped him navigate several corporate transitions while providing stewardship through 9/11 and its aftermath.

Of course, Baseline's 9/11 story is not unique for Ground Zero. There were many other firms that were horribly impacted. However, in the maelstrom within Two World Trade Center that day, the line between life and death arguably sat between the 77th and 78th floors. Our two floors. The demarcation between life and death that day was crystal clear. It sat with us. This is our story.

The written narrative had its origins on a cold, snowy Saturday in February of 2005. I sat inside the warm confines of my home and reflected back on the horrible day. I wrote down everything I could recall about my own 9/11 experience. I didn't want my daughters, or my descendants, to ever forget 9/11 or the heroics of my coworkers. I soon discovered that other colleagues of mine had done the same.

As I compiled a few of those notes, I sensed a connection between our 9/11 experiences and our company's cultural development. I quickly realized there was a larger story to be told. Unfortunately, paying bills and saving for upcoming college tuitions kept me busy. I simply didn't have time to devote to such a project. Fast forward to 2017, and I found myself retired and living in Florida. The 20th Anniversary of 9/11 was approaching, and I felt the gravity of that day was slowly slipping from our collective American conscience. Suddenly, I had the overwhelming sensation to share the story. Ironically, my multi-year efforts were aided by the occurrence of another human tragedy—the COVID-19 pandemic. Because of the widespread global lockdown in 2020, I was able to reach more of the people who add substance to the story of Baseline.

While *Undaunted* will provide a general overview of 9/11, it is not meant to serve as a history of the day and all its horrors. Rather, it is a recap of one company's journey before, during, and after the horrific events. My objective is to show how elements of the human spirit can create a successful business, overcome near-death certainty, transcend disaster, and bind a team together at a time of great crisis. I will share details about the courageous acts of colleagues, the dedication of first responders, and the emotional toll of losing friends. I will also recount the risk-taking of an entrepreneur, the funding of his business, the refining of his vision, the management of accelerated growth, and the grit and determination of an entire firm to rebuild. Simply put, this story is about leadership and overcoming adversity.

Undaunted intertwines the story of 9/11 with the story of Baseline, and describes how its corporate culture helped influence its employees' reaction to the events of the day and the months that followed. Leaders existed at all levels of the organization. Together, they refused to allow enormous adversity to stand in their way. Lastly, I will share an astounding tale of irony. While 9/11 served as an overwhelming obstacle, Baseline would soon encounter another challenge.

Naturally, the trials and tribulations of a business pale in comparison to the loss of innocent life and the devastation at Ground Zero. However, from my perspective, both 9/11 and Baseline are indelibly linked. Forever.

CHAPTER 1

THE INFAMOUS MORNING

THE ENGINEER SKILLFULLY navigated the switches as we pulled into Hoboken's large train station. My body swayed left or right depending upon the switch we encountered. It was 8:45 AM on Tuesday, September 11, 2001. I had made this journey more than three thousand times since beginning my career. The trip often felt robotic. This particular commute was no different. It was yet another uneventful arrival into the bustling terminal that sat on the western side of the Hudson River. Once in Hoboken, commuters from all over New Jersey would then scramble to find a seat aboard trains, buses, and ferries that would escort them into New York City. While my arrival into Hoboken was uneventful, the remainder of this day would prove to be quite different.

Sunrise had bestowed a beautiful day upon the New York area. A few wispy clouds dotted the sky, and a slight breeze added to what was a near perfect late summer day. The sunshine and 70-degree weather likely tempted even the most devout workers to play hookey. However, it was post Labor Day which unofficially meant that it was time to get back to work. The crowded streets and busy offices of the Wall Street area confirmed that notion. In retrospect, anyone who wished to harm the multitudes would also have known that New Yorkers were back at their desks.

As my train from the New Jersey hamlet of Radburn came to a stop, I found myself fixated on my business trip to San Francisco scheduled for later in the day. Prior to my afternoon flight, I planned to visit my office at the World Trade Center (aka The Twin Towers) in lower Manhattan. Eight forty-five AM was not my normal arrival time into Hoboken: because I was going to have a late night on the west coast and didn't have any scheduled meetings in New York that morning, I had purposely delayed my morning departure from home.

I grabbed my briefcase and garment bag and proceeded to the PATH[a] trains, where I walked through the labyrinth of century-old, musty smelling hallways and then down the stairs and through the turnstiles. I planted myself in a seat aboard the PATH train that would take me under the Hudson River and directly beneath the Twin Towers. In contrast to Hoboken, there was a very modern and clean PATH station right under the World Trade Center (WTC). The ride from Hoboken would last about twelve minutes. However, something wasn't right that morning. An announcement proclaimed a troubling situation.

> *Your attention please. Your attention please. Service to and from the World Trade Center is suspended due to a police action at the World Trade Center. You are advised to take PATH to 33rd Street in midtown Manhattan, and then take city subways downtown.*

Such were the words emanating from the loudspeaker aboard my WTC-bound PATH train at about 8:50 AM. I had often heard similar words reflecting a disruption in service, but the "police action" comment was a new twist. My initial internal reaction was *What kind of police action would shut down the rail service?* I quickly thought about the disruptive gangs I had occasionally witnessed over the years in the New York subways. Petty theft, loud rants, and even physical altercations were my recollections. But the unfolding truth that morning was beyond my comprehension.

Those redirecting words squawking through the loudspeakers

---

a   PATH. The Port Authority Trans Hudson transit system. The PATH is a subway-like rail system that carries passengers between Hoboken and New York City under the Hudson River.

caught me off guard and were frustrating to this commuter set in his standard ways. It was a rare occasion to have PATH trains shut down completely. Delays, on the other hand, were commonplace, but not a wholesale suspension of a train line that required me to make alternate plans. Since I was carrying travel bags, I wasn't in much of a mood for undoing what I had just accomplished—getting a seat (which was another rare occurrence). But another plan was necessary. As I saw it, I had two choices. The first would be to head across the platform and grab the 33rd Street PATH train to midtown Manhattan, as instructed. The other option was to head back upstairs and catch the NY Waterway Ferry, which would get me fairly close to the World Trade Center. I opted for the ferry. It was a tad more expensive but much faster and far more relaxing than traveling underground all the way up to 33rd Street, and then fighting for a strap to hold onto aboard a NYC Subway heading downtown. That circuitous route via underground trains could take forty-five minutes or more to make the complete trip to lower Manhattan. *No thanks!* I uttered to myself. Besides, it was a beautiful day to sit atop the ferry as it would make its way across the river with a grand view of the entire New York skyline.

Between 1973 and 2001, the twin towers of the World Trade Center dominated New York's skyline reaching over 1,350 feet high, and eclipsing the Empire State Building as New York City's tallest structure. In fact, when it was built, the WTC was the tallest man-made structure in the world. The World Trade Center was, and still is, owned by the Port Authority of New York and New Jersey. It is a governmental agency that oversees the flow of individuals, goods, and services throughout the area of New York harbor that borders the two states. It oversees all three New York area airports, the local seaports, the PATH train system, the Port Authority Bus Terminal in Manhattan, as well as the tunnels and bridges between the two states.

Because I made the decision to jump on the ferry, I grabbed my heavy bags and went back through the turnstiles and up the stairs. I still recall begrudging the darn $1.50 I was forfeiting by abandoning the PATH trains. At the top of the stairs I spotted a long line forming for ferry tickets. Apparently, my reassessment of options wasn't lost on a hundred other commuters who had already lined up to buy their tickets. Luckily, I had a ticket in my wallet from a previous purchase and was

The original Twin Towers of the WTC were the tallest buildings in the world when they opened in 1973. They were home to 50,000 workers, and housed the headquarters of Baseline from September 1999 until September 11, 2001.
[Photo Credit: iStock.com/ihsanyildizli]

thrilled I didn't have to get on that line. But above ground, something else was different. The people in the ticket line were spellbound as they all looked to the east. From my particular vantage point I couldn't yet see what they were staring at. I was still in a good frame of mind as I kept my eye on all the unfortunate folks lined up to purchase a ticket.

When I came to an opening between the train and ferry terminals, I immediately saw what they were so keenly watching: the North Tower of the World Trade Center (One World Trade) was on fire. The flames were near the top of the building. The smoke plume was not overly intense—yet. It looked like a scene from the movie *Towering Inferno*, and I thought that maybe a small plane had hit the building. Maybe a Cessna. The Empire State Building had once suffered such a fate back in 1945. But then again, that was during a bout of thick fog.[1] The sky on the morning of September 11th, however, was breathtakingly beautiful.

I thought, *How could a plane hit the building with such good visibility?*

It didn't appear plausible. However, no one in the immediate vicinity knew any differently. A quick survey of witnesses revealed the sense that a small plane had indeed hit the building. As the crow flies, the train terminal in Hoboken is almost two miles from the World Trade Center site. It's conceivable that a larger plane would appear small. I wondered if there had been any deaths. *Oh no!* was my gut reaction. However, I concluded with certainty that the fire would be put out quickly. I remained optimistic, especially because I was headed for the "other" tower of the World Trade Center (the South Tower). I worked there as the chief operating officer of a financial software and information company called Baseline. My office sat on the 77th floor of Two World Trade Center facing south. The view of the harbor and Lady Liberty from that perch was stunning.

Since my destination was the other building, I quickly designed a plan by which I could arrive in Manhattan via ferry and navigate around the developing chaos. My office building was clearly safe and intact. But, as I got closer and closer to the pier, a disrupting thought occurred to me:

> *It's going to be a mess in there. The New York police and fire departments never skimp on emergency responsiveness. Blocks and blocks will be cordoned off. I'm only going to the office to do light work and catch up on emails. I don't really have to go in there! I'm not going to chance it. I'll jump back on a northbound NJ Transit train and go home, and then take a car service to the airport this afternoon.*

Before I left Hoboken, I decided to call my office to see what my colleagues knew. Certainly, my team would know something. I was very curious, but not yet terrified. I entered the old stately Hoboken Terminal building. Built in 1907 by the Lackawanna Railroad, it is a wonderful tribute to pre-war (WWI) architecture. Its magnificence had just recently been restored in a 1997–99 renovation project. Embellished with Victorian grace and moldings, and adorned in copper that had turned green through the years, the terminal was something to behold. Along its internal southern wall was a bank of pay telephones. Remember those? They were technologically sound that day, given that cellular networks had been severely curtailed by extremely heavy demands on their bandwidth. After an unsuccessful attempt with my cell phone, I grabbed one of the available pay phones.

I first placed calls to Bob Levine and Nick Webb. Bob was our chief financial officer, who had his office on the 78th floor, while Nick was my head of sales, who sat on 77. Both their offices were in or near the southeast corner of their respective floors. Baseline occupied the entire 77th floor and a portion of 78. Neither man answered his phone. I left messages—but not frantic ones, as I knew their building was safe. I wanted to establish what had happened and how chaotic it actually was on the streets below. Their horrendous day had just begun, and unbeknownst to me, their harrowing experiences were well underway.

I then proceeded to call my wife. I thought, *Maybe she might know something, but I should certainly tell her I'm coming home instead of trying to enter the city.* But, again, unbeknownst to me was the fact that a second plane was hitting my building as I was dialing her. She answered the home phone and literally started screaming the moment she heard my voice.

"Oh my God! Where are you?"

She had just watched the second plane, on live television, tilt its wings and fly directly into my building from the 78th to the 84th floor—on the same south side of the structure as my office. From her viewpoint, it must have hit my office on 77. She hadn't focused on my purposely delayed commute that morning, and so believed that I was sitting at my desk.

"Come home immediately! It's a terrorist attack, Eddie! We're under attack."

I still had confidence that what I had seen was simply an accident and that she mistook which building was mine. I began to dissuade her of her information.

"Oh, no hon. That's not my building! I'm in the other one, and it looks like a Cessna—"

She cut me off harshly. "No! Two jumbo jets have just flown into the World Trade Center! They were probably hijacked. This is horrible. Get home now!"

My mind went instantly to mush. My wife's emotions and vehemence were clear. She repeated the cold hard facts. I dropped the phone and just left it dangling by its cord. Anger, fear, and sadness gripped me all at once.

I instantly thought, *How are all my teammates?* I hadn't spoken with Bob or Nick. *Are they okay?*

We had approximately 170 of our 215 employees in that office space. *How many were in there?* I considered the worst-case scenario. *Did they all make it out? What about all the other people that worked in both buildings? Oh my God!*

I began to curse loudly inside the terminal—like I had never done before. People waiting quietly for trains looked at me, mystified. The harsh reality of the day greeted people in waves. I was trying to come to grips with a wave of information that was probably the worst news ever to reach my ears. Those patient travelers around me were still in the dark.

I darted outside to the trainyard. It was only about 9:05 AM. The big board showed that my next train wouldn't depart until 10:30 AM. But I couldn't wait that long. Good thing I didn't, as all trains were soon cancelled. The entire country, in a state of shock and looking to prevent more tragedy, soon shut everything down. Within the hour, planes would additionally crash into the Pentagon and into a Pennsylvania farm field. Even then, we didn't know what might be next. Other airplanes? Bridges? Tunnels? Trains? The mind easily raced ahead.

What had just unfolded across the river was completely unconscionable. Two commercial airliners had separately been hijacked from Logan Airport in Boston. Both flew south in simultaneous villainy with the sole intent of flying both planes into the Twin Towers of the World Trade Center. They succeeded on an unprecedented scale. The first of the two planes hit One World Trade Center (the North Tower) at 8:46 AM. Hijacked and flown by Al Qaeda terrorists, it struck the building on its north side at approximately 465 mph, impacting floors 93 through 99.[2] It was American Airlines Flight 11, a Boeing 767 which was intended to be a cross-country flight to LAX in Los Angeles. Its insurgent pilot was Mohamed Atta.[3] On board with Atta were 4 other hijackers, 11 crew members, and 76 passengers.[4] At the same time, United Airlines Flight 175, also an LAX-bound aircraft from Boston, altered its flight plans in the same manner after it had been hijacked. It was piloted by an Al Qaeda operative by the name of Marwan al-Shehhi.[5] On board the Boeing 767 with al-Shehhi were 4 hijackers, 9 crew members, and 51 passengers.[6] It traveled south, and as it reached New York air space, it circled lower Manhattan and struck Two World Trade Center (the South Tower—and my building) from the south at

9:03 A.M. It was travelling at approximately 590 mph as it impacted my building on a slant, hitting floors 78-84.[7]

On the morning of September 11, as I frantically tried to leave Hoboken, the intricate details of this sinister operation were still unknown to me. As I raced outside and into the streets, catching a simple taxi was my goal. The scene outside Hoboken Terminal was reminiscent of an old Godzilla movie. People were running frantically in every direction. Fire trucks and police cars, sirens blaring, were zooming by. I saw a taxi and hailed it. However, before I could get in, someone grabbed me from behind. It was a police officer who said, "Get off the street and get in the taxi line!"

How I had completely ignored, nor even seen, the 200 people already queued up for a cab ride was a shocker to me. A subliminal desire to survive and get home apparently had me block those very visible and dutiful commuters from my conscious mind. Anyway, now dejected and facing reality, I slumped back towards the curb. Incredibly, as I crossed the median the same cabbie pulled up alongside me and said, "Get in!" He knew I had intended a longer ride and probably concluded a larger fare and tip would be forthcoming. Possessed with feelings of getting home, I didn't reflect too long on the line behind me. As I opened the door, however, I was knocked completely into the taxi by the same throng that wanted the next available cab ride. Shortly, there were seven men in this cab—a picture right out of the Guinness Book of World Records, often involving VW Beetles! None of us were sitting in any recognizable position. I was lying prone across the drive train on the floor of the backseat. The cab driver yelled, "I'm not going anywhere!" Some guy on top of me in that scrum suggested we'd each pay him $30, and the cabbie shifted the car into drive and said, "Where are we going?" Good ole capitalism. Fortunately, we were all from Bergen County and so northward we went.

As we drove along the New Jersey Turnpike, the two buildings were very visible and very much ablaze. They were occupying the horizon, the radio reports, and our minds. Tensions were high in that cab. Someone insisted that we immediately send missiles with nuclear warheads to obliterate Iraq, Libya, and other then-current non-conformant states. Given my rage and despair at the moment, I told him (in a very direct and non-tactful way) that wouldn't be prudent, and that we shouldn't jump to conclusions. I thought he and I were going to come to blows. Others in the cab intervened and we all realized we were on the same team. When they learned that I was from Two World Trade Center and was worried for my 170 teammates, everyone became a giant support group.

While the taxi raced northward, I couldn't help but think that everyone I knew and loved at Baseline was gone. With my then state-of-the-art flip phone, I called Larry Hirschhorn in San Francisco. He was the manager of our west coast office. It was he I was going to see that evening to prep for client meetings on September 12th. I told Larry I would not be coming given the gravity of the situation. His response was a politically correct version of the phrase "no shit, Sherlock!" He informed me that my decision was likely moot given that the FAA had just shut down all air space over the United States.

As the day wore on it became increasingly clear that cell phone connections within the New York area were nearly impossible given all the demands on the carriers' respective bandwidths. Cellphone networks were still in their relative infancy in 2001. However, long distance calls were somehow more easily achievable. I was able to reach Larry, and he could likewise connect with many people I needed to contact. Over the course of the next 36 hours, Larry became the hub of our communication wheel. If anyone heard of someone else being safe, it was relayed, one way or another, to Larry. He kept a spreadsheet. Thanks to a back-up data center in Philadelphia, our email system was alive and well. That helped immensely.

While Larry handled the tracking of my colleagues, incredible stories were unfolding at the World Trade Center. Stories of tragedy. Stories of valor. I would hear many stories in the months following 9/11. There must be countless stories of bravery, many still untold. The nearly 3,000 souls that lost their lives did not go down without a fight. God bless them and their families.

During that taxi ride, however, I had no idea how many people were dead, alive, or injured. The prognosis looked very bleak. As I stared blankly out the window, I started thinking about Rob Patterson, my boss and the CEO/founder of Baseline. He was in Key West with his wife, Mickey, purchasing a vacation home. I wondered if he knew what was happening. I couldn't fathom his probable shock, fear, and sadness. The business he had built was in peril, as were all the employees he considered his family. No matter what he was doing, he'd be helpless. As I later learned, Rob and Mickey had closed on a bungalow in Key West the day before. They were at the Key West airport waiting to board the first leg of two flights to return to New Jersey when the horrors unfolded. Clearly, they were not going anywhere either.

As I headed home in the cab, my building in flames behind me, our world would be forever changed. Suddenly, the normal challenges of a business day became irrelevant.

CHAPTER 2

A DOUBLE TWIST OF FATE

MY COMMUTE INTO lower Manhattan that morning had been inordinately delayed due to my California travel plans. Ironically, I wasn't even supposed to be traveling that day: a trip planned for the previous week had been pushed to September 11. Since I normally would have arrived at my office just after 8:00 AM, my wife had understandably presumed I was in my office on the 77th floor, given my usual commuting schedule.

The primary purpose of my trip to the west coast that day had been to see the Chief Investment Officer of Wells Fargo Private Client Services. Headquartered in San Francisco, Wells was our largest client. Larry Hirschhorn was coordinating. I was originally scheduled to fly out west on September 4th. Our annual review with Wells had been scheduled to take place the first week of September, but the client had called Larry and asked if we could move it one week. We obliged. When your top client asks you to move a meeting, you just say "yes sir!" That meant I needed to change my flight to September 11.

San Francisco was a frequent destination of mine. Our west coast office was gaining ground in terms of both customers and headcount. My goal was to be there quarterly, and always as needed. I generally chose one of three early morning United Airlines flights out of Newark that arrived in San Francisco in the late morning—in time for a client lunch, or prepping for afternoon customer meetings with the team. When I tried to re-book the original United flight for a 9/11 departure, the travel agent at Valerie Wilson Travel informed me that with such minimal notice I'd be looking at $2,000 for a round-trip coach ticket instead of my usual fare of $500. All three United flights on 9/11 were now ridiculously expensive. It wasn't my personal money, but there was principle involved. I told her, "I can't do that. Please find me something else!" Those highly desirable United flights were no longer an option. One of those three flights that day was United 93, which would find itself etched in history as one of its passengers said, "Let's Roll."[8]

On the morning of 9/11, United's Flight 93 departed Newark for San Francisco at 8:00 AM with forty passengers and crew aboard. It would be one of four equally improbable hijackings that day by Al Qaeda terrorists under the direction and support of their leader, Osama bin Laden. Flight 93's likely target was suspected to have been either the White House or the US Capitol Building. This notion was confirmed during the interrogation of Khalid Sheikh Mohammed, who was alleged to have been the mastermind of the entire plot.[9]

Because of the heroic efforts of its passengers, Flight 93 did not complete its perilous mission. Instead, after what appears to have been a valiant effort by the passengers and crew to regain control of the aircraft, Flight 93 crashed violently in a remote region of western Pennsylvania near the little town of Shanksville in Somerset County. It was 10:03 AM. Due to the widely broadcasted events of that morning, and with the help of cell phones, the passengers of Flight 93 became instantly aware of their likely fate. Since it was known that previously hijacked planes had sacrificed everyone aboard to achieve an evil mission, the passengers and crew of this flight knew they had no choice. They had to fight; otherwise they would be pawns in the ugly ambitions of Al Qaeda. The safety of the Capitol Building may have been secured by the fact that United 93 was forty-one minutes late for take-off due to heavy tarmac traffic that morning in Newark.[10] This tardiness clearly enabled the news of the World Trade Center attacks to reach Flight 93's passengers in time for them to make a stand.

The names of all the brave souls on board United's Flight 93 who physically assisted in the attempted midair coup may never be fully known. What is clear are the last words of one passenger who, among others, took matters into his own hands. The last words heard during a cell phone conversation from the lips of Todd Beamer were, "Let's Roll." It is believed that Todd and other passengers decided on a plan of attack: to storm the cockpit and retake the airplane. Given the outcome, it appears that the passengers successfully disrupted the Al Qaeda plan for Flight 93. These brave individuals likely saved countless lives on the ground in Washington by paying the ultimate sacrifice with their own lives. There were many heroes aboard that flight. Vice President Dick Cheney, upon hearing of the crash while in the White House bunker said, "I think an act of heroism just took place on that plane."[11] Cheney and other aides in Washington had been quickly escorted by Secret Service agents into the bunker underneath the North Lawn, a facility known as PEOC (the Presidential Emergency Operation Center). It dates back to World War II and is designed to protect the president from an incoming attack.[12] While Cheney was theoretically secure, President George W. Bush was visiting an elementary school in Tampa, Florida. He would eventually make it back safely to Washington, DC by evening.

When Flight 93 crashed into that rural field, it had only been 15 minutes from impacting Washington, DC.[13] The passengers on Flight 93 undoubtedly saved countless lives on the ground and also prevented damage or destruction of an iconic American landmark.

The final dastardly act involving commercial airliners that day came when American Airlines Flight 77 struck the Pentagon. Flight 77 departed Washington Dulles International Airport for LAX in Los Angeles on time at 8:10 AM. Thirty minutes after take-off it went radio silent and made a very quick adjustment in its flight plan to head back to Washington. At 9:37 AM, it crashed into what is known as "Wedge I" of the western side of the Pentagon at 530 mph.[14]

The quick action taken by the FAA to shut down the American airspace likely saved many lives. While not proven, there is evidence to suggest more attacks were planned that day. One story involves another LAX-bound aircraft. That morning, United Airlines Flight 23 was taxiing at JFK airport in preparation for its own journey to Los Angeles. While the plane was sitting in the number 7 spot for takeoff, Ben Sliney of the FAA ordered a Ground Stop for all US-based aircraft, given what had already transpired. No more attacks from the air would thus be possible that day. However, as the ground stoppage was called, a suspicious thing occurred aboard United 23.[15]

According to author Mitchell Zuckoff, in his book *Rise and Fall—The Story of 9/11*:

> Aviation and law enforcement officials told reporters that when the captain announced over the intercom that they were returning to the gate, four young men sitting in first class who appeared to be Middle Eastern became agitated, stood, and consulted one another. They reportedly refused attendants' orders to return to their seats. When the plane reached the gate, the men apparently bolted before they could be questioned.[16]

Among the four actual hijackings, no crew or passengers survived that day. September 11, 2001 was a day that rivaled Pearl Harbor in infamy but exceeded it in the number of fatalities. On December 7, 1941, over 2,400 people, military and civilian, perished at the hands of Japanese naval forces.[17] At the World Trade Center, the Pentagon, and in a Pennsylvania field, over 2,900 lost their lives.[18] While mostly an American event, the day's tragedy was felt globally. The victims of 9/11 represented citizens of 90 nations.[19]

Incredibly, the individuals who flew those missiles of hate had successfully learned to fly right here in the very country they aimed to attack. The two men who piloted the planes that flew into the World Trade Center had gained their certifications in a piecemeal fashion. Atta and al-Shehhi received their commercial licenses at Huffman Aviation in Venice, Florida. It was owned and operated by Rudi Dekkers. According to Dekkers in his book, *Guilty by Association,* their arrival at his school was after they had received some training at Jones Aviation in Sarasota. Apparently, their unknown dissatisfaction with the Jones program prompted them to approach Dekkers. In a most unusual fashion, the two walked into Huffman Aviation on July 1, 2000 inquiring about flight lessons. According to Dekkers, walk-ins were a very uncommon application process. However, it was the slow season and, by Dekkers' own account, the newfound training fees looked appealing. By mid-December, both terrorists had passed their Instrument Flight Rules (IFR) exams and gained their commercial licenses. They then departed for Miami to learn to fly bigger jets.[20]

In what appears not to be coincidental, the pilot of United Flight

93 that crashed in the hills of Pennsylvania also trained in Venice, Florida. Ziad Jarrah, a 26-year-old Lebanese man, had gained his education in close proximity to Atta and al-Shehhi. He had taken courses at the nearby Florida Flight Training School.[21] Perhaps the group split up to avoid scrutiny.

In prepping for my own travel on 9/11, I had finally heard back from my travel agent. She had good news/bad news. "I've got you a flight, but it's out of JFK. How about American Airlines to Oakland at 4:00 PM on 9/11?" My immediate reaction was "JFK? Ugh!" JFK Airport sits on the far eastern edge of Queens County—a Borough of New York City. Because I lived in northern New Jersey, flights out of Newark were far more preferable than JFK, and even better than LaGuardia, especially at rush hour. Going from northern New Jersey to JFK could sometimes feel like going all the way down to Trenton. On the other hand, it was only $400. "OK, book it!" I had successfully located a more cost effective round trip, although it would likely cost me time and convenience.

As some solace, my thinking was that if I was flying at 4:00 PM, I could break up the trip to the airport by working a half-day in the WTC office and continuing on to JFK via taxi at around 2:00 PM. Because I knew it was going to be a long day, including a late night of dinner and final team prep for our Wells Fargo meeting, there was no need to get into the office early. I made the decision the night before to pack in the morning. Thus, the plans were hatched for my delayed commute.

Soon after 9/11, I curiously checked to see if I had been booked on Flight 93 the previous week (the original plan for a September 4 departure). I had not. My ticket specified one of the other two flights. And for this particular rescheduled trip, I'm glad my frugal manner prevented me from playing a form of Russian Roulette with the three United flights. If the price had stayed at $500 (instead of $2,000) when I attempted my rebooking, Flight 93 might have been my aircraft. Instead, for $400 I was off to the other city by the bay—Oakland.

Normally, I would catch the 7:09 AM express train each morning out of the Radburn train station in the Borough of Fair Lawn, NJ. It zipped me into Hoboken in twenty-three minutes. On 9/11, due to my travel plans and morning packing, I attempted to take the 8:02 AM semi-express but missed it because traffic at that time was heavier than I was used to. My expected ten-minute drive to the train station became fifteen minutes. I ended up on the 8:08 AM local train and thus did not arrive in Hoboken until 8:45 AM. On that morning, a set of coincidences kept pushing me later and later, and onto a local train—a blessing in disguise, as it turned out.

When American Airlines Flight 11 hit the North Tower (1 WTC) at 8:46 AM, I was still a river away from the unfolding tragedy.

To this day, I often reflect on the word "luck." A neighbor of mine recites the same phrase every time he sees me: "There he is, the luckiest man alive!" Undoubtedly, he's referring to the two seemingly proverbial bullets I dodged that day. First, as a result of my travel plans, I wasn't in my office at the moment of the first plane's impact. And second, given the late postponement of my Wells Fargo meeting and the high price of rebooking, I wasn't on one of my typical early morning United flights to San Francisco.

While the neighbor's phrase might seem on the surface to have merit, I dislike it. I can't disavow that I was alive and relatively well at the conclusion of that horrific day, but why would I be lucky and so many others—nearly 3,000—be deemed wholly unlucky? The notion of being lucky seems unfair to all those who lost their lives that day— even unfair to the families of all who perished.

CHAPTER 3

THE ASCENT OF BASELINE

ON THE MORNING of September 11, Baseline had become a well-oiled machine and was in the midst of several consecutive years of over 20 percent revenue growth. It employed 170 people at its World Trade Center headquarters. It also sported a corporate culture that was widely respected in its industry. In 2001, Baseline's revenues would exceed $47 million, its overall employees numbered 215, and it had two remote offices—a software development team in Philadelphia and a sales office in San Francisco. At the time, it was a wholly owned subsidiary of the Thomson Corporation, which later became known as Thomson Reuters after Thomson acquired Reuters in 2007. Like many successful small companies, Baseline saw several iterations of product evolution and ownership transition over the years.

Baseline's relative success was based on a laser-focused vision. Its purpose was simple: to provide institutional portfolio managers with a user-friendly, software product that made researching stocks easier. Its value proposition was to make fairly complex financial statistics and ratios easy to understand, by making them visually revealing through the utilization of graphs and tables. Baseline employed the KISS[b] principle to the fullest—not through a lack of sophistication,

---

b   KISS. Keep it Simple, Stupid.

but in its user interface and presentation of data. It wanted its users to make better-informed buy/hold/sell decisions when it came to managing stocks. Baseline integrated many different sources of information about stocks without the user needing to worry about multiple user IDs or subscriptions to third-party data providers. And, because it was designed for one particular workflow, that of the institutional stock picker, sales pitches were well streamlined.

The brains behind this enterprise from the beginning were those of Robert "Rob" Patterson. Harvard-educated, with an MBA from Stanford, Rob was a creative genius. His ambition was to create a stock picker's workflow tool for the desktop. The product by the same name, Baseline, was an interactive application available on the PC that visualized and demystified a fairly quantitative subject, which previously was the realm of hardcore statisticians. Rob wanted his product to provide insight, as opposed to doing what most purveyors of equity analysis systems were doing at the time—which was simply making data, lots of it, available for general screening and reporting. Users of most other systems were often hardcore computer aficionados. Rob wanted to widen the playing field to appeal to the mainstream of institutional investors by developing an easy-to-use tool.

The fundamental challenge for most systems of the day was that they offered powerful computing capabilities to search vast arrays of financial data. Unfortunately, an average user could quickly become lost in most of those systems—in myriad of databases, mnemonics[c], time periods, and even wrong answers. A user would first need to have a good grasp of the difficult user interfaces of such systems, and either have memorized the mnemonics or have a detailed user guide at their disposal. He or she would also need to fully understand the problem they were looking to solve, and ensure the answers were fully compatible with the questions being asked. To Rob Patterson, the currently available process to do that was too complicated.

For the most part, information providers at that time like FactSet, Interactive Data, and CompuServe chose not to focus on any one specific area of capital markets. In fact, early on they were disinclined to take a bet on any one group of users for fear of missing an opportunity.

---

c   Mnemonics. The abbreviation codes for data elements within the more complex data access systems. For example, the code for "3 year revenue growth rate" might be abbreviated as REVGR3.

Therefore, systems were generally designed to accommodate all user types within the capital markets industry—including analysts, portfolio managers, investment bankers, wealth managers, securities traders, and investor relations professionals. The information providers had to offer extremely deep databases with an enormous range of computing capabilities to satisfy the various needs of all those user groups.

In the 1980s and 1990s it was common to see vendors sporting "financial data solutions" to anyone who would listen. . . one size fits all. And that's where Baseline took its best shot. Rob Patterson took aim with a rifle approach at one specific segment of the capital markets world, namely, portfolio managers. Based on personal experience with institutional investors at Standard & Poor's, Rob made several assumptions of what these users were looking to achieve. By narrowing down the likely requirements of a specific user group, Rob's solution made screening and reporting of key data points much, much easier. Further, Baseline did not require users to input mnemonics, user codes, or database login credentials.

As an executive with Standard & Poor's (S&P) in the 1970s, Rob helped advance the famed *S&P Tearsheet*—a one-page overview of a public company loaded with key data relating to that firm's common stock. It was well laid-out, with data and a price chart. However, it was in book form, and was updated annually in what was known as the *Standard & Poor's 500 Guide*. The Guide with its 500 tearsheets was expensive to produce, and therefore expensive to buy. Its subscriber base was mostly institutional investors and high-end retail stockbrokers—all with deep pockets. The *S&P Tearsheet* was specifically honed. It displayed various aspects of a public company's data (e.g., stock price chart, earnings growth, and revenue figures, to name a few). The term "tearsheet" originated from the fact that stockbrokers in the pre-electronic world would "tear" pages from the Guide in order to give to a client. The tearsheet's general concept would later serve as a foundation for Baseline.

As his career progressed, Rob became a group vice president at S&P and was responsible for most of their print products.[22] He also served as their chief financial officer.[23] [24] His CPA credentials from an earlier career proved helpful to understand the financial statements of not only S&P, but also the 500 stocks his firm followed. While working at S&P, Rob acquired an Apple II computer and played with

Apple Inc. (NasdaqGS:AAPL)

Technology Hardware, Storage and Peripherals   Employees: 147,000   Incorporated: 1977 in California, US

S&P Issuer Credit Rating FC LT:
AA+

One Apple Park Way
Cupertino, California 95014
United States
Phone: 408-996-1010
www.apple.com

Apple Inc. designs, manufactures, and markets smartphones, personal computers, tablets, wearables, and accessories worldwide. It also sells various related services. The company offers iPhone, a line of smartphones; Mac, a line of personal computers; iPad, a line of multi-purpose tablets; and wearables, home, and accessories comprising AirPods, Apple TV, Apple Watch, Beats products, HomePod, iPod touch, and other Apple-branded and third-party accessories. It also provides AppleCare support services; cloud services store services; and operates various platforms, including the App Store, that allow customers to discover and download applications and digital content, such as books, music, video, games, and podcasts. In addition, the company offers...

Key Statistics

	12 Months Sep-28-2019A	12 Months Sep-26-2020A	12 Months Dec-26-2020A	12 Months Sep-30-2021E	12 Months Sep-30-2022E
Total Revenue	260,174.00	274,515.00	294,135.00	333,546.07	348,393.44
Growth Over Prior Year	(2.0%)	5.5%	9.9%	21.5%	4.5%
Gross Profit Margin %	37.8%	38.2%	38.8%	39.7%	39.5%
EBITDA Margin %	29.4%	28.2%	29.0%	29.9%	29.5%
EBIT Margin %	24.6%	24.1%	25.2%	26.6%	26.2%
Net Income Margin %	21.2%	20.9%	21.7%	22.5%	21.9%
Diluted EPS Excl. Extra Items	2.97	3.28	3.69	4.46	4.70
Diluted EPS Excl. Extra Items...	(0.3%)	10.4%	17.1%	35.9%	5.4%

EPS Estimate (USD)

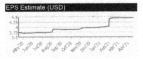

Estimates

Recommendatio	Buy(2.00)
Target Price	152.50000000
LT Growth %	14.69%

Revenue by Business and Geographic Segments (USD, mm)

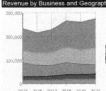

* Segments with negative values, such as corporate eliminations, are excluded from the total and percentage calculations and do not appear on the charts

Forward Multiples

	FY2021	FY2022
P/E	30.16x	28.61x
TEV/REV	6.52x	6.24x
TEV/EBITDA	21.82x	21.15x
PEG	2.05x	1.95x
P/BV	43.53x	43.95x

Competitors - NTM TEV/Fwd EBITDA

Walmart Inc. (NYSE...   Amazon.com, Inc. (N...
Volkswagen AG (XTRA...   Toyota Motor Corpor...
Daimler AG (XTRA:DA...

Top Holders

Holder	Common Stock Equivalent Held	% of Total Shares Outstanding	Market Value (USD in mm)
The Vanguard Group, Inc.	1,255,155,794	7.48	164,726.6
BlackRock, Inc.	1,056,461,286	6.29	138,650.0
Berkshire Hathaway Inc.	887,135,554	5.28	116,427.7
State Street Global Advisors, Inc.	638,166,552	3.80	83,753.0
FMR LLC	341,189,418	2.03	44,777.7

Holders as of Wednesday, April 14, 2021

Capitalization

Share Price as of Apr-13-2021	134.43
Shares Out.	16,788.10
Market Capitalization	**2,256,823.75**
- Cash & Short Term Investments	76,826.00
+ Total Debt	112,043.00
+ Pref. Equity	-
+ Total Minority Interest	-
= Total Enterprise Value (TEV)	2,173,295.75
Impl.Shares Out	-
Impl.Market Cap	-
Book Value of Common Equity	66,224.00
+ Pref. Equity	-
+ Total Minority Interest	-

Market Data

Last (Delayed)	133.26	Market Cap (mm)	2,256,823.7
Open	134.94	Shares Out. (mm)	16,788.1
Previous Close	134.43	Float %	99.9%
Change on Day	(1.17)	Shares Sold...	107.0
Change % on Day	(0.9%)	Dividend Yield %	0.6%
Day High/Low	135.00/132.57	Diluted EPS	3.69
52 wk High/Low	145.09/66.36	P/Diluted EPS...	36.46x
Volume (mm)	42.72	Avg 3M Dly Vlm...	108.53
Beta 5Y	1.22		

Share Price & Volume (USD)

Key Executives and Board Members

Levinson, Arthur D.	Independent Non-Executive Chairman of the Board
Cook, Timothy D.	CEO & Director
Maestri, Luca	CFO & Senior VP
Williams, Jeffrey E.	Chief Operating Officer
Kondo, Chris	Senior Director of Corporate Accounting

Events

Date/Time	Event
Apr-28-2021	Estimated Earnings Release Date (S&P Global Derived)
Apr-28-2021	Earnings Call
Jun-07-2021	Conference

Date Created: Apr-14-2021

S&P popularized the concept of the "tearsheet." The current day offering from S&P is electronic, provides far more detail, and is known as the Quick Report. It is available within S&P's Capital IQ platform. See page 248 for Disclaimer. [Provided with permission by Standard & Poor's Global Market Intelligence LLC.]

various ideas for advanced products to make the *S&P Tearsheet* an electronic product for institutional investors. To pursue his dream, when it appeared that S&P was not interested in a technological direction, Rob resigned and founded Baseline in 1981.

Early on, Baseline was simply a product that tracked the S&P 500 stocks, and Rob initially set out to automate the concept of a one-pager. His plan was to generate a monthly booklet containing 500 pages (one for each stock in the S&P 500) that institutions could purchase. But he went beyond just visual facts. He added the notion of valuation to his stock charts. He often cited the work of Graham & Dodd[d] as being inspirational. The word *Baseline* was, in fact, derived from the actual charted earnings of a company. It was that "baseline" earnings of a stock upon which price movements would be compared graphically. The early product was a hard-copy deliverable that graphically depicted a sophisticated analysis. Generally speaking, it involved the relation of a stock's price movement to the growth of its earnings and the impact of dividends. Based on the quantitative results of this model, Rob could easily break the 500 stocks into ten deciles, each containing 50 stocks. The deciles ranged from 1 (very expensive stocks) to 10 (cheap stocks). Over time, and after Rob expanded his valuation model to thousands of stocks, it bore out that the 7th decile was the most attractive from an upside investment perspective. The bottom three deciles were ostensibly too far gone to ever recover.

To help scale production, Rob seized upon the early capabilities offered by Apple Computer. The Apple II was not an end-user tool for clients. Rather, it was a manufacturing resource for Rob. A program was written in Apple Basic to overlay price and earnings on a chart, add some descriptive data on the page, and queue them for printing. A COBOL program ran the backend to crunch the numbers and create the deciles. All of this was designed in the quietude of Rob's basement at his home in Madison, NJ.

Sales were slow at first, but within a few years Rob Patterson was able to attract serious clients including the Bank of New York. Sam Wang, then Director of Research and Chief Equity Strategist

---

d   Graham & Dodd. Columbia Business School professors, Benjamin Graham and David Dodd, pioneered the work of "value investing" in the 1920s. Simply put, they came up with a method for valuing stocks, primarily looking for deeply depressed prices based on several fundamental factors.

for the bank, became one of Rob's first clients. According to Sam, "what Rob was trying to do was quite different than what Wall Street brought to institutional investors." Sam was very open minded to new approaches. "I saw a lot of people in those days. People came to me with lots of ideas and thoughts. Wall Street is never absent of novel ideas. What Rob brought to show me wasn't anything I had seen before." What Sam was referring to was Rob's skill of simplifying a complex subject concerning quantitative data into visually revealing insight. "I remember the first time he came to see me. He was very enthusiastic about the whole concept. I enjoyed his association over the years, and was always very impressed with him." Sam left the bank in 1993 and founded Runnymede Capital. His new firm was a client of the constantly evolving Baseline service for over twenty years.[25]

Rob added to his sales arsenal in 1986 by bringing in a longtime friend. Ogden White was both a prep school and Harvard classmate of Rob's. He had just finished a 27-year career at the Bank of Boston. In his last position with the bank, Ogden ran the bank's "Edge Act"[e] offices including New York, Chicago, Miami and Los Angeles. Given his background and experience, "Oggie" had an exceptional understanding of the portfolio management process surrounding stock picking, including the concept of valuation models. Ogden's contacts and activity also proved helpful in generating business and gaining market feedback.

During the 1980s, Baseline's pricing was set at $2,000 per month for a one-year commitment. However, there seemed to be a glass ceiling of about forty clients. New clients would be gained, but some would not buy into the model with its monthly updates and would cancel. Either the valuation model with its deciles didn't ring true with some customers, or the monthly updates of a *Tearsheet*-like product weren't useful. It was a frustrating cycle, and revenues plateaued at about a million dollars annually. That wasn't bad for a fledgling idea in a very specific niche market. But therein laid the challenge—it was indeed a very niche strategy.

Rob was an outstanding listener, which would help him redefine his strategy. He wasn't proud. Others could supply ideas if it helped

e   The Edge Act. A 1919 amendment to the United States Federal Reserve Act of 1913, which allows national banks to engage in international banking through subsidiaries chartered by the Board of Governors of the Federal Reserve System.

him further his Baseline product. Over time, feedback from clients was plentiful. Part of Rob's brilliance was his ability to leave his ego at the door, at least when it came to product ideas from clients.

The feedback coming in was useful, but overwhelming. Rob's own ideas were voluminous. To freely implement what customers were suggesting while adding his own flair would require far more effort than Rob's initial implementation. He knew that whatever he might release as a new product had to be interactive, and the client had to gain control of the output. The ideas for enhancement were plentiful:

- Go beyond the S&P 500, and beyond the valuation model. Customers were beginning to look at the Russell 2000 universe or even smaller equities.

- Provide additional valuation ratios. Early on, many clients were Value Investors looking for highly discounted, but reliable companies.

- Offer access to growth statistics, and show a full range of fundamentals for each stock. The 1990s brought with it a new eye towards equities—the arrival of the Growth Investor.

- Provide an ability to search through the data using filters.

- Make the price charts interactive, and allow users to play "what if" analyses on the charts. For example, "what if" the PE[f] ratio for this firm rises to its industry's average—what will the price be?

- Provide a capability for customers to upload their own portfolios and lists of followed stocks.

- Let customers build *ad hoc* reports across their portfolios, around their filtered results, or on an entire industry. And let them weight any fundamental characteristic based on holdings.

---

f   PE. Price to Earnings ratio. The ratio of a stock's price to its earnings; namely, stock price per share divided by the trailing four quarters of earnings per share.

And on and on. The ideas were mounting. But how to put these ideas into production, and in the Rob Patterson format, i.e., visually revealing and also easy to use? One thing Rob knew for sure—he had to hand over the reins to his customers. In other words, make them the users of an interactive experience and not simply readers of a static booklet.

As the original business reached a modest level of success in the 1980s, Rob knew that his five-person enterprise headquartered on 3rd Avenue in midtown Manhattan needed to expand to realize his product's full potential. He embarked on a mission to seek several million dollars in funding. But first, he needed a well-structured strategic plan. That required him to articulate what exactly his product would do, and also identify its specific target audience. Other questions occupied his mind in those days: What would be the value proposition? What would he charge? What would be the size of the target market, how much market penetration could be garnered, and what distribution strategy would be employed? Rob had all the answers at the ready. Despite his intellect and high-end education, Rob was a very informal guy. He was so "chill" that he preferred to simply know his agenda and not write it down for others to debate or even judge his plans. That's why a friend became the best vehicle for quickly providing him the funding he was seeking.

When Rob was at S&P, he befriended a senior executive of another firm that occupied the same building at 345 Hudson Street in Manhattan. Rob often rode the elevator with Dick Koontz, who at the time was executive vice president of Bowne & Co. They became friendly acquaintances. Both were responsible for their respective finance departments. Rob was aware that Bowne, squarely focused on financial printing as a business, was looking to diversify in the late 1980s. Much of what was printed by Bowne, namely 10-Ks, 10-Qs, and prospectuses, was read by the very same audience that Rob's Baseline reports targeted: institutional investors. Initially, Rob was seeking $3 million in funding. By the time 1989 rolled around, Dick Koontz was CEO of Bowne, and Rob didn't hesitate to make that phone call. After a few private meetings with Dick, Rob successfully gained an audience with Bowne's board of directors to seek an investment in Baseline.

In recounting his meeting with Bowne's board, Rob told me of a very spirited exchange he had with them on the day he made his pitch for the money. This meeting in 1989 was two years before I even met Rob Patterson. While I no longer have access to his actual presentation to the Bowne board, it was humorous to say the least. According to Rob, he made plenty of tongue-in-cheek parodies about entrepreneurs seeking money from venture capitalists—whom Rob referred to as "vulture capitalists." The chief financial officer of Bowne was not particularly amused with the casual approach of Rob's presentation. In particular, the CFO directly questioned Rob about an asset on his balance sheet.

"What is this refrigerator? I didn't see a refrigerator when we toured your tiny office!"

Rob matter-of-factly replied, "Oh, that's my home refrigerator."

According to Rob, a pall fell over the room. The CFO was getting redder in the face with each passing second, while others in the room found it quite comical. "You are telling us that you have mixed your personal business with that of the firm! How can we possibly accept that or even trust you?" the CFO exclaimed with a lot of emotion.

Rob simply countered with a statement that seemed most reasonable. "Look, put yourself in my shoes. I funded this entire business on my own dime. Profits are next to zero, client turnover is high, and I pay my salespeople on a commission-only basis. It's a struggle, but I know what I need to do! If you notice the income statement you will see "Officer Salary." Do you see the figure? I pay myself $25,000 per year. It's been that way from Day One. How would that compare to your salary? And if you could ever imagine having my salary, do you think you could afford the new refrigerator that your wife was screaming that you needed?" A quiet came over the room. A minute seemed like ten.

The CFO then asked. "So, you're asking us for a lot of money. What if your big plans and dreams fall on their face, and this is a complete failure? Then what?"

Without hesitation, Rob said, "Then I guess you lose three million dollars."

Rob had his commitment the next day, except that Dick Koontz told him they believed he would require $4 million. In exchange, they asked Rob for a whopping 90 percent of equity. For a long time, I remained baffled as to Rob's acceptance of that request. Whenever I posed it to him over the years, he always said to me, "Ed, I just wanted to have fun, create a magnificent product, and be a company where I offered meaningful employment to a good group of people. And, I really wasn't sure if we would really be successful. I had only gotten to $1 million in revenue over 8 years, and it was often a slugfest just to tread water."

In defense of Rob, research shows that raising capital in 1989 was quite difficult for entrepreneurs. According to an article in the *New York Times*, "Venture Capital Loses its Vigor," dated October 8, 1989, start-ups were challenged to find money that year. Despite the growth of venture capital (VC) funds in the previous decade from $3 billion to $31 billion, money was tight in the late 1980s. For starters, the failure rate of the IPO surge of 1983 made venture firms far more selective with their money. More importantly, the stock market crash of 1987 added greatly to the difficulty for VCs to cash out when they wanted. The net result was a more short-term return focus by the VC funds brought on by the demands of the institutions investing in those funds.[26] Rob's pitch to Bowne, on the other hand, clearly involved a longer-term investment horizon. To be fair to would-be investors at the time, Rob had only achieved a $1 million run rate without much recent growth. He was seeking an investment worth 3 times revenue on a flat revenue curve. In retrospect, Bowne was a godsend.

While equity stake is one variable in the mix regarding an investment, there are other issues that can protect a burgeoning enterprise. Certain items, such as the make-up of the board of directors and right-of-first-refusal when it comes to the sale of the business, can help stave off unforeseen consequences. In my opinion, Rob was so overjoyed at receiving this funding, and thus having more road on which to operate, that he may not have covered all the bases. It is only a supposition on my part, but it appears that Rob did not negotiate additional governance provisions. Although the Bowne investment did indeed propel Rob to greater glory, the lack of protections would come into play in later years.

Given the newfound capital in Baseline's bank account, the specifics of Rob's plan etched solidly in his head could proceed. He would immediately expand the software development effort, and make his product interactive by creating a PC DOS-based software program that would update nightly. Further, he would no longer rely solely on data from the outside, and would begin to collect earnings figures through a larger team dedicated to data integrity. And, he would hire a head of technical operations to oversee product deployment.

For the better part of the 1980s and into the 1990s, Rob had outsourced his software development to a firm in Philadelphia. Minority-owned Wilson Hewitt was a very capable software house. Phil Wilson was its managing partner. Upon receiving his additional funding, Rob pushed Phil to provide dedicated resources. John Sharp, one of Wilson's top developers with intimate knowledge of Baseline, was tapped to lead the dedicated development team. John had already been actively converting Baseline code from Apple BASIC to Microsoft BASIC for the new PC application. In the coming years the team would grow, and by 1995 Rob Patterson would strike a deal with Phil Wilson to extricate these programmers and make them full-time Baseline employees. In addition to John Sharp, talented software engineers by the names of Brian Coffin, Bill DiPierre, Sam Hillard, Matt Horne, Barry Levine, Mike Powers, and Dan Stranick joined the Baseline ranks.[27]

As for data integrity, Rob began the arduous task of creating Baseline's own quality-assured database of earnings figures and securities prices. Rob termed this key information his "primary data." It was the set of data points most critical to his mission. End-of-day prices were key because of all the valuation ratios. Earnings and earnings estimates drove stock prices up or down, so they too, along with dividends became "primary" data points. Great care would govern their acquisition and maintenance. All other data points were outsourced. Financial statements of public companies, for example, would be labeled "secondary data" while textual data like business descriptions for each stock would become "tertiary data." Priorities were always established in that order. Rob hired Barbara Tripp to oversee this monumental effort. Barbara was previously a project manager in information systems for Aetna Life & Casualty in their Pension Investment department.[28]

Rob also decided to aid the user experience by shipping the entire database and software application to each client on a dedicated IBM PC XT computer, a state-of-the-art personal computer at the time. This would ensure fast data retrieval into his product. A common complaint about other systems at the time, which often included dial-up access, was the delay in receiving data over the phone line due primarily to network bandwidth issues. This was pre-internet. Data transmission rates in 1991 were painfully slow relative to today's standards. Additionally, Rob would begin to offer salespeople a draw against commissions to help solidify longevity in his sales ranks. And he would hire a savvy head of Systems and Operations to manage all the needed logistics. That last point came to fruition with the hiring of Simon Chen in 1989. He had been a systems analyst at Toys R Us and had built a labor scheduling system using Lotus 1-2-3 macros, and oversaw its roll-out. Simon's success with a system roll-out, along with his Master's degree in Operations Research from Columbia University, were very attractive to Rob. For Simon, it was the project management role, Rob's "eye for visual presentation of financial data," and the founder's personality that attracted him to Baseline.[29] With all these changes in place, "New Baseline" was released in 1991. The initial release of this new Baseline was still far from Rob's ultimate vision, but it had a technological framework upon which to build over time. And, that's exactly what would transpire.

A boost to Rob's efforts in the 1990s was the explosion of mutual funds. The trend of corporations moving from defined-benefit plans (i.e., pension plans) to defined-contribution plans, like 401Ks, fueled the mutual fund industry. Additionally, an exemption from the Glass-Steagall Act of 1933 gave commercial banks the ability to create and market proprietary mutual funds, as long as they did not participate in underwriting or distributing the fund.[30] The sudden popularity of mutual funds attracted the attention of many commercial banks, which greatly expanded the market for Baseline. One of the earliest proprietary funds created by a bank was that of Midlantic Bank in Edison, New Jersey. That fund, the Compass Capital Growth Fund, was managed by portfolio manager John Lee. Being local in New Jersey, he provided Rob with another key voice for valuable input. According to John:

> Rob was a great help. He was polite, personable and smart. We were a pretty good springboard for ideas at the bank. On more than one occasion Rob would pick up the phone and call me, and we'd occasionally grab a hot dog. He never questioned "what" I was

asking about, but did want to know "why" I cared about X, Y or Z. For example, why dividend growth rate mattered to me, or why my work with Michael Milken at Drexel Burnham had me focus on EBITDA[g] as a key screening element.[31]

John Lee, who remained a client of Baseline for more than twenty years, also praised the teamwork of Rob and Simon Chen as they worked together to build the new and improved Baseline product. When the initial phase of New Baseline rolled out, John recalled being asked what key data points would be of interest:

> I said something as simple as "PE ratio is great, but how about a company's relative PE (i.e., in relation to the market itself), and let's do that with companies to show their relative valuation to their sector (e.g., Consumer Staples). And, I want to see companies with PEs less than the market. I'd love a PEG[h] ratio. I want to see dividend yield, EPS[i] growth and market cap." I remember working with Simon on those things, and it was like once a week he'd cater to my needs.[32]

Simon recently recalled working with John and other clients. "John Lee and other early users had numerous suggestions which helped Rob and me understand that investment decisions were usually relative. [Based on that], we implemented industry and sector aggregates for various fundamentals and momentum values to compare a stock to its industry or sector. It was a great combination of quantifying user ideas, then serving them back in a very intuitive and visual way!"[33]

In a 2018 interview, Lee harkened back to those days of the early 1990s. "Everything was unwinding and being developed. Rob's grasp of how the investment management field was changing was such that he saw a whole new market for his product. The commercial banks were becoming pretty good competitors to the investment

---

g   EBITDA. Earnings before Interest, Taxes, Depreciation, and Amortization.
h   PEG ratio. The ratio of P/E to the Earnings Growth rate.
i   EPS. Earnings per Share.

banks—the sell-side. The sell-side[j] will always be the sell-side, with their products *du jour*, but the buy-side[k] was such a bigger market."[34] Baseline capitalized on the growth of the buy-side.

At the same time, another such buy-side firm taking notice of Baseline was Heartland Capital of Indianapolis. Tom Maurath, then a portfolio manager with Heartland, recalled that "Baseline was easy to use and intuitive." Later on, when Maurath had moved to Goelzer Investment Management, he brought Baseline with him. According to Tom, "We relied on Baseline for all our equity research needs. Baseline was great for me because I wanted it to steer me in the right direction for broad characteristics, and then I would personally do more in-depth research either from the Qs and Ks, or [Wall] Street research."[35] Rob Patterson's ambition to aim directly at portfolio managers was gaining real traction in the early to mid-1990s.

Competition for the buy-side's budget dollars existed, but no one did exactly what Baseline did. A smaller competitor by the name of *Stockval* featured a well-respected valuation model, called the G-model, but it lacked wider utility. *FactSet*, the primary competitor, had deeper data and wider computing power than Baseline. However, it was more expensive, more difficult to use, and often required its clients to subscribe to third-party databases. FactSet also focused more on serving equity analysts as opposed to portfolio managers. Founded in 1978, it was also bigger than Baseline. During the 1990s, Rob Patterson was fond of saying that Baseline was tracking to FactSet's growth rate, just five years behind it.

As time progressed, and Baseline's business grew, a pseudo-competitor appeared on the scene, namely the *Bloomberg Terminal*. Originally designed for fixed income traders, Michael Bloomberg had slowly expanded his desktop kingdom with additional capabilities and a wider variety of securities. When equities finally made their debut inside the "Bloomberg," smaller buy-side firms took notice. For tight-budgeted asset managers, which invested equally in stocks

---

j   Sell-side. The segment of the Capital Markets that is involved in the creation, market-ing, and sale of securities including stocks and bonds. Examples are Broker Dealers and Investment Banks.

k   Buy-side. The segment of the Capital Markets that is involved in the purchase of stocks, bonds, and other financial products based on the needs and strategy of their company's or client's portfolio constructs. Examples include Mutual Funds, Hedge Funds, and Insurance Companies. Also known as the "Asset Management" industry.

and bonds, Bloomberg became a possible choice. On a feature-by-feature comparison basis, Baseline and Bloomberg looked like they came from different planets. Baseline was a stock selection tool for long-term equity investors with specially honed visual analytics, while the Bloomberg terminal was a real-time[1] quote, news and communication tool primarily designed for fixed income traders. However, in the battle to win over small firms where economics played a large part in the buying process, the two very different products occasionally found themselves to be competitors.

As a product exclusively designed for long-term equity investors, Baseline did not focus on fixed income instruments or real-time information. As such, Baseline fit into the market segment known as Equity Analytics. This market segment was a subset of the larger playing field called Financial Information Services. The biggest segment in that overall market was "Real-Time News and Quotes." Initially, in that large corner of the market sat Quotron and ADP. During the 1990s, Bloomberg and Reuters joined the fray and vendors fought tooth-and-nail for supremacy of their terminals on the desktops of sell-side securities traders and retail stockbrokers. Those customers cared mightily about intraday movements. In the 1990s, adding to the mix of real-time information players was a surging, upstart player by the name of ILX[m]. The Thomson Corporation, wanting to gain a toehold in this large market segment, took an early stake in ILX with a $30 million investment.[36]

Meanwhile, Rob Patterson's fledgling outfit, with its focused strategy towards equities and portfolio managers, would grow from 20 employees and $1 million in revenue with zero profit in 1991, to a national enterprise ten years later with a staff of 215, serving over 1,000 money management firms and more than 12,000 users. It would also sport a 25 percent pretax margin on revenues north of $47 million by the end of 2001.

At the time of that fateful day in September of 2001, Baseline was in the midst of its greatest growth period. It had come a long way since

---

[1]   Real-time. Referring to the nearly instantaneous provision of information surrounding financial markets. Most often used in reference to stock or bond quotes and news stories.

[m]   ILX. A real time quote, charting, and news service founded in 1988 by Bernie Weinstein. By the mid-1990s, Thomson owned all of ILX.

BASELINE ANNUAL REVENUE

Millions of Dollars

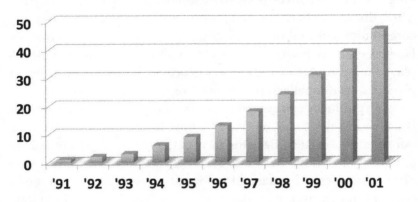

With newfound capital from Bowne, Rob Patterson released "New Baseline" in 1991, and portfolio managers coast-to-coast found it addictive. Revenue soared.

its founding in 1981, and especially since its reincarnation thanks to the infusion of $4 million from Bowne. With that investment, Rob Patterson found a new lease on life. His original idea of visually representing the valuation of the 500 stocks in the S&P index had decidedly taken a positive turn. The eventual product greatly surpassed the S&P's finite set of stocks, and incorporated far more utility. Baseline received broad market acceptance as it appealed to the wider asset management community. Rob's vision had come to fruition.

CHAPTER 4

A SPECIAL CULTURE

THE FIRST TIME I met Rob Patterson was in 1991. He was already two years removed from that fateful Board presentation when he secured $4 million of funding. He had implemented his new processes and had just released Version 1.0 of New Baseline. At that first encounter, I was immediately struck by two major themes about the man: informality and vision. In October of 1991, approximately two years before I joined his company, he and I had a very important lunch date. I was really looking forward to meeting the man who had not only created a new product which was getting good reviews in the industry, but who also had just stolen my best sales rep, Chris Tresse.

I phoned Rob to introduce myself and, with my tongue firmly planted in cheek, suggested that he owed me lunch for stealing my best guy. After some mutual chuckles, I got straight to the point during our phone chat. I was interested in learning more about this new product and the tiny company that was making a lot of portfolio managers stand up and take notice. I said, "Clearly, you're doing something better than I am, and I'd love to learn what it is." He invited me to come by the office and talk over lunch.

When I arrived at Baseline's modest office at 61 Broadway in lower Manhattan, I was surprised that he answered the front door's bell. While it wasn't a large organization by any stretch of the imagination,

I at least expected some semblance of a receptionist to greet me. But the greater shock was that he wasn't wearing any shoes! *Okay, this is different,* I thought. His informality was only exceeded by his graciousness. Shoes or no shoes, this gentleman was indeed a gentle man. He was happy to see me, and thrilled to tell his story. He seemed genuinely appreciative that I took the time to research him, and to determine why my sales rep had left me.

My second instant impression was that of his vision. Taped to the top of his computer monitor was a small figurine of Mickey Mouse. I couldn't help but inquire as to the meaning. It turned out that Walt Disney was a great inspiration for Rob. He explained that Disney was a non-conformant visionary who liked to think outside the box. Rob saw himself in a similar light.

At the time, I was the managing director of CompuServe's Financial Services Group—a team dedicated to providing financial data solutions to investment bankers and money managers. CompuServe's prowess in this particular sector was waning. In the 1980s, we had built our relative success on capturing the lion's share of New York's investment banking data needs. Goldman Sachs, Donaldson Lufkin & Jenrette, Dillon Read, and Shearson-Lehman were a few of the places where we fulfilled almost all of the data and analytic computing needs regarding public companies. However, while CompuServe had its origins in providing such computing services to big business, its more prominent success was becoming a pre-AOL[n] standard for personal information access, as well as selling excess network bandwidth (pre-internet) to corporate computer applications with remote users. Its shift in emphasis resulted in tremendous corporate growth.

Although my business segment generated an impressive pre-tax profit margin, and a top line of $12 million, it was of decreasing interest to CompuServe whose overall revenues were already north of $200 million in 1991.[37] That contrasted greatly with its results of ten years earlier of just $27 million. My Financial Services Group didn't scale like their new target market of tech-oriented consumers, nor was my group's growth rate comparable to this blossoming global information service. Aimed at the savvier side of the consumer market, the *CompuServe Information Service* had already eclipsed all of the firm's

n   AOL. America Online.

traditional commercial businesses in revenue. While top management liked the profit margin from my group, the inability to leverage our software development efforts to other areas of the firm spelled the end to our niche business as a growth engine. Product evolution slowed and customers started walking.

I first became aware of Baseline in May of 1991. I accompanied one of my sales reps on a visit to a prospective client. Chris Tresse had been with me for three years and was doing exceptionally well. We went to see a portfolio manager at Marine Midland Bank. The prospect listened to our sales pitch, but then proceeded to tell us about a great new service called *Baseline*. He was effusive in his description of the service and how it reflected his workflow as a portfolio manager, while "your solution is simply an efficient data gathering tool."[38] Chris appeared spellbound. I was seeing the proverbial crystal ball spell T-R-O-U-B-L-E.

According to Chris, the prospect's "enthusiasm for Baseline was infectious. Baseline seemed to be way ahead of its time in terms of user interface and the simplicity of getting things done." In his exploratory meetings with Rob Patterson, Chris learned of Baseline's specific market focus. Chris added: "Rob had decided to go straight to the decision maker—the portfolio manager—with a tool that they could grasp, relatively immediately, so it became engrained in their daily workflow. The elegance and simplicity of Baseline was unbelievable. The interface was intoxicating. I fell in love with a pretty face." After three years with CompuServe, Chris made the choice to join Rob Patterson and Baseline in the summer of 1991.

Soon after Chris's departure, and desiring critical market intelligence, I made that phone call to Rob. His greeting me in his socks was a telltale sign of his corporate culture—one that I would eventually join and help reinforce. However, I still had two more years of CompuServe work—and wearing shoes—ahead of me.

Within a year of our first lunch, Rob's success would catch him off guard. The market was welcoming his product with open arms. Suddenly, as more and more portfolio managers acquired desktop PCs, the ability to serve them with an easy-to-use tool for researching stocks became far easier. For the most part, these users were not computer aficionados. They were, however, sophisticated investors. Rob had tapped an emerging niche. His growth, and the waning interest of CompuServe in my business segment, put us on a collision course. In August of 1993, I happily joined Rob Patterson as his new head of Sales. My written goals included scaling the sales team to enable faster growth. My unwritten goal was to help Rob further the already strong corporate culture he was forging.

The term "corporate culture" has been gaining more and more prominence since the turn of this century as an often critical factor in determining a firm's success or failure. According to a 2018 article entitled "The Leader's Guide to Corporate Culture" in the *Harvard Business Review*, "culture is the tacit social order of an organization. It shapes attitudes and behaviors in wide-ranging and durable ways."[39] The authors, Groysberg *et al*, further assert that cultural norms define what is encouraged, discouraged, accepted, or rejected within a group. They stipulate that culture can, in fact, "unleash tremendous amounts of energy toward a shared purpose and foster an organization's capacity to thrive." Additionally, they argue that culture in a business is a shared phenomenon where the intentions of a founder can easily blend with the knowledge and experiences of frontline employees. It is also "pervasive, enduring and implicit."[40] From the first day I met Rob Patterson, I could see that he possessed an undaunted passion for his business. He purposefully had created a company with a familial, informal culture, yet with a very focused vision and a well-laid-out strategy for action. The development of a very special corporate culture was well underway.

I would argue that the "tacit social order"[41] that Rob Patterson created unleashed tremendous amounts of energy and increased our capacity to succeed. Let me expound.

On the people side, Rob knew that he was only as good as the individuals he and his managers hired. From the beginning, he dubbed all his employees "associates." He disliked the term "employee." He felt employees worked for all the mediocre companies that dotted the globe. To Rob, associates saw themselves as family who cared deeply about each other and, most importantly, the clients. Rob also instructed his managers to "hire people smarter than you." He wasn't necessarily talking about IQ, as it would have been difficult for Rob to practice what he preached from that perspective: from my view there weren't many people with his intellect. However, what he was speaking about was specialized knowledge and experiences. Best-in-

Class knowledge. He often cited Simon Chen, who became our chief product and technology officer, as someone who could figure out technological solutions to his vision's requirements more effectively than Rob could himself. He also once commented to the Bowne board that "with Ed, I knew I was getting someone who understood sales and salespeople. It wasn't just that I didn't have enough bandwidth, although that was part of it. It was that I needed someone who would do a better job managing sales than I would." As such, he constantly urged his management team to "hire above your weight class!" His feeling was that weak managers don't want to be threatened, and thus they hire marginal people. Regarding the overall workforce, he would stress team orientation as a critical hiring attribute.

In terms of his direct management team, Rob called us the "Operating Committee" or "Ops Team" for short. By the mid-nineties we had built a management team with critical mass. In addition to Rob, the Ops Team consisted of Bob Levine (CFO), Simon Chen (CTO), Jonathan Weinberg (VP, Technology), John Sharp (Director, Product Development—Philadelphia), Barbara Tripp (Director, Data Integrity), Carl Boudakian (Director, Client Support & Marketing), Ron Perez (VP, Product Management), Helen Byrne (Human Resources & Office Manager), and myself. Later on, it would add Nick Webb as head of Sales as I transitioned to COO.

In my opinion, Rob's magic with his Ops Team was a simple phrase—abject accountability. Each month the team would gather. After each person gave a two- to three-minute update on any major news, the team settled in for a prolonged discussion. First, all associates due for a performance review that month would be discussed openly. Each associate's manager would have completed the review, and the relevant Ops member would share the manager's sentiments. Then, the Ops member would propose a salary raise in line with company expectations and we would discuss the raise and vote on it. In this manner everyone in the company was treated equally. Additionally, this reduced the often-described grind of performance reviews by managers whose companies conduct them at one particular time of year. It was Rob's opinion that a crunch period of performance reviews resulted in a degradation of effort as it related to the very important, and very personal, nature of a performance evaluation.

Secondly, we would review an 11x17" sheet of paper entitled

"Operational Priorities." These were a running list of key items per Ops member that had been agreed to the previous month as having the most tactical or strategic importance to Baseline. We would all review our relevant items, and the group would comment. Rarely was there a need for alarm in terms of any one team member falling behind. Based upon the overall discussion, a new list of priorities would be generated by Rob himself (on a new 11x17" sheet) and personally hand delivered the next day for follow-up at next month's meeting. Everyone on the Ops Team received the same 11x17" paper. Of course, while the Ops meetings were monthly, there were many iterative talks during the month to ensure compliance or to update challenging issues. Rob's style was incredibly collaborative. He wanted all his associates to be apprised of the company's progress, but he too required updates on all tactical and strategic items of importance. He never wanted a surprise—good or bad.

To prove himself worthy to his associates, Rob backed up his words with action. There were numerous gestures of good faith that Rob brought to his business. In the 1980s, as a fledgling enterprise and located on 3rd Avenue in Manhattan, Rob paid for lunch every day for his five employees. That may not seem like a lot until you realize that the company was still providing daily lunch in 2001 to 215 associates in three cities.

It was Rob's ardent belief that going outside for lunch in New York was a distraction. He valued the need to take a break, to take a deep breath, and to eat well. His words led me to believe that he possessed some fear that a one-hour lunch could become ninety minutes. However, Rob always ensured a healthy fare through the efforts of the administrative staff—not bags of Cheetos washed down with a sugar-filled Coke. Sandwiches in the early days were augmented as the years passed with a variety of salads and hot meals including such dishes as Chicken Cordon Bleu served with broccoli. In exchange, Rob politely asked that associates either congregate and socialize while eating, or at least eat at their desks and continue working when done with their meal. No one was ever prohibited from going outside for an hour in lieu of the provided meal. I'm sure today's Human Resource departments would be a little nervous about offering such a plan for fear of being called out for unfair labor practices. But nothing at Baseline was meant to comprise a slave-driving mentality.

Rob's generosity in the name of efficiency didn't simply end with lunch. The reason he wasn't wearing shoes on the day I met him was not simply because he was more comfortable in his socks, but because it was also the weekly Shoe Shine Day at Baseline! From the earliest of days, Rob always desired his representatives to the outside world to look their best, and so he provided those people—usually sales people—with a free weekly shoe shine right in the office. It was a low-cost item to Rob, but one that saved his people from needless worry about finding the time and place to do such. It ensured for Rob that each person would always look presentable—at least from the ankles down. Bobby, the always affable, kind gentleman from Brooklyn, was there every Monday at 11:00 AM.

Ninety miles south of our New York operations was our software development office at 1601 Market Street in Philadelphia. Those associates benefitted from lunches as well. And, while there weren't any salespeople from that office leaving each day to see customers, the software engineers were hunched over at their PCs grinding out very valuable code written exactly to spec to help advance Baseline's business. In lieu of shoe shines, that group received a weekly visit from a chair masseuse. Tensions were ostensibly relieved, and as theory has it, better code got written—or the programmers just felt better about working for this distant enterprise in New York called Baseline. In either case, it created good karma.

Beyond epicurean delights and massage therapy, Baseline was also an environment of diversity. There was no ethnocentricity. At least that was my perspective. While Wall Street firms were typically made up of white males, this Wall Street software company was a place of many races and creeds. Baseline was a kaleidoscope of colors representing the four corners of the world. Males and females. Over the years, two of our top four performing sales executives were women. Our associates included Buddhists, Christians, Hindus, Jews, Muslims, and non-believers. Yes, many corporations today are made up the same way, but this was true when Baseline was perhaps only fifty people strong. In the early days, the administrative staff was made up primarily of Jehovah's Witnesses. While Rob forbade them from any proselytizing, he appreciated their custom of not celebrating things like birthdays and holidays. Rob was about celebrating the team. He didn't necessarily like increased focus on any one person. Although he was raised Christian,

Rob did not permit a Christmas tree in the office. He felt strongly that it sent an uncomfortable signal to those of other beliefs. Rob and I rarely discussed religion. He simply felt that it shouldn't be part of the workplace. Not that it was a bad thing, but rather he didn't want any one group to feel they were being influenced by any one particular belief set. The only belief set Rob instilled in his associates was that the client was Job One.

Former product design specialist, Allan Unger, offered his view in a 2019 interview. "Everyone was open to different cultures. Half the people I was friends with were Filipino. I had lunch almost every day with six people in the conference room. Baseline was a friendly atmosphere. It was very collaborative. I think it was very progressive. If you look at organizations now, this is what they're striving for. And, I think, Baseline had it twenty years ago."[42]

In 1994, Bernadette Ross was a 24-year-old Irish immigrant who had just arrived in the United States. Baseline was her first job in America. She recently recalled that "I was welcomed [at Baseline] with open arms for my first job as a young, inexperienced immigrant. It was so easy to make friends, and it wasn't just with the other Irish girls I met. I had never talked to Jewish people, or Muslim people, or Jehovah's Witnesses ever in my life. That's how closeted I was brought up." Bernadette shared how she would awkwardly ask questions about their cultures and religions. "They were so honest and open, and I would apologize because I didn't really know. Talking as an immigrant, it was a huge learning experience. I was welcomed and nurtured at Baseline." Bernadette would eventually progress to be a manager within our Data Integrity department, ultimately spending twenty years with Baseline and, subsequently, Thomson Reuters.[43]

In addition to the separation of church and state, so to speak, Rob also believed in the separation of business and personal lives. He ardently subscribed to the notion that there should be no fraternization among the families of management. I learned this quickly during my first month on the job. One evening, I was walking to the ferry with Rob in lower Manhattan. We both took trains out of Hoboken. I had come from a very open culture at CompuServe where holiday parties and summer barbecues, with beer and other libations, were shared with employees and significant others. While we were in lockstep heading towards the ferry terminal along the

Hudson River, Rob mentioned his wife, Mickey, by name for the first time. I quickly responded that I looked forward to meeting her one day. Suddenly, Rob was no longer at my side keeping pace with my strides. I stopped and looked back. He had come to a dead halt. I walked back ten feet to his position.

"Is everything okay, Rob?"

"Oh, yeah, Ed. Sure. But, please know that you will never meet my wife. Don't take it personally. I just don't believe in mixing socially. Nothing good comes of that."

Wow. How could I not take that personally? I was still a young, impressionable 34-year-old. I had just spent eleven years with CompuServe where the culture was very social. CompuServe may not have been as diverse, nor as amenity-filled, but it was very open to familial connections. I had always enjoyed meeting the significant others of my colleagues. I never saw it as a desire to learn something negative or to find ways to undermine my fellow associates. Rather, it often provided me a better glimpse into the person who I worked with day in and day out. But, *Whatever!* was my internal response. I was surprised that such a little suggestion—that I meet his wife— might stop him dead in his tracks.

As time wore on, I made it my goal to help him ease into a more open attitude towards socialization. I knew that "all work and no play" within a growing corporate entity would result in a "dull boy" culture. I had help with my endeavor from two members of my sales team. My former CompuServe teammate, Chris Tresse, and his fellow sales executive, Danna McCormick, made it their objective to get an annual, off-site, social gathering on the calendar. We would succeed, but not for three more years.

That little encounter with Rob on the way to the ferry represented one of a few examples during my first month on the job that had me initially question my decision to join this man and his small firm. What I came to later appreciate was that this pleasant visionary wasn't always comfortable in social settings. It was easy for Rob to limit social encounters, especially as the leader of a small firm. What he would come to understand was that with success he would need to be more visible, and more communicative. His growing management team would help him ease into that role. And getting to know people and their families would help bond this firm closer together.

Other cultural differences with my personal expectations began on the first day of my employment in August 1993. It was just the second "first day of work" in my life. I had just left a senior management position at a well-respected national information services company. I had been with CompuServe for eleven years. I was now joining a twenty-employee pseudo-startup. At CompuServe, pressure on me to relocate to their headquarters in Columbus, Ohio, and the company's lack of emphasis on financial information services had given me little choice but to leave. At a relatively young age, I was willing to take a risk. I liked what I had heard on the Street about fledgling Baseline, and liked the informality, intellect, and pleasantness of Rob Patterson. Additionally, Chris Tresse was there and he provided helpful insight. However, I encountered two quick bumps in the road on my first day on the job.

First, the day had hardly begun when Rob was seriously managing my expectations. He had hired me as his vice president of Sales—the national sales manager. He congratulated me on starting the job and pushed my new box of business cards across the table in my direction, while never taking his hand off them. As I reached for them, he pulled them back. "Ed, you need to know we have no titles here. I'm the president and that's pretty much it. I know you wanted a title given your corporate background, and I will give you these cards, but please put them in your desk and don't use them."

What?

Okay, now that's just plain weird, I thought.

What was his motivation? I would later learn that Rob was a man who cared little about his own title. He was against corporate politics. He felt titles created power struggles. He wanted me to know he trusted me enough to be his head of sales, but that I should act that way in spirit and generate credibility with my actions, not my title.

It was another idiosyncrasy of Rob's personality. Deep down I understood—let's not create fiefdoms and worrisome pecking orders. But I also realized that his perspective would not scale well if we were eventually successful. In my opinion, people need to know how they fit into a corporate culture and organizational hierarchy. With twenty people it's okay to have one boss and nineteen workers. In fact, I grew to appreciate the lack of politics and hierarchy in those early days, given our very small size. However, if a business grows to a hundred or more employees, structure becomes critical. We did grow, and we added titles as the years passed. But even in 2001 with 215 associates and a given hierarchy, the business remained familial and very horizontal. I learned to see that as a very positive aspect of the business. Everyone felt very plugged in, and important. I credit Rob Patterson for the continuity.

The second oddity of my first day soon followed in the same room. Rob proceeded to tell me that while he planned to give me an office, he only had two that could possibly work. One was for his office manager, Helen Byrne, who had been with him for years, and he couldn't remove her. The other was for his top performing salesman. He stipulated that the salesman's office was a condition of employment as that particular salesperson desired a very private space in which to make cold calls. That left Rob with no options for me. I don't think I entirely expected an office, but the assertion from Rob felt unsettling, especially on the heels of the business card discussion. In the end, however, I would have declined an office that required me to displace someone. Small firms are no place for big company politics.

At the time of my arrival, Baseline had revenues of about $3 million and was not yet profitable. Rob's perspective was that the whole company should just work hard as teammates and not worry about rank or office. I was shown my desk in an open room along with the head of customer service and her team of three customer support reps. It was a sort of come-uppance for this managing director from CompuServe. I had come from a company where rank and office meant a lot—rightly or wrongly. This small company approach would take some getting used to. This very fact is why small firms need to be very careful when hiring talent from larger firms. The culture is different. The expectations are different. The support infrastructure is often minimal. I was very cognizant of Rob's concern in this area during my own interview process. However, I was happy to have received the job offer and willing to give it a shot. I knew this small company had legs.

During my first year at Baseline, I was often asked if the notion of a sales rep having an office, while I sat in an open bay area, presented an awkward situation for me or the senior salesman. The question often came from individuals who had experienced standard corporate life. While it may have been initially unsettling, my answer was easy. "Hey, this is still an unproven, unprofitable enterprise. If we are successful, then this issue will take care of itself. If we are unsuccessful, it won't matter." Baseline was practically a start-up. The fabric of its culture was still in development. There was absolutely no need to interfere with its momentum until I had the time to take its measure as a company.

In retrospect, fellow Ops Team member Ron Perez recently said "this flat culture with lunches and no titles predated by years the entrepreneurial culture of Silicon Valley startups. Rob was years ahead of his time in his beliefs and practices." While I agree with Ron's assessment, it took me several months to understand that my choice to join Rob Patterson was the correct one. In the end, it was the egalitarian culture, the quality of the product, the enthusiastic responses from customers, the goodness of the man I worked for, and the firm's clear need for help managing its accelerated growth that told me I would be happy at Baseline. I was also confident that I could make a positive difference. And I wasn't giving up on the wife thing either!

Success cures all ills. Within a year we would climb from 200 clients to over 300. Contracts averaging a recurring $25,000 annually were pouring in at the rate of almost 10 per month by the end of 1994, and a needed office expansion had finally provided me with an office. The growth of the business also necessitated additional account managers, whom I hired enthusiastically. As success begot success, Rob's tendency towards magnanimous behavior continuously showed itself. At each centennial milestone of customers (100, 200, 300, etc.), Rob gathered the company for an "all hands" Town Hall Meeting. He reviewed the recent success stories, commented on how product evolution or data item additions had fueled our progress, and congratulated particular salespeople for large account contracts. Most importantly, he handed each associate a plaque commemorating that new centennial milestone. The plaque simply said, for example:

BASELINE
400th Client
December 8, 1995

Rob was becoming more comfortable with larger groups of people and sharing his success story. He often asked the Ops Team for feedback prior to Town Hall Meetings to be sure he touched all the appropriate highlights. And, because those sessions were centennial milestones, Rob made sure each associate received an envelope with a crisp $100 bill in it. Rank, title, or tenure did not matter. $100 for each person. In later years, we shifted away from celebrating the number of clients, in lieu of recognizing the growth in users. Since many customers had Baseline networked across their local-area-network, those "desktops" that were authorized for Baseline access were counted. Wells Fargo, for example, had nearly 300 users. Yet, it was one client. It could not reasonably be put on a par with say, a small, one-user money management firm. The last milestone we celebrated prior to 9/11 was the achievement of 10,000 desktops on April 7, 2001.

Milestones such as centennial achievements of client numbers were wholly celebrated at Baseline. Town Halls, plaques, and envelopes with cash that drove employee morale were the centerpieces of such celebrations.

The culture that Rob created often caught people off guard when they joined the company. During his first month on the job in 1998, newly hired sales manager Nick Webb kept telling his wife that Baseline was "too good to be true. The other shoe has gotta fall soon." One of Nick's favorite stories was that on his first day of work he received a plaque along with a $100 bill. "Something is wrong. This isn't meant for me. I got someone else's!" he exclaimed.[44] We assured him. Nope, it was his. Welcome to Baseline.

During the early years, the cash required for centennial celebrations was minimal. As the years went on, it became more challenging, given the level of cash. Parent companies got nervous, then angry, and then shut down the practice in 2001. I'm sure it was an income tax reporting concern, as well as a fear regarding the logistics surrounding the withdrawal and transport of $100 bills. However, from a cultural standpoint the provision of crisp Ben Franklins was pure brilliance. While $100 per employee over an average period of a year was negligible, it had a very positive impact on morale and it made people proud, wanting to do more. It also resulted in all our associates keeping a watchful eye on our client count.

One of the veterans of Baseline's operations was Alfredo Guzman, a manager in Data Integrity who joined the firm in 1994. He recently commented on his recollection of the Baseline culture:

> Literally, it felt like you're on top of the world. From the beginning, we were made to feel welcome. As we grew it was always a pleasure to come to work. It was always an atmosphere of "How can we all help each other?" Everyone came in and did their job. That was expected, and you knew everybody was doing it. Even from the top. You knew the president was doing what he needed to do, giving us the tools we needed, and motivating us [by being] always present, always smiling, and the $100 bonuses were great![45]

It was a revelation hearing the $100 bill make it into a personal reflection of Baseline's culture. It shows the impact it had. Rob used this small piece of motivation to drive home the notion of the Client being Job One. To be sure, even on the very first day I met him in 1991 for that chat and a sandwich, Rob was proudly displaying the names of each of his clients. He had two adjoining white boards on his office wall. Rather than free them up for the scribbling of product ideas or sales strategies, those white boards were fully dedicated to prominently displaying the valued names of all his clients. The display of client names remained a constant theme with Rob during my entire tenure with him. During that first encounter, I commented on his boards. He said, "Ed, I want all my staff to know that I value our clients most of all. I want everyone that comes in here to know that the only reason we exist is to serve our clients." Since Rob's office doubled as a conference room, many meetings were held there. One couldn't help but notice the client names. In later years, as the list became much longer, it became digitized but was frequently re-printed and still displayed on Rob's walls.

One of our administrative assistants, Lorena Munoz-Udik, was often charged with the task of updating Rob's client wall. She recalled the specifics of that assignment:

> His client board was super important. He was very particular about it. You had to get it exactly right, but if I made a mistake, he was always great about it. He'd say "Take it as a learning experience, and do it the way I want from now on." We would keep adding paper as we'd go. He wanted each name always written down. That's just the way he wanted it. It was always important to make sure you didn't mess it up and forget a name, and to be sure to immediately add a new client. He valued his clients. That was the whole point.[46]

While Rob didn't naturally feel that social gatherings were necessary, he always valued the intermingling of associates from different departments. From the earliest days of Baseline, Rob would hold monthly lunches in his office and he would invite one person from each department. They were small, intimate sessions that were very educational for those involved. People who wouldn't come in contact with Rob on a daily basis would find themselves breaking bread with the president, and meeting other associates from other disciplines. Everyone wanted an invite. In later years, the monthly lunches took place in upscale restaurants.

As the mid 1990s arrived, the culture started to become more social. A non-denominational Holiday Lunch always occurred at the office each year in late December. It often meant an expanded lunch menu and perhaps a Grab Bag. Employees only. But in 1995, the holiday party included families. Even spouses were invited. And, Santa Claus arrived to distribute whatever presents we associates had brought in (already wrapped) for our kids. Of course, to my chagrin Mickey Patterson did not attend. But, as mentioned, I wasn't done with that goal.

There was no liquor at these holiday luncheons. Rob had shared stories of corporate party experiences in an earlier career that he had witnessed turn ugly. He was resolute that no one would consume alcohol at any Baseline event. For that reason, he was firmly against any after-hours function. But in 1996, we used his own success against him. "Rob, your 15th anniversary is coming up. How can we not celebrate that?" Later that year, the entire firm cruised around lower Manhattan at sunset. Two sales executives, Danna McCormick and Chris Tresse, had spearheaded the effort with great help from Helen Byrne and her administrative team. Associates only, and no liquor, but what a breakthrough that was. Within a year or two, beer and wine would be served. The boat trip continued annually until 2001 when it morphed into our special 20th anniversary party. Open bar that night.

From a cultural standpoint, senior executives at Accenture[o] recently labeled the "workplace culture" as the secret to innovation. Based on the results of a 2018 global study, Julie Sweet and Ellyn Shook assert that people need the right culture to flourish, and that the type of culture best able to drive innovation is one of equality. "No matter who or where they are, if people feel a sense of belonging and are valued by their employers for their unique contributions, perspectives and circumstances, they are empowered to innovate more." The study undertaken by Accenture resulted in the listing of specific workplace factors that contribute to a workplace of equality.[47]

The culture that Rob created, and we as a caring base of associates helped steer, was indeed egalitarian. As mentioned, it was certainly ethnically diverse. The average associate at Baseline also felt fairly empowered. He or she was treated well, had a voice, and knew Baseline was truly an equal opportunity employer. Further, internal communication was frequent. Each associate knew quite well how the company was doing and where we were going. As a result, creative ideas came from all ends of the organization. Innovation was a constant theme. Several examples will be shared in future chapters.

Even outsiders who fulfilled consultant roles felt plugged in. In 1996, Bob Levine, our CFO, hired Cutting Edge Consulting to

---

o   Accenture. A large global consulting company that originated in the Big 8 accounting world. Upon the dissolution of the public accounting firm of Arthur Anderson, its consulting arm was spun off as its own entity and named Accenture.

implement a full-blown accounting system. The decision was made to purchase an open-source software package called SBT[p], and modify it to fit our needs. Brian Branco, the consultant on the project, spent two to three days per week with us implementing the system. Brian recently commented about the Baseline culture:

> It was really an amazing place to work. I've always done consulting work here and there, and I talk about that (the Baseline culture) to this day. Being a consultant—and I've done it for twenty-five years—you always feel like an outsider. You're never included in anything. The culture of Baseline was not that. The culture of Baseline was "Hey, you're here . . . Come to the party!" or "Hey you're here . . . Do you want lunch?" or even "Hey, you're here . . . Let's go out after work." The whole culture and how I was personally treated. . . it was just amazing. Just the whole concept of the family spirit. To this day, I tell people about that, because there's never been anything like that again.[48]

Over time, many of Baseline's associates came to greatly respect Rob Patterson and the environment he fostered. It wasn't simply because he bestowed wonderful amenities upon them, but rather because he took a measured, long-term approach to his business. He wasn't out to squeeze profit margins out of each calendar quarter, nor did parent companies place such edicts upon him. His first investor, Bowne, gave him free rein. His second suitor, Primark (by way of acquisition in 1997) had more stringent expectations, but they were not onerous. Nonetheless, he demanded accountability for stated goals. However, the achievement of those objectives was based on an expectation for measured and deliberate actions by the various staff members. Knee-jerk reactions to business challenges were never tolerated. Adding to the evidence of Rob's long-term approach was the fact that he did not come to work each day to maximize his own wealth. Recall that he relinquished 90 percent of

---

p   SBT (Software Business Technologies). A suite of accounting and business management software with an open architecture designed for small to mid-sized businesses.

the company in 1989 to Bowne when he solidified the investment to turn Old Baseline into New Baseline. Rob just wanted a new lease on life to continue honing and executing his vision, creating that visually revealing stock picker's tool that could be embraced by an increasing number of buy-side firms. Rob also endeavored to provide a terrific environment for a diverse workforce. And, he loved his workforce—his associates.

One of the key reasons we were able to maintain that familial sense was Rob's own ability to connect with everyone. He made it a point to know everyone's name and how they contributed to our overall mission. The Ops Team's monthly performance reviews were certainly one way for him to stay in touch with details, but he had a knack for knowing who these individuals were—as people—who worked tirelessly towards our overall goals. Lystra Archer, who ran Accounts Payable for us, joined Baseline in 1997 as a temp. She recently recalled her first week on the job. She was walking down the hallway and noticed Rob approaching her. Before she could utter a word, Rob exclaimed "Hi Lystra! How are you? How do you like working here?" That stunned Lystra, and caught her off guard. She was thinking of how to say hello, and was completely pre-empted by the master of names. "I was surprised at that, because here was the president. I came in as a little temp, and he was calling me by my first name. He made me feel so welcome. It was like I was just one of them." Lystra stayed with Baseline, and subsequently Thomson Reuters, for seventeen years. In a 2019 interview, Lystra said that Rob "was the most beautiful soul I have ever met."[49]

Similarly, Jyoti Dave Vyas, a member of our Quality Assurance team, was getting into the elevator in 1999 to go home during her first week on the job. We were still at 61 Broadway at the time, but had well over a hundred associates. As she relates, Rob jumped aboard before the doors could close. Jyoti decided that it was a good time to introduce herself. She said to Rob, "Hello. I work for you. I just joined the company."[50]

Rob replied, "I know. I know who you are. You joined Jenny Green's group."

Jenny ran the QA (quality assurance) team in New York for Baseline. According to Jyoti, "I was very impressed. He remembered people. After 9/11, when we all got together for the first time, he came in and hugged me and said 'So glad to have you here!'"[51] That was significant in that Jyoti was seven months pregnant on 9/11, and was one of a dozen Baseline colleagues who treacherously descended 77 flights together after the plane hit our building.

Ray McCombs, an account manager, shared a story from our World Trade Center days. He had just joined the sales team and while on the lunch line in 2000 he happened to chat with Rob. Rob kept referring to him as Roy. Not wanting to embarrass the CEO, Ray thought that discretion was the best approach and kept quiet. When Ray was back at his desk eating lunch, Rob popped his head into Ray's workspace. "Hey, Ray! I think I called you Roy, and I just want to apologize." Ray said it floored him, because he was impressed that Rob had it close with Roy.[52]

Rob's ability to connect with everyone went far beyond knowing names. Casual hallway conversations could be lengthy, and impressively could pick up right where they left off, whether it was a day later or three months removed. The manager of our Earnings Team in Data Integrity, Bernadette Ross, highlighted Rob's ability to be personable with just about everyone:

> He was always so absorbed in everything you had to say. Whether you met him in the corridor or in the canteen for a cup of coffee, he was so absorbed in your day, and then the conversation would twirl off into something about my family or what's happening in the world, or what I did back in Ireland. He was so intrigued, so interested in your life. He was so personable. It wasn't just about the company and making the company successful. It was his personal level, one on one, individually to each single person that made the difference.[53]

While Baseline clearly portrayed a warm and friendly environment, it also possessed standards of performance. Peter Haller, our manager of System Quality and Distribution who oversaw server deployment to clients, recently shared his feelings that Baseline was like "a shining city on a hill—the best company I ever worked for." When pushed to answer why, he explained:

Because it was led very well from the top. Because you felt it, and you felt it at each level that there was a demand to treat people well. There was a demand to make it a meritocracy. There was a demand that discussions ended up with information that then ended up with decisions, and that that was what it was all about. There was an awful lot of right stuff to go and emulate.[54]

Baseline was indeed a meritocracy. The immigrant, Bernadette Ross, declared that she had "a chip on [her] shoulder" when she arrived from Ireland. "I wanted to prove that an Irish immigrant girl could come to New York and not be a nanny or a waitress. I wanted to be on Wall Street." She soon learned that hard work was recognized and rewarded at Baseline. Bernadette rose quickly from an inexperienced data analyst into our management ranks. By 9/11, she commanded the entire Earnings Team within Data Integrity. She recently relayed that "I didn't have to struggle for years with a glass ceiling or anything over my head. Hard work and dedication was recognized pretty quickly at Baseline."[55]

All levels of managers at Baseline prided themselves on a cooperative and open office environment. Performance reviews were standardized and consistent, communication of our goals and results was ongoing, and our commitment to hiring top candidates was relentless. Outside sales recruiter, Mike Ehlers, who specializes in software and information sales roles, recently commented on the culture:

Recruiting for Baseline for many years gave me the chance to witness an amazing dynamic. I first observed it at Baseline, and have only truly seen it three or four times in my thirty-year career. Whenever a candidate progressed though the interview process, it was always observed that everyone they met at Baseline was on the same page—whether a salesperson or an account manager or a C-level executive. The candidate was given a consistent set of positive information about Baseline without any prodding. It was clear that it wasn't rehearsed, but actually a belief system. While it was a small thing, it was extraordinary. The effect it had on impressing candidates was real, and that translated to a high conversion rate—good for me, and ultimately good for Baseline.[56]

The Baseline culture was well-defined: focus on the customer, communicate often, hire diverse, team-oriented people, and treat them well. It also expected results and held people accountable for their assigned tasks. A large majority of people looked forward to coming to work, because it wasn't just seen as "work." It was fun. It was stimulating. It was rewarding. People were motivated to innovate. Empowered to care. The culture, using the words of the *Harvard Business Review* article, was certainly "pervasive, enduring, and implicit."[57]

CHAPTER 5

A DIFFICULT FLASHBACK

AS I WAS racing northward in that overcrowded taxi and away from the burning buildings on the morning of 9/11, the first bombing of the World Trade Center flashed before my eyes. It had occurred on February 26, 1993, and 20/20 hindsight was haunting me at that moment: *Why did we relocate there?*

I was reliving the day in early 1999 that the Baseline Ops Team visited the space and was discussing the subject. Baseline was then a subsidiary of Primark, and I was the head of sales and marketing. Our lease at 61 Broadway was soon to expire, and we were exploring options. The Port Authority of New York & New Jersey owned the World Trade Center and had spent time and money to better protect the property. Tank traps and other fortifications had been installed at the World Trade Center and surrounding areas in the years after 1993. As we walked around the unfinished 77th floor in early 1999, it was a discussion point.

The real estate agent had the Port Authority representative tout all the special changes made to prevent such attacks in the future and to make the two buildings safer from major catastrophes such as large-scale fires. They had spent more than $90 million on safety improvements.[58] Evacuation drills were held every six months, and Fire Wardens were recruited on each floor as volunteers to help educate all tenants' workers in the two towers. According to journalist Dennis Cauchon, in an article for *USA Today* on December 20, 2001, entitled "For Many on Sept. 11, Survival Was No Accident," the Port Authority had "added a second source of power for safety equipment, such as fire alarms, emergency lighting, and intercoms. It also built duplicate fire command posts, one in each tower." They additionally placed batteries in stairwell lights in case of power failure, and installed loudspeakers so that building management personnel could reach tenants in their offices or in the hallways.[59]

In addition to considering all those changes made by the Port Authority, the members of the Baseline Ops Team agreed that the other options we had considered were suboptimal. Fourteen Wall Street was simply too old for a technology-laden company, despite a swanky little restaurant at its summit. Two Broadway was off the beaten path for salespeople to come and go, and the Century 21 building on Church Street involved four small, non-contiguous floors. Further, we knew that cars or trucks with explosives couldn't get close to this refortified World Trade Center complex. It was unfathomable in 1999 to consider the reality that was facing us on this September day in 2001: that human beings would coordinate a terror plot where they could all somehow simultaneously avoid security detection and hijack four large commercial airliners from three different airports, while at the same time easily sacrifice their own lives for their sense of some greater purpose.

Yet, here I sat gazing out a taxi's window with a pit in my stomach and a sense of despair I had never experienced before. Despite all the reasons my colleagues and I had for moving to the World Trade Center, I could not escape one unrelenting feeling that morning: *I wish we had picked one of the other choices.*

It was a haunting flashback.

Based on reasonable decision making, Baseline moved to the World Trade Center in September 1999 from 61 Broadway, which was only blocks from the Towers themselves. Prior to our tour of the unfinished space in the WTC, Rob Patterson had been contacted by his favorite real estate broker with an attractive offer. The investor relations consulting company, Georgeson, which apparently had negotiated a sweetheart deal with the Port Authority, was being acquired by Shareholder Communications Corporation. As a result,

As the taxi with seven exasperated passengers raced northward along the New Jersey Turnpike at around 9:30 AM on the morning of 9/11, both towers of the World Trade Center were ablaze and in structural peril. The South Tower, home to Baseline, is the tower on the left. [Photo Credit: ROBERT GIROUX via Getty Images]

they were backing out of their contract, but had negotiated many leasehold improvements that would make our landing there seem like we had skipped a step in our corporate evolution. We would assume their lease.

Baseline was going to leave a Class B building at 61 Broadway and land in Class A space that would be fully decked out with new offices, conference rooms, state-of-the-art computer facilities, and mahogany trim. It seemed a bit of a stretch for us. We had been a no-frills entrepreneurial effort for the six years I had known Baseline. I was accustomed to ripped carpets and wires lying about the floors. No more. The new office became a source of pride for our associates. The general consensus was that our space had finally caught up to the success of the business and the tremendous culture that Rob had created.

Baseline secured approximately 58,000 square feet in that real estate transaction. We assumed Georgeson's lease and would not have to worry about primary space again until 2009. It was actually a terrific fit for our business, and very nicely accommodated our workflow.

Each floor of the WTC buildings was one square acre—200 feet by 200 feet. We took the entire 77th floor of Two World Trade Center representing 40,000 square feet (not all usable), plus an additional 18,000 square feet on the 78th floor. An internal escalator moved our associates between the two floors. Our reception area sat right off the 78th floor Sky Lobby. That made access from below easier for employees and guests. The WTC had 110 floors in each tower, which made it impractical to have banks of elevators that could serve each floor from the ground floor lobby. Instead, the design called for "Sky Lobbies." From the ground floor, riders could reach floors 2 through 43, as well as the pinnacle floors that offered access to the Windows on the World restaurant in the North Tower and an Observation Deck in the South Tower. However, floors 44-107 in each building would be reached via large express elevators to the Sky Lobbies on 44 and 78, where smaller elevators waited to take riders even higher. The elaborate elevator design placed 99 elevators in the South Tower alone. This design required many workers at the WTC to take two elevators to get to their jobs. Having our office entrance on floor 78 afforded our associates immediate access from the express elevator into our reception area, which was right off the 78th floor Sky Lobby. Only one elevator ride. It was so quick your ears would pop.

In addition to our reception area, the smaller space on 78 included a large conference room overlooking New York Harbor. It also housed the Finance and Accounting department, as well as Rob Patterson's office. One floor below, on 77, was where all the product and client action occurred. The square acre was perfect for the business. Sales, Marketing and Client Support occupied the southeast corner. Product Management and Consulting Services took the southwest corner, while Data Integrity sat in the northwest quadrant. Our Computer Room, Systems Distribution Lab, and our Technology staff occupied the northeast side. The layout greatly facilitated working relationships.

We moved in during September of 1999. At first, it was a bit intimidating working so high above the ground. The windows throughout the World Trade Center practically went from floor to ceiling, intensifying our awareness of the altitude. On that first day, a top performing sales rep, Ken Robinson, called me and asked if I could see the blimp. I looked out and about. "I don't see it, Ken."

Knowing that I had likely done exactly what he had done, he laughed and said, "No, look down!"

Wow! We were higher than the Fuji Film blimp circling lower Manhattan. My knees buckled a bit. The windows didn't help. It was easy to sense the height, although after a few weeks the altitude issue faded away for most of us.

On 9/11, the location and layout of our floors had a profound effect on the outcome of that day. The second plane to strike the World Trade Center, United 175, hit the south side of our building from floors 78 through 84. At the moment of impact, there were still four Baseline employees on 78, and twelve on 77. Horribly, the four souls on 78 did not make it, while the twelve individuals on 77 all survived but endured a harrowing journey as they desperately looked for ways out. On that day, the group of twelve on the 77th floor—amazingly—found each other amidst utter chaos, banded together, and frantically searched for a viable escape route. I credit the nurturing culture of Baseline, as well as the innate human spirit of the twelve that propelled them downward.

The four brave souls of Baseline on the 78th floor who lost their lives that day were Bob Levine, our CFO, Steven Weinberg, our controller, Jill Campbell, our executive assistant to Rob Patterson, and Ruth Lapin, a senior systems analyst. Each was a special person with God-given talents that both aided Baseline's advancement and made people smile. Each had established wonderful relationships within the company, and their close friends remain devastated to this day. It was a pleasure knowing each of them, and the firm benefitted greatly from their contributions.

As I sat, utterly stunned, in that northbound taxi on that infamous morning, my sentiments changed from anger over our selection of the World Trade Center to complete despair over what was my new reality. While I didn't yet know the extent of our losses, I tried to gather my thoughts. I mourned for all my friends who had likely just lost their lives. I mourned for our country to think such a tragedy could occur, regardless of the perpetrator. I mourned for the reaction that would beset Rob Patterson as he would undoubtedly witness the devastation from Florida. And, I mourned for the loss of a business that had required the sweat equity of so many people. I was enormously proud of our success, and knew our results had their foundation in the people, culture, and vision of Baseline. I realistically presumed I had just lost all three, and I couldn't get the image of Disney's little mouse out of my head.

CHAPTER 6

A VISION WITH EARS

THE PROMINENCE OF Mickey Mouse atop Rob Patterson's PC was more than symbolic. Rob adored the creative juices that Walt Disney poured into his business, as well as his non-conformity. Rob found Disney, the man, to be wholly inspirational. Walt was a pioneer. In 1928, he introduced sound for the first time in a motion picture with his animated movie, Steamboat Willie.[60] Rob saw his own colorful, graphic portrayal of financial ratios and growth statistics as similarly groundbreaking, albeit not as sociologically impactful. Disney's full-length motion pictures in stunning animated color, including *Snow White*, *Pinocchio*, and *Fantasia* set new standards in the industry. As the years passed, Rob would see each of his additional product enhancements as presenting Disney-like advancement. He prided himself on uniqueness.

Rob used the metaphor of an "Air Fleet" to visually describe his strategic vision. His presentation to the Bowne board of directors way back in 1989 incorporated an 11x17" sheet of paper with a sketch of several different sized airplanes on a tarmac. Each plane had a "B" emblazoned on the tail. Each aircraft represented the forecasted evolution of Baseline into a suite of products and services. There was the original valuation model, but there was also the much larger plane (New Baseline) along with other aircraft meant to depict future services, such as portfolio integration and macroeconomic analysis.

Rob once offered an opinion that the Air Fleet was akin to Disney World. He had planes depicting various services, while the fantastic park had areas of different themes (e.g., Main Street, Fantasyland, Frontierland, etc.). To this day, the irony of planes, Baseline, and the World Trade Center is a bit surreal to me.

From a product design perspective, Rob Patterson's vision was to provide the portfolio manager with an easy-to-use, colorful user interface that made researching stocks, or presenting results, both insightful and fun. Rob had three overriding criteria for his ongoing design ambitions. First, the display of results needed to be "visually revealing." In expounding upon this, Simon Chen shared that "Rob felt passionately that 'a picture is worth a thousand words,' and he would spend hours to ensure the right color, font, and placement of a letter was perfect in his eyes before he would sign off on a new design."[61] In other words, he wanted the graph or chart to quite easily reveal the insight behind a trend or sudden change in a stock's worthiness. Second, to the extent possible, the feature should be unique. Simon added that Rob "was relentless to look for uniqueness and would always opt for long-term sustainability over short-term quick wins." Third, the product could not be overly complex to operate. Rob drummed the notion of the KISS principle into every software development discussion. A perfect example of this occurred with one of the eventual airplanes on the Baseline tarmac—"Portfolio Snapshot." One of the lead software developers in Philadelphia, Bill DiPierre, shared how Rob would evaluate complexity:

> I remember on the Portfolio Snapshot feature we offered a few different visualizations. A couple of them were pie charts. I told Rob we could do a lot more sophisticated analyses pretty easily with some of the built-in functionality of Visual Basic. He said, "No! Our customers are portfolio managers who need something to show their clients. They are not looking for in-depth quant-style analysis, and their clients certainly are not." (It was) another lesson from Rob: know your customers, stick to your vision, and do not over-complicate with things that might seem cool, but are ultimately just noise.[62]

As Rob Patterson built New Baseline, he was acutely aware of the need to personalize information access. He knew all too well that a portfolio manager cared not only about what stocks he or she should own, but also how ownership of individual stocks fit within the overall portfolio and the weighting of a particular industry versus a portfolio manager's chosen benchmark. Rob chose to call all lists of stocks *Queues*. He had grabbed the term from an early assistant at Baseline. She was British, and when Rob one day talked about a list of stocks (i.e., ticker symbols[q]), she replied, "Oh, you mean the queue?" Rob was so enamored with the colloquialism that he decided that all lists of stocks within Baseline would, henceforth, be called Queues. Rob was keenly aware of branding implications and being unique. These lists of stocks, or Queues, might be the result of a screen—perhaps, two dozen or so stocks that made it through various filters. Alternatively, the Queue being examined by the user might be all 500 stocks in the S&P, or an industry's constituents. More often than not, a favorite Queue was a client's portfolio that had been uploaded in order to perform fundamental analysis, or to prepare for a customer presentation.

As for matching the non-conformity of Walt Disney, Rob was a rebel at heart and travelled to the beat of his own drum. In 1937, Walt quickly acquired land and commenced construction of the large Hyperion studio while his brother and partner, Roy, was away in Europe. I believe that was analogous to Rob's own desires to do whatever he felt was right regardless of pressures or involvement from above. Soon after 9/11, Baseline's parent company, Thomson, was insistent that we move into their headquarters at 195 Broadway in lower Manhattan. We had been acquired by Thomson in June of 2000 as a result of our previous parent, Primark, being purchased by Thomson. In the year following that acquisition, our success rate, and small size, afforded us a continuation of business-as-usual. However, 9/11 brought our existence front and center, as we tragically found ourselves without a home office.

Rob countered Thomson's insistence with alternate plans to move Baseline into space in midtown near the Empire State Building. Part of this activity was to have something in his pocket to reject the

---

q   Ticker Symbol. The one to four letter abbreviation for stocks based on the Exchange where they are traded. For example, C=Chrysler, IBM=International Business Machines, TSLA=Tesla.

Thomson edict, because 195 Broadway was immediately adjacent to Ground Zero. Rob fully understood that relocating there at that very moment would have been very difficult for Baseline associates. In my opinion, Thomson had a hard time understanding how the Baseline culture still existed and why we did not see ourselves as Thomson employees, as opposed to Baseline associates.

A compromise was ultimately reached with Thomson. Baseline would not, under any circumstances, enter into its own real estate transaction for midtown space. In exchange, Thomson would locate suitable space somewhere in New York in a Thomson-occupied building. In late January 2002, Baseline moved into decently appointed office space at 395 Hudson Street in the West Village[r] of Manhattan, where Thomson's Legal & Regulatory division had offices. It was over a mile from Ground Zero. Rob had effectively stood up to Thomson. In an interesting twist of fate, this new home for Baseline was only three blocks from where Rob Patterson and Dick Koontz of Bowne had met in the 1970s.

But in the meantime, after 9/11 and until January of 2002, Baseline operated out of its software development office in Philadelphia, with many associates commuting the 100 miles for four-day stints each week. It was not an easy time. I will delve more deeply into our reconstruction period in a later chapter.

Non-conformity was often a trump card that Rob would play. In the early years, when we were owned by Bowne, Rob asserted that "a once per year Board meeting will be sufficient," despite requests for more frequent updates. With Primark, he pushed back on frequent cash sweeps from our checking account, settling on monthly, then weekly as time marched on. As an additional example of Rob's defiance, after having been a subsidiary of Thomson for more than a year, he refused to tell them about our planned 20th anniversary celebration of Baseline's founding. The party took place on July 24, 2001 at the American Park restaurant in lower Manhattan without a single Thomson representative present. That fact caused quite a stir afterwards. However, because the details were discovered only three

---

r   West Village. A reference to the west end of Greenwich Village, which for years has been a center for artists, cafes, and low-rise apartment buildings. It sits in Manhattan between the downtown financial district and the midtown area of Times Square and Park Avenue.

days after 9/11, there was little consequence for the reeling staff of Baseline. Clearly, Rob enjoyed being the proverbial "fly in the ointment."

In addition to creativity and non-conformity, Rob also shared the pursuit of perfection with Walt Disney. During the making of *Snow White*, Disney became notorious for regaling against all attempts to make deadlines. Disney refused to compromise on quality for economic justifications. According to Eames Yates and Shana Lebowitz, in an article penned for *BusinessInsider*, Walt Disney's "exacting demands meant that production (of *Snow White*) moved at an excruciatingly slow pace."[63] Rob would often lament over design issues. For example, I recall him worrying deeply about which gradation of royal blue should be used as a backdrop for a chart. While the salesman in me could easily become frustrated over such deliberate study, I couldn't argue with the results he delivered. Rob was famous for uttering a phrase that I must have heard him recite over a hundred times: "No wine before its time!"

Being in charge of sales, it was natural for me and my sales force to want new product enhancements sooner rather than later. Clients and salespeople were always clamoring for updates on new features and capabilities. Rob and the product team were often pushed for delivery dates, but they would only offer a "window of likelihood," and that was never guaranteed. The only time Rob Patterson ever raised his voice at me in anger was related to a delivery date. In 1995, I had convinced him we should revisit going to the annual AIMR conference sponsored by the accrediting bureau behind the coveted CFA (Certified Financial Analyst). The American Institute for Management and Research (AIMR), known today as the CFA Institute, was holding their annual conference in Washington, DC the following May. In an effort to speed up product delivery, I attempted to slip a deadline into the mix to enable a conference announcement: "What a great thing it would be, Rob, if we released our new Windows platform at the Conference. We could make a big splash announcement!"

We had already begun our development effort on the conversion from our DOS-based platform, and April was the internally discussed, expected release date. Rob's response to my suggestion was quick and direct. "Don't you ever, ever push me to a date on such a release. No wine before its time. And, Ed, that's a public spectacle. We could be embarrassed in front of competitors and clients alike. No way! I am going to forget you even suggested that!"

While we did indeed return to the conference, we did not formally announce anything to do with Windows, although our sales reps on site certainly made known it was coming. The ensuing reality was that the new version was not ready at the time of the May 1996 show. We released our first Windows-based version of Baseline in September of that year.

While he oversaw the development of the user interface, Rob Patterson was able to strike an effective balance between the macro goals of the firm and the minute details of the product. According to sales executive Chris Tresse, "His ability to agonize over the user interface and make it elegant, and at the same time powerful, was the secret sauce. He had incredible attention to detail, and the minutiae, but could also bring [his focus] back to the marketplace and the big picture. He bounced back and forth effectively."[64]

Armed with Disney-like creativity, non-conformity, and a perfectionist bent, Rob Patterson pursued his dream with undaunted passion. From the outset, Rob was fixated on his vision of creating the perfect mousetrap (pun intended). And in that pursuit, he saw two aspects of his business as unilaterally critical: customers, and employees. As his small business started to grow, he tirelessly drummed the notion of customer service into his associates. The Client was Job One. Period. Rob would constantly say, "Service them well, and they will stay with you."

Through the years, Baseline would experience a fairly constant 95 percent renewal rate among its clients. As a business with a recurring revenue model, the high retention rate was critical in building year-over-year success. We would unleash sales executives on "new logo" sales, while relying on account managers and the Client Support department to lock in customer satisfaction. Rob Patterson was a stickler for outstanding customer service.

Rob's vision ensured that Baseline became a customer-centric culture. It was not a software development culture, although it might easily have morphed into one given the nature of the business. It was not a data culture. No one at Baseline ever uttered the words "content is king." We believed that the application, which integrated disparate sources of content for the purpose of aiding customer workflow, was the real king. Baseline was also not a sales culture, although Rob did recognize, from his own pounding of the pavement in the early years, that salespeople make a B2B (business-to-business) service grow. But even the salespeople were acutely aware of Rob's predilection with outstanding customer service. He often recited that "it doesn't matter who you sell if they are not satisfied and do not renew the annual contract." He referred to customer service as the "second sale."

In 2003, the commitment to outstanding customer service was officially validated in a measurable way. As one of many products within the Thomson organization, Baseline was put to the test. A survey was conducted to measure customer satisfaction with many individual brand names under the Thomson umbrella. Nearly 20,000 surveys were mailed to users of Thomson products in the Investment Management industry. My recollection is that approximately 1,500 were returned completed. The surveys asked the users to rate more than a dozen separate products on four different scales: Account Management, Help Desk, Product Training, and Overall Satisfaction. The results were displayed on four key slides presented to senior Thomson management. I proudly recall that Baseline stood at #1 for Account Management, Help Desk, and Overall Satisfaction. In the case of Product Training, Baseline was still in an enviable position at #2.

While Rob placed the clients on the top pedestal, and enjoined his associates to do the same, his real enjoyment—his passion—came from creative expression with the product. He relished retreating into his Madison, New Jersey basement to advance the product specs, and then traveling to Philadelphia to see those ideas through to completion.

It is not far-fetched to state that, despite his corporate beginnings as a CPA and then as a senior executive with Standard & Poor's, Rob Patterson was not a corporate guy. He eschewed corporate politics and the brassy, well-manicured executives of corporate America. He often poked fun at the stereotypical executive. That perspective came front and center one day in December of 1997. It was the day of our holiday lunch party, and I was bringing my wife and daughters into Manhattan for the gathering. A mishap with a local car service that left me stranded at Newark Airport one chilly December night had afforded me the opportunity to receive a complimentary trip. I opted to treat my family to the car service, rather than putting them on the local train circuit on the way in to the holiday luncheon. However, the night before the office event I received a phone call from the car service informing me that only a stretch limo was available, but the charge would still remain at zero. Well, I knew my three ladies would greatly enjoy that. My reaction was "Bring it on!"

The next day, as the limousine approached lower Broadway where Baseline was then located, I asked the driver to drop us off a few blocks away from the office. I knew how Rob viewed such displays of grandeur. "Nonsense," said the driver. "I can take you right there!"

"No, drop us here," I barked. Well, before I could counter his insistence, we were smack dab in front of 61 Broadway, and who did I see on the steps of the building? Rob Patterson and Helen Byrne. *Oh great*, I thought to myself. *Just what I wanted to avoid!*

Well, upon exiting the white, elongated vehicle of high bourgeoisie status, and getting my ladies onto the curb, I couldn't help notice that Rob and Helen were doubled over in laughter.

Oh good, I thought. *They're preoccupied with a joke and hopefully didn't pay much attention.* When I got upstairs, I made my way to Rob's office. Upon seeing me he broke into uncontrollable laughter.

"Okay, chief, what's so funny?"

"Oh Ed, I saw this white stretch limo coming down Broadway and said to Helen 'Hey, get a load of this thing. Let's wait a second, and see what kind of asshole gets out of it!'"

It was a very funny moment for both of us, although I probably counted to three before laughing. His amusement was that one of his own would actually board such a vehicle, but he understood when I told him the story. To me it was good he saw it as funny. Perhaps Rob knew at that moment that his firm may have had a bit more "corporate" leanings than he might have thought. One thing was for sure—thank goodness that occurred in the fifth year of my tenure and not in the first.

As mentioned, Rob was definitely not your average "corporate" stereotype. He was much more closely aligned with the portrait of a classic inventor. While he greatly desired success, he did not seek any kind of public persona. In fact, he tended to easily fall back into a very private existence. While Rob was perfectly able to be engaging and direct when necessary, he preferred to sit quietly and invent new ways to portray complex data to enhance our clients' portfolio management workflow. That detailed focus, bolstered by the team he hired to execute his vision, paved the way for great corporate success.

While Rob always had a product vision, he also adopted an organizational vision that further drove customer satisfaction. Let me simply call it the "Three T's." Rob was particularly struck by an article in the *Corporate Board* magazine in 1994 entitled "Teamwork, Technology and Talent."[65] He was quick to tell me and Simon Chen that "this embodies much of what I stand for." The article was written by Bill Koch, the 1992 winner of the America's Cup race, and the founder and CEO of the Oxbow Group, an energy development holding company. Koch sports three degrees from MIT in Cambridge, Massachusetts, which include a PhD in Chemical Engineering.[66]

Bill Koch's article on the Three T's put forth the notion that managing a company is like captaining an America's Cup sailing team. His principle was that in each case, whether at the helm of an enterprise or a sailing vessel, everything starts with people. And, with respect to people, it is ultra-critical to hire team-oriented individuals. According to Koch, the "T3 approach strives to balance the best of human emotion, skill and intelligence."[67] The article's title was a listing of three key items in priority order. Teamwork. Technology. Talent.

In his article, Bill Koch foremost emphasized the need to approach everything from a team perspective. Similar to the Accenture requirement for an "equal" culture, Koch stated that "all members of an organization must be seen as equally important, because every job must be done well, and every job counts."[68] He also implored simple but achievable goals that can be monitored and that everyone can see. Koch was clear: "The glue that holds a team together is a clear focus."[69] Rob's vision, his wall of clients, his Town Halls, and his non-hierarchical philosophy mirrored this advice perfectly.

Koch then advised that a team with clear goals should utilize technology for competitive advantage. He implored the reader to think outside the box and suggested that traditional rules of thumb can be ignored in favor of simply looking at what makes products better. According to Koch, "to win, you have to combine art and science."[70] If you follow the Baseline narrative, Rob's artistic vision of new ways to portray data combined with Simon's technological implementation was exactly such a path.

Regarding talent, Rob would often say "no assholes, please" to describe our firm's recruiting activity. What he was referring to, beyond the obvious elimination of troublemakers, was the oft-used phrase of the 1990s, namely "the war on talent." It is often thought that the global consulting firm McKinsey coined the phrase in that decade.[71] Rob was pleased to think that competitors might simply be grabbing "talent" without regard for their team orientation. Koch's article talked plainly about hiring people with the right attitude over those candidates who possessed overachieving attributes who might describe how they alone conquered the world. Such overachieving attributes might include, for example, signing the largest deal within their company, or achieving the highest score on a computer programming aptitude test. However, those candidates sometimes came with a "me first" perspective.

The Baseline Ops Team coached our managers to examine how candidates described their past success. Regarding an applicant, were their responses all about them, alone, or was there a sense of team achievement and pride in their answers? Further, we employed a personality profile service from Caliper, a Princeton, New Jersey firm that helped affirm a person's likely affinity for a team environment. While

it was initially used at Baseline to identify sales characteristics among sales candidates, it was eventually deployed to all serious employment candidates across the firm.

At the aforementioned 20th celebration in July 2001, we presented Rob with a silver plate from Tiffany's. On it was inscribed the three interlocking T's, along with Rob's name, the dates referring to the twenty years, and our appreciation for all his efforts. We attempted to hang a pair of Mickey Mouse ears off the left T, but Tiffany's balked at that idea. They claimed it was bordering on trademark infringement on Disney's rights. *Oh brother! Okay, no ears.* It still went over well.

Rob Patterson speaking at the 20th anniversary celebration of his original founding of Baseline. The evening of July 24, 2001 was a momentous occasion, yet it would be followed just weeks later by a far more momentous, and horrific, event.

As I stood at the microphone as the emcee that evening, I looked around at quite a spectacle. While it was an associates-only gathering, Rob's wife, Mickey, and daughter, Molly, stood with proud smiles on their faces. The 215 associates, including those who flew in from San Francisco and those who rode Amtrak up from Philadelphia, beamed with pride as Rob received his silver plate from all of us. We then showed a short video hailing Baseline as *Simply the Best* to the sound of Tina Turner. The band then took over, and we danced the night away—Rob and Mickey especially. As I watched them dance, I had to wonder if it was mere chance that Rob had married a lady named Mickey.

I was very proud of what Rob had created, and what we all had contributed by way of establishing best practices, hiring the right people, and establishing a terrific camaraderie among the staff. Rob's deep product vision had become a reality—honed by an enduring culture, three T's, and a mouse with big ears.

And, by the time that momentous evening rolled around, I had recently enjoyed the opportunity to check the Bucket List box that simply read "Meet Wife."

CHAPTER 7

MANAGING GROWTH

MANY OF THE people who toasted Rob Patterson on that special anniversary evening probably didn't fully comprehend the toils and troubles that he had weathered over those twenty years. In fact, I could only conjure up visions of difficulty, dread, and despair that Rob had likely endured. I was very fortunate to have met Rob and joined him, but only after he had already established a business with legs. One thing was certain. Everyone at the celebration that night had their jobs and career-enriching experiences at Baseline due to Rob's perseverance in the 1980s, and his constant resolve to succeed.

The turning point for Baseline may have been a hot August afternoon way back in the summer of 1988. Rob stood on a corner in Shawnee Mission, Kansas waiting for a bus. He was in between sales calls. He was still pushing his valuation model via the monthly booklet service. The temperature was over 100, and he could sense the beads of sweat rolling down his legs inside his pinstriped suit.

Where did I go wrong? he murmured to himself, exasperated.

He often shared that story with his teammates. It was perhaps the defining moment of Rob's first iteration of Baseline. He returned to New York after a mediocre sales trip with great resolve to fix the situation—to either create the Baseline "Air Fleet" or else call it a day. Keep in mind, this was the former CFO of Standard & Poor's hocking his wares across the Plains States—by public transportation no less. That experience would be tough enough for a veteran salesperson, let alone someone who had achieved success as a senior executive at a well-respected firm like S&P. Rob's patience, combined with his incredible drive and lack of ego, made him the perfect entrepreneur. He was clearly patient, having waded through the weeds for the first ten years, but his drive to succeed kept him going. And, his complete lack of concern for his personal reputation in the marketplace allowed him to keep marching forward. Many others would have quit without the ego-stroking events of promotions and positive publicity. Rob had received none of those things for nearly ten years as he tried to grow the initial version of Baseline. Upon returning from that gut-checking moment in Kansas, Rob pulled himself up by the proverbial bootstraps, outlined his plan, and made that fateful call to Dick Koontz of Bowne.

One of the greatest aspects about Rob Patterson was that he always understood the need to listen to customers. In the early days, that meant personally getting on planes, trains, and automobiles. But, he was also smart enough to hire salespeople even in the early years to help drive meetings, close business, and generate feedback. Rob believed his path to success included keeping close tabs on the market's pulse. It also involved having the salespeople report directly to him.

During my initial lunch meeting with Rob in 1991, he may have misconstrued my intent. He quite plainly, and resolutely, told me he did not need any sales management help. That was okay with me. I just wanted to know what made him tick, and to determine what had attracted my top salesperson, Chris Tresse, to his firm. Besides, I wasn't ready to jettison CompuServe for what was still a tiny firm, Baseline, but our respective agendas would clearly change soon thereafter. It was obvious my world was changing as CompuServe was shifting its emphasis, but what was it that made Rob Patterson change his mind over the next two years to feel he might benefit from a sales manager? The answer was his success. New Baseline was getting tremendous traction and his personal involvement in the sales process didn't scale. Rob's primary challenge in his first decade at Baseline was establishing the right formula for success. In his second decade at the helm, his chief test would be managing the growth that was beyond his expectations.

From the release of New Baseline in mid-1991 through the end of 1992, his customer count rose from that historical plateau of 40 to over 125. Suddenly, more clients were bringing feedback to the table, and Rob's ears were hearing about product enhancement ideas much more frequently from the sales team. As the business grew, Rob also learned about territory disputes and commission debates. Naturally, he saw some aspects of the sales management process as distracting; the requirements of that role robbed him of the time he needed to focus on product design and corporate strategy. The management of demanding, and at times vocal, salespeople was a challenge for him. After joining Rob in 1993, I soon came to realize that one of the reasons he hired me was to put space between himself and potential confrontations. Within six months on the job, and specifically after flying to and from Los Angeles in one 24-hour period to comfort a frustrated client and support an exasperated sales executive, Rob said, "Thanks for handling that, Ed. You know, I think your appointment has added five years to my life!"

With a smile I thought: *Whatever it takes!*

From the day I joined Baseline my task was to scale the sales team. That meant better defining the roles within the sales organization, hiring the right people, examining the sales compensation plan, implementing a better communications system, and improving our customer service acumen. It also meant embracing the culture and the existing sales staff. Rob had done a marvelous job recruiting veterans of the financial industry as well as younger, energetic talent. My arrival on the scene was challenging for the sales team. The veterans wanted no one in between Rob and themselves, but with Baseline's growth, Rob found himself getting more and more fervent feedback from his reps.

While Rob didn't mince words with me about the Philadelphia software development office, he rarely, if ever, publicly divulged a key reason why he placed his software developers ninety miles away. From the get-go, he continually reminded me of his concern of co-locating salespeople with developers. "Ed, ever hear of the Feature of the Week Club?" That was his response the first time I asked him why the programming staff was in Philadelphia. He simply let me know that his opinion of sales feedback was that it was primarily driven by a salesperson's next sale or recently lost sale. He felt that with a sale on the line, the average salesperson would not think strategically about the product from a big picture perspective. While he loved and coveted the fire-in-the-belly tenacity of his sales reps, the last thing he wanted was to turn that energy loose on eager, impressionable programmers in casual hallway conversations. Rob was specific about the product specs he would create, and wanted no one to alter the thinking of those individuals responsible for reading and implementing his designs. The salesman in me rejected the notion, but I understood his perspective. Rob enjoyed hearing the market's feedback, and greatly valued sales input. He just wanted that input to be amassed over time and properly prioritized. However, once the input had been gathered and debate had concluded, no changes (i.e., no "scope creep") regarding the next software version would be permitted.

The distance between New York and Philadelphia increased Rob's confidence in that regard. However, there is a delicate balance to strike between keeping developers on their appointed mission and making sure that market feedback is critically gathered—if not for the imminent software release, then surely for all subsequent releases. As Rob's head of sales, it was my job to constructively channel my team's input to him, while keeping Simon Chen always in touch with our collective feedback. I also made sure that our most senior sales reps always had access to Rob, and, of course, Rob was equally interested in their viewpoints (albeit occasionally and without verve). Time and success would show that the ninety-mile distance from Philadelphia didn't hurt the business. From a 20/20 hindsight perspective, Rob's adamancy regarding the physical separation of the two groups proved to be utterly fateful. Without that second office, there would have been little chance to resurrect the business following the events of 9/11.

As far as the senior reps perceiving me as a bottleneck preventing their access to Rob, the flack actually started on the first day of my employment. It was August 1993. Soon after Rob pulled my newly minted business cards back across the table, a senior salesperson took me aside and said, "I have no idea why he hired you. We don't need any head of sales. We are nearly tapped out at 200 clients: 300 will be tops." However, Chris Tresse, who had left me to join Baseline two years earlier, wasn't echoing that doomsday scenario. Further, a reality check now shows that we surpassed 1,000 clients in 2002. I simply chalked up the affront to a top sales rep not wanting anyone in between his market feedback and the founder and product guru. It was worth a shot to scare me off. To that end, another challenge to my authority occurred a few weeks later. On a visit to Deutsche

Bank, I noticed our account manager was not comfortable with me in the meeting. I got those "stop talking" glances whenever I chimed in.

After the meeting, I constructively challenged her as to what was wrong. Her response: "Look. I don't need any sales manager telling me what to do. I'm fine on my own. We were all fine before you came!"

When I simply said I wasn't here to critique but actually learn from her, and through that education become better able to represent her needs to Rob, she relaxed.

"Oh, okay. Thanks. Well, I probably shouldn't tell you this, but I've been told by [a senior rep] to ignore everything you say."

I chalked that one up to classic Sales Management 101 stuff. Funny now, looking back on it. A bit tense at the time.

Over the years, the sales team benefitted from having veterans of the industry on the staff. I, too, benefitted. I learned as much from them as I did from the customers, and that says a lot because I visited clients in twenty-one cities in my initial year on the job. Those valuable veterans on the sales team included:

- A former executive of the Bank of Boston;
- An equities trader from a broker/dealer;
- A senior product marketing executive from Standard & Poor's;
- An entrepreneur who had built a business measuring product shelf-life in retail stores, and selling that data to securities analysts.

These top sales executives had fun doing their jobs at Baseline. They applied their market knowledge to help prospects and customers quickly understand how newly enhanced Baseline could help them pick stocks, maximize their portfolio's return, or simply aid them in marketing their services to clientele. But their fun was not my aim. I had to ensure the growth of the firm continued while keeping them engaged. Learning from them, yet leaving them alone. Ensuring they continued to earn good commissions, yet not tipping the scales of future territory alignments too heavily in their favor. Keeping them focused more on new business than customer support, and making sure they could reach Rob without any stranglehold.

As time went on, the sales team continued to supply meaningful input to the product development process on an ongoing basis. Quarterly sales meetings became the most effective sessions for idea sharing and debate. They were, at times, boisterous, but constructive. Danna McCormick, one of our sales leaders, offered her take on the meetings:

> I loved the fact that when we did disagree on what would be in the product, there was banter. Sometimes, fierce banter. But, he [Rob] wouldn't shut it down. He would listen. It was all being absorbed. He was very much a consensus person, and would say "let's hear from everybody around the table." Maybe that's why he was so successful, because it wasn't "his way or the highway." It was genuine committee input.[72]

While Rob graciously accepted input from his sales team, albeit in an orderly fashion, the feedback had to parallel his overall vision for it to be acted upon. Rob's Harvard classmate, Ogden White, said, "Part of Rob's discipline was that we all stayed on message." Oggie shared that Rob would occasionally steer him away from certain ideas, such as adding a specific new source of information to the product that Rob didn't consider mainstream to the mission. The buck clearly stopped with Rob Patterson.

Rob's control of the product also translated into a very efficient software development cycle. Sales executive Chris Tresse, shared his view:

> The feedback loop from the end user in the marketplace, back through the sales channel to Rob, and then to the development group wasn't a painfully long process. Product development was pretty swift. It was energizing. There was a high bandwidth connection between the end user, product development, and Rob overseeing all that. He was the boss. The president and CEO was in charge of the next [software] release. Things just got done.[73]

By 1994, the business had an overall framework that was very scalable. We ushered in new roles in the sales force. Sales managers, the internal name for hunters, would focus on new business, while account managers would focus on customer satisfaction, account growth, and renewals. And, never the twain shall meet. Previously, it had been everyone's job to do both. Rarely did anyone accomplish both well, so we made it official. One could not do both. It was a variation on the old hunter/gatherer model.

We also introduced a new sales compensation plan with the help of DG McDermott Associates out of Red Bank, New Jersey. The existing comp plan was fine for a small static firm, but a growth firm's success would quickly turn account management into a cash annuity under the old plan. We left handsome, entrepreneurial commission rates in place for larger sales and implemented lower rates for tiny relationship deals. Accounts were classified as Platinum, Gold, Silver, or Bronze, and first year sales commissions varied depending on the level of the client. Commissions had previously been at a fixed rate for all contracts. Bronze accounts, our tiniest relationships, cancelled 30 percent of the time after Year One, while new Gold accounts cancelled only 10 percent of the time. Therefore, we would welcome the Bronze accounts, but pay a smaller stipend for bringing them on board. And, in the same vein, we would further incentivize the sales of larger, more stable accounts. Additionally, Bronze accounts made up the lion's share of our inbound inquiries, which meant that there was technically less sales work to be done. This fact strengthened the argument for less of a payout. The stratification of accounts helped steer new business efforts and customer service activity. The account demarcations were based on total annual revenue under contract. Prior to this stratification, it was noted that account managers would often spend equal amounts of time with all their clients, regardless of size or growth opportunities. The new plan helped steer activity.

As we grew, we added to our ranks of salespeople through our own network of contacts, and also through the efforts of talented recruiters like Mike Ehlers, Jim Riely, and Bob Bernikow. Since we had financial industry expertise in-house, we began to look for more sales-oriented people versus deep Wall Street knowledge. This strategy contrasted with Rob's initial method, which called for deeper asset management expertise among his sales ranks. Early on, it was smart of Rob to utilize professionals with industry contacts who would need little training to understand the value proposition. The new recruitment approach was based on the fact that we had learned what sales pitches worked. We simply needed to train smart, energetic, competitive individuals. The new slant on recruitment was also easier and more cost effective. To assist us, we employed the personality profile service from the Caliper Corporation that Rob had earlier brought on board. According to Caliper, the profile "is an objective assessment that accurately measures an individual's personality characteristics and individual motivations in order to predict on-the-job behaviors and potential."[74] While the profile itself was not a knock-out variable, it often helped steer our thinking toward new business or account management. Upon my arrival, I was extremely skeptical of this personality profile which I had also taken as a requisite for my job. It wasn't until I matched my own observations about individuals with their particular Caliper profiles that I became a believer. I could write volumes on this subject. Caliper was founded by the late Herb Greenberg, a blind entrepreneur from the Princeton, New Jersey area. He authored two best-selling books, including *Succeed on Your Own Terms*. Mr. Greenberg passed away in 2016,[75] and Caliper was subsequently sold in 2019 to PSI Services LLC—a global company that specializes in online employee assessment tools and consulting services.[76]

The Caliper Profile, created in the 1960s, was designed to help ferret out the right attributes for sales success, looking for things like empathy (the ability to read others), ego drive (the desire to persuade others), abstract reasoning (the ability to think outside the box), and the mix of aggressiveness and assertiveness. These are only a few variables, but with years of experience of seeing positive correlations, the Ops Team at Baseline came to greatly appreciate its value. By 2000, we were using it across the company for all positions. The Caliper Profile didn't say that people were either good or bad, or right or wrong for the company. More often, it was about establishing what role would best fit a candidate, regardless of what their résumé touted. According to Herb Greenberg, "the real winners in the world are those people who are in positions that really let them play to their strengths."[77] And, that's what Caliper helped us achieve—placing the right people in the right roles.

The Caliper Profile, however, was only consulted when all other facets of a proper recruitment process pointed to a potential match with a candidate. Upon a person's hire into Baseline, and regardless of their Caliper feedback, they were quickly indoctrinated into the most important concept at Baseline—that the clients were Job One.

In my opinion, these changes that involved differentiating sales roles, properly incentivizing sales activity, and aiding our recruitment process helped drive average annual revenue per client. In a recurring revenue model like Baseline, it's not only important to maximize the annual renewal rate, but to also drive average client spend. Think of it this way: if you can convince a client to take on more users or additional services, they are, by default, happy with your service and will automatically renew. For an account manager to seek new revenue streams from a client, it was a foregone conclusion that they would first need to ensure customer satisfaction. Over the years, while client retention always hovered around 95 percent, the average annual spend per client rose from $26,000 in 1992 to over $53,000 in 2002.

To aid the sales team in its pursuit of revenue growth, the company additionally focused on better information systems regarding clients, a step-up in customer service efforts, and identifying best practice standards among the sales team itself. The first action we took in this regard was to increase common knowledge about the clients all throughout the firm. We implemented a communications system utilizing Lotus Notes to replace an outdated method of tracking client activity. In 1993, the sales team was using a CRM (Customer Relationship Management system) called Act![s] It was a DOS-based product that each salesperson used religiously, but it was a standalone offering. Each person kept track of his or her own account notes on laptops, but nothing was integrated or searchable. At month's end, the administrative staff would collect each salesperson's Act! notes for the month and a very large pile of paper would be circulated for review. Even if Rob read it all, there was much "garbage in, garbage out" inside that large pile. It was very inefficient.

While working at CompuServe, I had met a consultant by the name of Rich Mancini. Rich was representing Lotus Notes to the financial community at that time. Notes was the second major product to come

---

s   Act! A customer relationship management software application which is used to keep track of client and prospect details in a single database.

out of the Lotus Corporation, which had first released the global spreadsheet phenomenon of Lotus 1-2-3. Lotus Notes was one of the first "groupware"[t] products available in the market. It offered email as a key feature, but also offered a "powerful, programmable backend that let you create databases and workspaces for collaborative work, contact management, information sharing, and communication."[78]

In 1993, I introduced Rich Mancini to our newly hired technical manager, Jonathan Weinberg. Jonathan was (and is) an incredibly talented technology maven. Simon Chen, our chief product and technology officer, had hired Jonathan who was doing consulting work for Donaldson, Lufkin, & Jenrette at that time. Jonathan quickly went to work networking all our PCs, and improving upon our internal storage capacity. Adding a cross-company communications tool like Lotus Notes was a logical segue. Jonathan jumped in with both feet, along with direction from Simon, to analyze and implement Lotus Notes. According to Simon, "we built this whole client support system using Lotus Notes. Nothing in the market was good enough. What was unique about Notes was that it was a replication system. It wasn't always on."[79] That meant that the decision to utilize Lotus Notes saved hardware resources. Servers only needed to be connected to users when a "replication" was performed. It wasn't long before Jonathan was our VP of Technology and a member of the Ops Team.

In 1994, we converted Act! to Lotus Notes and had a real-time, integrated CRM with searchable notes. What a boost that was to me. It became immensely easier to be able to cross reference any account, or even search for the prevalence of a product enhancement request. With the help of the Finance Department under Bob Levine, we created an account overview page for each client with key statistics including total account billing, renewal date, and the number of contracted users. All correspondence with each user, whether by phone or in person, was also catalogued within this archival capability. Another added benefit of the Notes platform was that it brought email to Baseline. Having had it as a daily tool since 1982 at CompuServe, I went through serious email withdrawal during my first year at Baseline.

Another key technical achievement from a customer service standpoint involved closely tracking usage at each client. Our remote

---

t   Groupware. Software designed to facilitate collective working by a number of different users.

servers at client sites would be updated nightly with key market data, but would also send data back to us regarding usage statistics on every machine the previous day. We would append that data to a rolling history. We called it our "Keystroke Counter." It gave us the ability to see detailed usage data at any client—how often they used the product, by whom, and when. But, territory reports sorted by account manager were not initially available, and printouts only depicted one client per page. Based on input from the Sales team, Simon's staff created a daily territory report that listed all accounts (by account manager) and showed 1-, 7-, 30- and 90-day client usage averages. The one-page report listed one client per line in the new territory report. It helped streamline client support activity very quickly, and was a critical resource for account managers each morning. It enabled us to quickly detect falling or rising usage at any one client and, for that matter, to determine which clients were targets for re-training.

Speaking of client support, we were able to better align that department with the Sales team in 1995 due to this newly integrated Lotus platform. I was fortunate to meet Carl Boudakian of Value Line who brought us knowledge of the markets, a great service work ethic, and a friendly demeanor that fit well with our culture. He was hired as the manager of the Client Support department which oversaw the Help Desk, and our Systems Distribution Lab that fulfilled remote server deliveries and repair. He would eventually join the Ops Team as director of Marketing and Client Support.

As we grew and needed more support-oriented field personnel (as opposed to sales) we added a new position to the sales team: National Account Consultants (NACs). They were "bookend" roles. They helped train the hundreds of users at our largest (Platinum) accounts, and when in the field would visit the nearest smallest (Bronze) accounts. Our account managers had been crying for help to train their largest user bases. The account managers were completely capable of doing the work, but the training was drawing on their time needed to sell more services to existing accounts, and to network with our clients' decision makers. Carl's Client Support team became a marvelous feeder to the NAC program which, in and of itself, became a feeder for future account managers. The greatest aspect of Carl's value to Baseline was his process-driven mentality. Every task and responsibility had clearly laid out instructions, and training was extremely thorough.

In my opinion, this attention to detail across the entire spectrum of customer service activities was the reason the aforementioned Thomson Financial survey found Baseline to be its most satisfying product in the eyes of its buy-side customers.

Just as Rob Patterson needed help in 1993 to scale the sales force, I, too, started to feel stretched as we entered 1997. Our revenue had already grown to $13 million, our product line had widened considerably, and the sales force had grown to nearly twenty people— all reporting to me. I set out to find a smart, client-focused manager who was knowledgeable in financial markets, but also affable and collaborative. We were still entrepreneurial and moving at the speed of sound, which meant things were always in a state of flux, with occasional sonic booms. I needed a sales lieutenant who would be flexible with our evolving product, culture, and sales personalities. I was fortunate to locate Nick Webb with the help of an executive recruiter, Ed Kaminski. The search process took much of 1997. I had reviewed dozens of résumés and had four finalists among whom Nick shined brightly. Nick Webb started in January of 1998, having come to us from the econometric analysis firm of DRI. To create a smooth transition for Nick, and to improve his chances for success, I divided the sales force into two groups. Initially, he managed one half of the group while I handled the other half. This enabled me to witness Nick's skills firsthand without turning over the entire sales force to a new manager. It also provided Nick with additional career growth, if things went well.

Immediately, Nick went about working on standards. Best practices were something that Nick harped on, and his contributions quickly became obvious. First, he recommended we run our entire team through a sales skills program. After some interviewing we settled on Communispond.[u] It was a crash course form of boot camp for professional salespeople. The aim of the two-day course, which was customized for Baseline, was to create common language, and drill basics into the entire team including appearance, punctuality, and meeting agenda management. It also focused on the art of Socratic

---

u   Communispond. A firm engaged in providing corporate training in the areas of presentation, writing, sales and leadership skills.

Selling[v] skills, which was the primary goal of the course. According to Communispond, sales productivity can be enhanced through the art of dialogue. That requires asking clients the right open-ended questions to determine pain points, and properly relating needs to product benefits. One of the biggest fans of the program was Ogden White, the classmate of Rob Patterson who had joined Baseline twelve years earlier in 1986. He had been long aware that selling was not about demonstrating features, but of solving problems and improving upon the client's process for the purpose of making money or avoiding losses. According to Ogden, the program helped reinforce that, when in client meetings, "you didn't first talk about the product. You sought to learn about the client's process. You aimed to get the client to open up about what their problems were or what their aspirations were, by asking the right questions. Only then would we try and find a solution to those problems with the product."[80] Lectures, role plays, and video feedback ruled the two-day Communispond program. At its conclusion, we had a new level of expectations amongst the sales staff—one of standards. Or, one might say a "baseline."

Nick took that notion of standards to a higher level. In future sales meetings (two contiguous days per quarter), we devoted time to "Best Practice Discovery" whereby associates of like-duties (e.g., sales execs, account managers, field trainers) would meet for a couple of hours and discuss new ways of making their roles more efficient. For the sales execs, that might constitute new ways of researching a prospect's investment strategy. For the account managers, it might be discussing strategies to locate additional users across a client's local area network installation. Or, for the field trainers (NACs), it might involve creative ways to maximize the number of people trained per hour.

Another reason for greatly expanding the sales team and its leadership was a product breakthrough that occurred in 1997 with the release of Spreadsheet Link. Over time, feedback from the sales team was building that clients were looking, more and more often, to do their own custom analyses. Microsoft's Excel was being installed everywhere within the asset management community. While Baseline provided a full set of visual representations of a portfolio manager's daily analyses, we were nonetheless a finite set of tools with fixed

v   Socratic Selling. Refers to the practice of asking open-ended questions to reveal more information about the customer and their challenges.

graphical displays. Excel greatly expanded our customers' curiosity and gave them a platform to explore their own ideas. Customers relied on Baseline for standard daily analyses, but they also started to request more and more tools that were, frankly, beyond the production ability of our relatively small development staff.

The number of enhancement requests was increasing exponentially. Simultaneously, Excel was driving the advancement of creative ideas by clients. Getting Rob to explore, and ultimately agree to, a product evolution that would go beyond his controlled environment was very difficult. He often cited the black-box nature of the Bloomberg Terminal as analogous to his solution. The financial information terminal created by Michael Bloomberg offered access to a wide array of real-time and historical data on global markets and companies. While its capabilities differed from Baseline, it was similar in that it sold for a flat price per terminal/user, and its capabilities were fixed. In 1995, neither Baseline nor Bloomberg offered an open architecture. Despite Rob's reticence, Simon Chen and I began a deliberate campaign to sell him on this additional need. We started by diligently sharing how an "Excel add-in" could leverage the burgeoning Excel phenomenon, greatly expand our capabilities in a shorter time period, and lessen the load on our development team over the long run.

One of the opportunities to close the gap on our differing perspectives was my introduction of Ron Perez to Rob and Simon in 1995. Ron was the president of a small financial information service called Infovest. I had met Ron in 1992 through my own networking campaign as I eyed a possible departure from CompuServe back then. Ron welcomed me to his firm's offices in New Jersey that year, and we agreed to meet shortly thereafter at the SIA[w] Conference in New York where my CompuServe team was showcasing a utility called the "Data Engine for Excel." (It received mixed results in the market.)

Unfortunately, CompuServe was devoid of portfolio management expertise as well as the data points and graphical objects that Baseline owned. It was at that 1992 conference that Ron and I discovered that we were on the same page regarding the general need for Excel compatibility in the market. The challenge was that we were both at

---

w   SIA. Securities Industry Association. Today, it is known as SIFMA (the Securities
    Industry and Financial Markets Association) having merged with the Bond Market
    Association in 2006.

the wrong place at the wrong time. Soon thereafter, I joined Baseline and Ron's firm was acquired by Track Data. In 1995, as I was recruiting Carl Boudakian from Value Line to run Client Support, I knew that Carl and Ron had previously worked together at InfoVest. In a dual agenda meeting, I introduced Ron to Rob Patterson. We were interested in his feedback about Carl, but we quickly dangled the idea of Spreadsheet Link being compatible with his skills and interests.

Culturally, Ron Perez was a perfect fit for Baseline. After meeting with Simon Chen, he was hired and immediately starting working on our Excel project with our Philadelphia team and a new hire of theirs by the name of Ed Bazzelle. We released Spreadsheet Link in 1997. We wanted a better name for the product, but in the end we decided that it had to be subservient to our core product, and, as such, should be viewed as utilitarian without a jazzy name. By 2002, over 65 percent of all our customers were using this add-on product that came with an additional charge.

While Spreadsheet Link helped us extend the application footprint of Baseline, another new capability, known as Portfolio Link, became the ultimate glue for customer loyalty. While Spreadsheet Link was a front-office, end-user tool, Portfolio Link was a back-end utility that made the front-end application of core Baseline more valuable. You may recall that Rob Patterson had colloquially dubbed any list of stocks to be a Queue. Over time, we added the ability to also allow the update of the number of shares held by our client's customers. This permitted the easy analysis of the fundamental characteristics of private client portfolios. As a result, the number of proprietary queues that sat on client servers grew exponentially. With this growth, clients began clamoring for better organization of their proprietary queues within Baseline, and also started asking for a streamlined process to get their client portfolios into Baseline. Manual uploads were increasingly unpopular, and untenable. This new request was simply due to the success of Baseline offering its clients the ability to analyze the fundamental characteristics of client portfolios.

As a result, Portfolio Link was born. It was a utility spawned by the increased frequency of manual uploads of portfolios by clients, and thus the need to do so in an automated fashion. It was an automated handshake between Baseline and a variety of third-party portfolio accounting systems. Examples included Advent, SEI, PAM and others. Ron Perez spearheaded this effort as well, which led to an interface being built for over fifteen different accounting packages. "The idea that customers could upload (daily and automatically) their holdings (not just ticker symbols, but shares) was a game changer," said Ron. One of our first beta sites was Fred Alger Management, conveniently co-housed in the World Trade Center. Ron recently recalled the beta install. "I remember when I installed it at Fred Alger for Selai Khoo, a senior portfolio manager who reported to David Alger. I worked with Dan Chung, who was then just an analyst, to get it set up on Selai's PC. It took over three hours to get it just right, with Selai coming by every so often to check on our progress."[81] Once Portfolio Link was established at a client, daily handshakes and transfers of identified portfolios became automatic. In assisting Fred Alger Management with the installation, Ron was aided technically by John Tabako, a key member of our technical support team. It was John's frequent visits in the days following beta installation that afforded him the opportunity to befriend Fred Alger's network manager, Mike Howell. On 9/11, the firm and people of Fred Alger, which was headquartered on the 103rd floor of the North Tower, were decimated. Mike Howell, Selai Khoo, and David Alger all lost their lives that day. As of this writing, Dan Chung is the CEO and Chief Investment Officer of Fred Alger Management.

The two different Links were indeed the "missing" links. They enabled far greater research and analysis without requiring Baseline to program every desired feature, and brought customized analysis regarding private portfolios to each and every user. To enable effective support of both the sales force and customers, Ron Perez built a new group of application consultants to oversee the deployment of both Spreadsheet Link and Portfolio Link. The team eventually grew to twenty consultants led by managers Brendan Minter and Mark McNasby. The release of Spreadsheet Link, and subsequently Portfolio Link, clearly helped Baseline avoid the traditional product life-cycle flattening effect.

To better service all of North America, we greatly expanded our west coast presence in 1997. Chris Tresse led the charge. Due to the Primark acquisition of Baseline earlier that year we were able to offer a new sister company, San Francisco-based Vestek, an east coast sales office. They reciprocated with space in their headquarters at the

By 1999, the Ops Team had grown to eleven members, but it had been stalwartly anchored for many years by Rob Patterson's earliest management hires—Helen Byrne and Simon Chen. This photograph was taken at a 2016 Ops Team reunion.

foot of Market Street near the Embarcadero. Chris's right-hand man in that west coast endeavor was Larry Hirschhorn, who had been a successful account manager with us in New York. They relocated west together. Within a couple of years, we had a staff of ten including sales executives, account managers, a national account consultant, and two Spreadsheet Link specialists. The dot-com explosion of 2000 wooed Chris away, and while I was sorry he left our employ, we were able to plug Larry right into that top role. As you will recall, Chris joined Baseline in 1991 when he left my employ at CompuServe, while Larry was instrumental on 9/11 as a communications hub for the entire firm.

Regarding our west coast success, it is important to note that our two transplanted associates were greatly aided by the successful pioneering sales efforts of Danna McCormick. Danna was our original West Coast sales executive. In the early days, she enjoyed working the west coast from New York. According to Danna, "pre-9/11, business travel was easy and fun and glamorous. I had no problem exploring these cities and dining by myself. I loved it. I was young; it was pre-9/11."[82] However, handling a territory from New York that spanned Denver to Honolulu and San Diego to Vancouver, eventually became untenable, given her level of success. In 1992, she requested a relocation to the Bay Area to help fuel revenue growth on the West Coast. As a lone soldier, Danna closed dozens of west coast clients including top-drawer institutional names like Wells Fargo, Trust Company of the West, and PIMCO. Chris and Larry inherited a good base of business upon which to build a team. When she married in 1995, Danna moved back east and continued her sales magic for us in the mid-Atlantic area.

By 9/11, Baseline's overall revenue run rate had soared to over $45 million, and it had a national following which was almost cult-like.

Nearly 20 percent of new account sign-ups were due to users landing at a new firm and demanding Baseline as a condition of employment. In late 1999, when Rob asked me to take the reins as COO, it was easy to hand the entire sales force over to Nick Webb. The sales team had grown to over 35 professionals, but we had also divided the country into four regions—each with its own sales manager. This success made it easy to toast Rob and celebrate his twenty years of perseverance and success.

Only six weeks after that marvelous 20th Anniversary celebration, the walls came crashing down. The events of September 11 provided a stark contrast to the euphoria and love felt on the evening of July 24. Despite the utter horror that rained down on the people of Baseline, I witnessed the company's strong culture take center stage. To this day I remain deeply saddened over the loss of our friends, but I credit the fortitude and caring attitudes of our associates for the lives saved that day.

CHAPTER 8

GROUND ZERO

IT WAS SUPPOSED to be like any other day at Baseline. At 8:46 AM, on the morning of September 11, 2001, early risers like Ron Perez and Nick Webb were already deeply engaged in the details of the day. They were sitting at their desks on the 77th floor of Two World Trade Center (the South Tower). Both of their offices were on the same south side of the building as mine. They looked out upon New York Harbor.

Suddenly, from out of nowhere, Ron felt an incredible jolt. His instant reaction was to utter, "What the hell was that?" When revisiting his experience with me, he recalled that "the whole building shook. Then I saw a big chunk of building fly by my office in flames and down towards Liberty Street below. It might have been eight to ten feet long." Ron added that "a barrage of paper then went by. Paper everywhere. It was like a ticker-tape parade. I was convinced a bomb had likely gone off above me in our building."

Two of Ron's consultants instantly appeared at his door inquiring as to the reason for the jarring sensation. Ron's reply was quick, "I don't know what that was, but I think we should leave." Ron had no idea that the other tower had just been struck.[83] The North Tower was not visible from his vantage point.

What my colleagues were experiencing was American Airlines Flight 11 slamming into the North Tower at approximately 465 mph, carrying 92 people and 10,000 gallons of jet fuel.[84] According to journalist Dennis Cauchon, "The jet exploded into the 93rd through 98th floors . . . with a force equal to 480,000 pounds of TNT."[85] The impact was so severe that many in our building were convinced the blast occurred in our tower.

Ron immediately went up along the west side of our floor towards the Data Integrity department and instructed anyone he met to start getting out. Before ascending to the Sky Lobby on 78 where he could catch an express elevator, Ron had a brief thought that he should grab a few things from his office. However, he quickly assured himself that his absence would not be long in duration, and so left all his materials behind.

Nick Webb also felt the jolt and he, too, saw the large cloud of paper waft mysteriously past his window. *This can't be good*, he thought. He immediately left his southeast corner office and also started telling people to leave. He quickly headed north along the east side of the 77th floor covering the sales and client support areas. With several people in tow, Nick ascended our internal escalator and made a beeline for the express elevators on the 78th floor Sky Lobby. As Nick tells it, there was not yet an abundance of people waiting for those elevators.[86]

Shock and curiosity ruled the moment, and the truth regarding the first impact and its location were not yet fully known. As minutes rolled on, many people started to determine that the best course of action was to leave the building. According to Nick, the elevators on 78 were still relatively open when he jumped aboard. However, all the people working above us had to first take elevators down to the 78th floor Sky Lobby, and then switch to the larger express elevators to descend to ground level. As that ensued, the Sky Lobby right outside Baseline's reception area filled up very quickly. By that time, however, Nick and company had already safely reached the first floor and had exited the building.

When Ron Perez reached the Sky Lobby he found it "was already like a sardine can—packed like a crowded subway." He had already seen Nick in the hallway herding his troops out. However, by the time Ron arrived at the Sky Lobby, there was little room to maneuver. This was only a minute or so after Nick had left the scene with several associates.

When the first hijacked jet hit the North Tower, there was no mistaking the sudden tremor for anything but something very ominous. Though both Ron and Nick recalled the sense that perhaps a bomb had gone off in our building, neither presumed the problem stemmed from the other tower, nor could they possibly conceive of the act that had just been perpetrated. According to Ron, "A plane was the furthest thing from my mind." In fact, it wouldn't be until Ron hitched a ride across the George Washington Bridge in the back of a bread truck hours later that he would be given rough details about two hijacked planes and other fallout from around the country.[87]

One of our volunteer fire wardens at Baseline was Alfredo Guzman, a manager in Data Integrity. His office was in the northwest quadrant of the building, which had a good view of the North Tower. Along with Building Management, Alfredo periodically led scheduled fire drills. They were mandatory. He was very process-oriented and knew what to do. That morning, he quickly assessed that fire was raging on both the southern and eastern sides of our sister tower. His training prompted him to act. Alfredo recalled the moment. "At that point, we needed to evacuate the 77th floor and go upstairs to 78 to see what's going on. I wasn't sure that an alarm had even gone off in our building, but I knew at that point what we needed to do."[88] Simon Chen was the other fire warden for the floor. According to Alfredo, the two of them grabbed their fire-warden whistles, checked the bathrooms, and had everyone go up to the 78th floor to await further instruction. That instruction was to come via the emergency "red phone" that hung on the wall in the public 78th floor Sky Lobby. However, upon getting to the designated emergency phone, a communications breakdown occurred. Alfredo recalled the situation: "I picked up the red phone. I'm holding onto the red phone listening for further instructions, and there's no instructions. No one ever answered the phone. No instructions were ever given."[89]

Alfredo was getting frustrated. "I have people looking at me wondering what they should do." With the receiver in his ear, he began to motion to these people to just leave. The World Trade Center's communications protocol was clearly overmatched by the magnitude of this emergency. There was no message to be received per the designated plan.

Meanwhile, Ron Perez was determining his own exit strategy. In the claustrophobic Sky Lobby with him were a few of his consultants as well as network manager John Tabako and sales team members Courtney Timms and Henry D'Atri. Alfredo was also there holding the red emergency phone while countless other associates stood by. Ron eyed a stairwell on the southern side (our side) of the Sky Lobby. He realized there could be a long wait for an elevator in that crowded lobby, and he also recalled something from past fire drills that suggested elevators should be avoided during emergencies.

As John Tabako heard Alfredo's inability to reach anyone via the red phone, something inside of him just said, *Forget this. . . . Get to the stairwell and walk out!*[90] He didn't even wait for Alfredo's signal. Ron Perez, Henry D'Atri, and John Tabako quickly encouraged the team to join them on the stairs. According to Ron, Courtney gave a look of major incredulity to the suggestion they would walk down 78 floors. But the group acquiesced and down the stairs they went. It was an exit route known internally as Stairwell C. It was in the southern end of the building's core. Henry described the scene as crowded but not chaotic. "It was two people per stair, and as they flowed past, you had to almost wait for a little opening to get in. It was pretty much that if you didn't jump in, there was always somebody coming. They weren't pushing or shoving. No one was running. It flowed very well."[91] Courtney, John, and some others had gone on ahead and had put some distance between themselves and the two managers. Henry and Ron continued down together.

Ron estimates that it was only a few flights down when they heard an announcement that our building was safe and secure. From Henry's recollection, the announcement was from a woman who sounded a "little unsure . . . She didn't sound official." Henry recalled that the announcement sounded something like:

> *Due to a smoke condition in One World Trade, that building is being evacuated. There is no reason to evacuate Two World Trade at this time. Tower Two is secure. If you want to leave, you can; if you want to stay, you can return to your office.*[92]

According to Henry, "She really left it to whatever everybody wanted to do." As for his reaction, Henry was seriously considering going back to his office. However, Ron Perez intervened. In a recent conversation, Henry empathically said, "I pretty much owe Ron my life!" He added:

> I was a very much get-back-to-work person. I was just giving up my territory to an account manager and was going to have a trip to Wisconsin with her, and needed to plan for it. When the announcement from the building occurred, a lot of people turned around and were heading back to their offices. I was pretty much going to turn around and head back. But Ron said, "You know it may not be safe, there's still a lot of fuel smell in the air, and it may not have been an accident." So, I just followed Ron's lead and we kept going. But I think if I had my druthers, since I had work to do, I was going to go back.[93]

In recalling the announcement and his own decision process, network manager John Tabako recently shared his thoughts at that moment. "I felt we were in a non-natural structure . . . I did not feel confident." John then turned to the team with him at that point and said, "We're going to stick to our plan . . . let's get out of here. We'll make sure everything's okay . . . and then we'll come back up. I don't care if it takes two hours, but we're going to do this." John also shared that immediately after the announcement the stairs opened up greatly, and they were able to accelerate their descent.[94]

While that group was making an orderly exit, our dutiful fire warden Alfredo finally hung up the red phone when the building-wide announcement was made over the loudspeakers. He quickly returned to the 77th floor via Baseline's internal escalator to see who had returned to their desks, or needed assistance. Simultaneously, Carl Boudakian, our director of Marketing and Client Support, was also scanning the 77th floor. Carl said he and other managers "decided to go to our respective areas to make sure that nobody else was on the floor before we left ourselves."[95]

The time between the first and second planes to hit the World Trade Center towers was only 16½ minutes. Ron Perez described it as "a very compressed timeline, although at the time it seemed to last forever."[96] There really wasn't much time to react. However, there was no reasonable expectation that a second disaster was imminent. Why would there have been? Further, most people in both towers after the initial impact were very much in the dark as to what had actually occurred.

While Nick and Ron decided to get out, other managers decided to stay put. They included technology leaders Simon Chen and Jonathan Weinberg, along with financial leaders Bob Levine and Steve Weinberg (no relation). In defense of their staying in the building was that famous (or infamous) announcement throughout the South Tower that the building was secure and that it was "okay" to remain in the building for safety reasons.[97]

At the same time, New York's police and fire departments were stepping into high gear. Just prior to 9:00 AM, realizing that what was confronting them was unprecedented, police chief Joseph Esposito issued an order for a "Level 4 Mobilization" to the World Trade Center. It called for 1,000 NYPD officers to immediately dispatch to the site. Level 4 is the highest level of alert for the NYPD. The FDNY was also signaling its highest alert—a Five Alarm response. In fact, the FDNY launched the biggest response in its history "drawing resources from across (New York's) five boroughs. Thousands of other first responders and government officials arrived on the scene as well, from local, state, and federal agencies."[98] Firefighters began to ascend the North Tower while EMT professionals set up triage centers, and police officers helped establish evacuation routes while keeping onlookers away from harm. All of this response, at that moment, was due to just one of the buildings being struck.

Up on our floors in the South Tower, confusion and trepidation reigned. Our finance and accounting team worked on the 78th floor directly behind our reception area. Myles Donnelly, who ran our Accounts Receivable effort and was a recent arrival from Northern Ireland, wasted no time dealing with the situation. When he felt the initial jolt, he quickly jumped down to 77 and surveyed the situation. He saw the holes in the North Tower and immediately proceeded back up to his boss's office, that of Steve Weinberg, and said, "Having some experience with some trouble over in Northern Ireland, this doesn't look good. I think we should leave."[99] Meanwhile, Brian Branco, the software consultant, had been with Steve that morning. An upgrade to the SBT accounting system was well underway and there was extra work to do. They both had arrived early that morning. As the first plane hit the North Tower, Brian recalled "feeling a little vibration and seeing paper fly by two minutes later." He was sitting in the complete opposite corner from the activity in the other tower and clearly unaware of the horrible details. Brian quickly developed a plan to go down to the main lobby on the first floor in order to "see what was going on, and then to come back up."[100] When Myles arrived with more detailed information, Brian and Steve Weinberg decided to join Myles and all grab an elevator.

On their way out, Bob Levine, our CFO, caught sight of them and asked, "Where are you guys going?"

Brian said, "Downstairs. C'mon!" Bob declined.

But as soon as Brian, Myles, and Steve headed toward the elevators, Steve uttered words that still resonate today. He told them, "I forgot something in my office. I'll see you downstairs." Brian and Myles then proceeded to the Sky Lobby elevators which were on the same floor.[101]

As Brian traveled quickly through the reception area, he spotted our dutiful executive assistant, Jill Campbell, on the phone. She, too, was likely trying to determine a plan of action given the conflicting aspects of fleeing associates and reassuring guidance from the building. As Brian exited our tall glass doors, he found the Sky Lobby just as Ron Perez described: crowded. A sea of humanity pushing and pulling on one another as elevator doors opened and closed. Brian recalls being pushed into one of the cars by several ladies who had locked arms and weren't going down without each other. Myles jumped aboard an adjacent elevator. They each made it down to the main lobby of the South Tower just minutes before it was hit. Police then quickly forced them out of the building and away from the fires and chaos surrounding the North Tower. Clearly, Brian was given no chance to "go back up" as he had envisioned. Of course, no one knew what was yet to come for people still inside the South Tower.[102]

On the northern side of the 77th floor in our South Tower, the data and technology groups had a better view of the proceedings over in One World Trade Center—the North Tower. Jonathan Weinberg, our VP of Technology, was just outside his office talking with a colleague when the first plane hit the North Tower. As far as Jonathan was concerned there wasn't any question as to which building had suffered a traumatic event. Unlike his colleagues on the south side of our floor, or those up on 78, he could see the gaping holes on the eastern and southern façades of the North Tower. According to Jonathan, word eventually filtered around his side of the office that a plane had hit the other building, but no one knew whether it was a commercial airliner or a Cessna-sized craft. He also believed that it was simply a horrible accident. Jonathan recalls knowing that some people were deciding to leave our building, but he decided to stay. He believed it was an accident and that he was in no immediate danger. Also, as head of technology for a financial information firm, Jonathan figured "it might be days or weeks before we could return to our offices, so there were many things I needed to attend to so that operations could be moved to an off-site location if necessary."[103]

Simon Chen, our chief product and technology officer, reflected back on the morning. He said, "Peering out my office window, which had an unobstructed view of the east side of One World Trade Center, I could see a gash with bright orange fire and black smoke across a few floors of that building just a few floors above ours."[104]

Florence Jones, our contracts administrator, added that the other tower "looked like a tuna can . . . like somebody took a really bad screwdriver or can opener and opened up the building. It was awful."[105] At their closest point, the two towers were only about 120 feet apart. The tragic views would have been dramatic. In fact, sensory perception wasn't limited to just sight. Florence was burned by simply touching one of our windows. "The glass was that hot that I burned the center of my hand."[106]

During her visit to the 78th floor as part of the initial evacuation process, Florence met Lou Williams and Bob Rasmussen from our sister company, Vestek. We had provided Vestek with approximately a dozen workstations (offices and cubicles) on the 78th floor to house their eastern sales and support office. Lou and Bob were members of the sales team and were in town for just one day for a scheduled Vestek national sales meeting. They were utilizing our main conference room for the day. Williams had flown up the night before from his home in New Orleans and planned to return again that evening or the following day. Similarly, Rasmussen, a Vestek sales rep from Chicago, had also arrived for the meeting.

Florence engaged the two gentlemen in a quick chat. She discovered that their sales meeting had already been scuttled and most of the attendees had quickly left the building about the time of Nick Webb's escape. However, Lou and Bob must have decided it was better to stay put rather than fight the throngs for a place in the sardine can of a lobby. Sadly, that was the last time anyone saw them alive. On an additional sad note, another Vestek employee was also lost that day. Tom Hynes, who had just joined their customer service team the previous month, also perished. Details are few regarding his whereabouts, but he was never heard from again. Clearly, he was somewhere within the confines of the World Trade Center complex during that fateful hour.

While visiting with Vestek's out-of-town guests on the 78th floor, Florence also encountered her friend, Jill Campbell. Jill was one of our sharpest administrators and served as Rob Patterson's executive assistant. She was also one of the most pleasant individuals at Baseline. That morning she was manning the phones for the company and serving as our receptionist. Florence noted that the phones were ringing off the wall. She asked Jill, "Why are you sitting here?"

The dutiful Jill Campbell responded, "Well, I have to man the phones."[107] Jill was incredibly conscientious.

Florence was never one to mince words. "You don't have to man no freakin' phones. Flip the thing off and leave!" Florence believed that the only people calling in that morning were other employees checking on "what was going on?"[108]

One of Jill's closest friends at Baseline was Lorena Munoz-Udik. From Lorena's standpoint, Jill's actions that morning were completely understandable. Jill was the daughter of a New York City firefighter. Lorena believes that Jill "was one of those people that would stay and wait to make sure that everybody was out before she would leave. It was in her nature. It's just who she was."[109]

As precious minutes ticked away, Florence entered the escalator to return down to 77. She looked back and overheard our CFO, Bob Levine, telling Jill that it was okay to leave. According to Florence, "They were right at the front door. Jill exited the glass doors into the Sky Lobby while Bob returned to his office."[110]

One of the Baseline associates that had also returned to the 77th floor after exploring the Sky Lobby was Jyoti Dave Vyas. You may recall that name from an earlier chapter as someone who commented on Rob Patterson's miraculous command of first names. Jyoti was a software engineer on our Quality Assurance team. On 9/11, she was seven months pregnant and clearly in need of assistance. While up on the 78th floor, she made the quick decision that returning to her desk on 77 was far safer than pushing and pulling with the crowd in the Sky Lobby in hopes of grabbing an elevator ride. Her manager, Rob Rothman, was aware of her situation and kept an eye on her. He, too, had decided to stay. Again, there was no indication that our building, the South Tower, was in imminent peril. Clearly, the building-wide announcement gave comfort to those remaining inside.

After his own trip up to 78, Jonathan Weinberg returned to his office on 77 and quickly called his wife and mother to let them know he was okay and to assure them it was the other building that was affected. Jonathan had a most gruesome view of the initial incident from his office, which had the entire North Tower in plain sight. Jonathan describes a very heart-wrenching scene over in that tower: "Smoke was pouring out, and while I don't recall seeing much in the way of flames, it was clear that there was a raging fire going on inside the building."[111] While on the phone with his mom, he witnessed people come to a large hole in the eastern façade of the North Tower and jump to their deaths. Utterly helpless were the poor souls above him in the other building. According to Jonathan:

> I saw a man and a woman come to the window, hold hands and jump. The feeling in my stomach is still there. It must have been unbelievably hot—to perceive no other way out. They certainly had no way out to make such a choice. And, of course, they couldn't have known that the buildings would eventually collapse. I watched them jump and then quickly turned away knowing their fate below. I preferred not to watch.[112]

At the same time, Simon Chen, whose office was adjacent to Jonathan's, was on the phone with his dad and then his wife. "I yelled and shouted trying to describe what was happening outside my window . . . people were losing their lives right in front of my eyes!"[113] Mesmerized by what he was also seeing, Alfredo Guzman shared that he looked up and saw "a man flying. Nothing wrong with him. Nothing wrong with him. I could see his white shirt. I could see his tie. There was nothing wrong with this guy. No blood. No guts. Nothing. He wasn't hurt or anything. He just jumped."[114] Alfredo witnessed this from our northwest corner conference room. It was the closest point to our sister tower. He was with fellow associates Allan Unger, James Magalong, and Eric Thompson. According to James, Eric brought the gruesome reality of falling bodies to their attention by screaming, "Oh my God! Oh my God! Oh my God!"[115] That experience stunned them all. At that moment, they all realized it was time to leave the building. But time was not on their side.

As mentioned, Florence had personally felt the heat of the fire from the North Tower on our window glass in the South Tower. The temperature at the point of impact inside the North Tower was reported to approach 1,800 degrees Fahrenheit.[116] According to a September 2002 article in *USA Today*, entitled "Desperation Forces a Horrific Decision," approximately 200 people jumped to their death that day. Journalists Dennis Cauchon and Martha Moore reported that "those jumping appeared to make a conscious choice to die by falling rather than from smoke, heat or fire. Ultimately, they were choosing not whether to die, but how to die."[117] The North Tower's three stairwells were unfortunately all destroyed, trapping everyone above the impact zone and leaving very little alternative. My associates had a clear view of the horror. From their perch on the 77th floor of our building (the South Tower), they were observing people on the 93rd through 98th floors of the North Tower.

According to Jonathan, "It's hard to express what I felt at that point, because I can only describe it as shock. Your mind cannot really comprehend what is happening—almost an overload state. You see it with your eyes, but you are somehow mentally detached from it at the same time." To this day, Jonathan admits that the visual of watching people jump is "one memory that is seared into my brain that will never leave."[118]

As this emotional maelstrom was occurring right in front of my friends' eyes, some were planning an immediate evacuation while others felt safe having a bird's-eye view from a comfortable distance. "We had no idea the clock was ticking at that point," said Jonathan Weinberg, who had chosen to stay. Alfredo Guzman, who was planning on leaving with Carl, Florence, and others said, "It seemed like we were safe. We didn't realize that we were in the most dangerous place in the world at that very moment."[119]

Down on the streets below, sales head Nick Webb had crossed Church Street and had met up with Bernadette "Bernie" Ross, the Irish immigrant who had progressed to a manager in the Data Integrity group. The two associates were chatting right near Liberty Plaza Park, now called Zuccotti Park, when they heard a loud roar above. By the time they looked skyward, the second hijacked plane had already disappeared into our building—the South Tower. It was traveling at 590 mph.[120] It was 9:03 AM. They witnessed a massive explosion. Glass, debris, fire, and smoke jettisoned out from the floors that were our offices. Glass shards rained down upon them. Nick's left arm received several cuts and abrasions from the falling glass. He and Bernie became separated and Nick decided to retreat towards Broadway to the east. He found a small convenience store whose workers helped bandage him up. He then returned to watch the tragedy unfold and to determine whether his next steps would be to aid people or seek a way home.[121]

As Bernie sought an escape route, she was struck with the horrible reality that terror attacks were now commonplace in the world. It was the second "act of terror" that she had encountered in less than a week. Just days before, she and her husband were in Ireland visiting friends and family. One afternoon, as they had approached the City of Derry, which is an island city on the west coast of Northern Ireland, both bridges that grant access to the city were closed due to bomb threats. Bernie and her husband sat in traffic for over four hours awaiting the "all clear" signal. At the moment she and Nick Webb had separated on New York's streets, she recalled the words that she had just recently shared with her husband while sitting motionless in that car: "These poor people have to live with these terror threats all the time." Less than a week later, while moving quickly away from the World Trade Center, Bernie realized that she and her soon-to-be fellow American citizens were also very much a part of the global terror phenomenon. Three days later, on September 14, Bernadette Ross officially became an American citizen.[122]

Of all the Baseline associates who viewed the events from afar, Kellie Kenny was easily the one most affected. As a member of Nick Webb's sales team, Kellie had a personal connection to both towers as she saw the entire tragedy unfold. That morning, she found herself stuck in traffic on the New Jersey Turnpike Extension that hovers over

Jersey City on its approach to the Holland Tunnel. She had a full view of the Twin Towers and witnessed both planes hit the buildings. Kellie began her career at Cantor Fitzgerald, a fixed income trading company headquartered on the upper floors of the North Tower. Admitted into their training program in 1994, she spent three years at Cantor making dozens of friends as well as meeting her future husband. On the morning of 9/11, Kellie was already with Baseline for three years and was a successful account manager. As she inched closer to the Holland Tunnel, she found herself in the unenviable position of sitting in full view of the horrific events which impacted her most directly. She witnessed two planes fly directly into the two floors occupied by her two beloved companies. Cantor Fitzgerald and Baseline were gravely affected. In fact, Cantor lost more employees that day than any other company. Fortunately, Kellie's husband had left Cantor just three months prior to 9/11.[123]

Kellie, who was always one of the first salespeople into the office every day, was inordinately delayed on September 11 due to her husband having a business meeting in Morristown, New Jersey that morning. In an unusual sequence of events, Kellie dropped him off as she commuted in from western New Jersey. That detour placed Kellie in heavier traffic, and she was not at her desk at her usual arrival time of 8:00 AM.[124] Kellie recently shared her memory of her inching along the turnpike's extension:

> I was listening to *The Howard Stern Show* on the radio, and I looked up and saw a plane crash into the North Tower. I saw the first plane go in. I proceeded to immediately start calling my friends at Cantor. I was frantically calling them, but I couldn't get through to them. Thank the Lord that I didn't! I hung up and immediately called my husband [Brian], who also had worked at Cantor. We met there. I left a message. "Hey, Brian, a plane just hit the building. I've been calling the guys and I haven't been able to get through to them." And, as I was leaving him that message, I'm watching the second plane come. I don't remember exactly what I said [in that message], but he deleted it, saying "that no one should ever hear that message again."

I just watched it. I watched it come in. I watched it
approach. I'm sitting on the side of the highway just
watching it.[125]

Understandably, emotions were high during my recent discussion
with Kellie. Nearly twenty years have passed as of this writing,
but the sensations and flashbacks are still raw and vivid for many
people. She recently shared that after the second plane hit, she found
herself on the shoulder of the road in a hysterical state. At that point,
she knew she had likely lost a lot of friends. In the coming weeks,
Kellie would sadly attend many funerals, but personal strength and
resilience would keep her moving forward.

As Kellie Kenny sat in her car by the side of the road on the morning
of 9/11, a horrific scene of death and destruction was unfolding inside
both towers. By the time the plane struck our building between the
78th and 84th floors, Ron and Henry had made it down the staircase to
about the 62nd floor. Ron said, "The impact knocked a few folks to the
ground right on the stairs. I almost fell over like I had buckled." He
described two ladies screaming at the top of their lungs. He believes
that it was due to fear and not injury. He asked everyone there to
remain calm. Everyone froze. The group of people had no idea if what
had happened was above or below them. They were totally unaware of
what was happening in the outside world. Ron said the stairwell was
"rocking back and forth. You could feel it and even see it."[126]

Henry, who was still with Ron, said, "I was walking along the
outside wall, and had my hand on the railing. The next thing I knew,
I was on lying on the stairs holding onto the railing. I looked around
and saw everybody on the ground. It was like a car accident where
you're driving along and get sideswiped. You don't even see it coming.
People quickly began helping others off the ground, but the stairway
was swinging like a Ferris Wheel . . . like when you're on the top and
it stops, and you're just rocking."[127]

Twenty-seven floors below Ron and Henry, the fleet-footed group
with John Tabako had made good progress outdistancing the two
managers. John said they, too, felt a mighty jolt, although far fewer
people fell as the building's sway factor was smaller on the lower floors.

Soon after the impact, Ron recalls the stairwell becoming extremely
hot. He described perspiring like he was in a sauna. In retrospect, Ron

believes that the stairwell ran parallel to the southernmost elevator shaft and that fire from the impact must have descended the shaft and they were feeling its presence. Ron was most likely correct. The two impacts sent massive fireballs down many of the elevator shafts. Jay Jonas, Captain of Ladder Company 6, FDNY, was one of the first responders to enter the main lobby of the North Tower—the first building hit. In relaying Jay's experience, author Mitchell Zuckoff wrote:

> Jay saw slabs of stonework and marble tile smashed on the floor, enormous windows shattered from their frames, and a bank of elevators destroyed by fireballs that had blown down the shafts and incinerated everything in their path. At a melted desk beside the elevator sat the charred remains of a security guard, his badge still visible on his burned jacket, his body fused to his chair. Other firefighters stepped over piles of debris in the lobby that they only later realized were human remains.[128]

These two plane crashes were not isolated events limited only to the top floors. The explosions were so powerful, and so hot, that even the first-floor lobbies and the streets below were not safe from danger. Parts of American Flight 11 tore through the North Tower and rained down on the streets, and the right engine of United Flight 175 went right through the South Tower. It exited the South Tower and landed 1,500 feet north of the building at the corner of Murray and Church Streets. The right landing gear also jettisoned through the tower.[129]

As several Baseline associates were witnessing or experiencing the impact from a "relatively" safe distance, Jonathan, Simon, and others were right there at the impact zone. Ground Zero was right inside our beloved Baseline. Personally, I cannot fathom the utter horror, noise, and destruction that confronted my friends that morning.

As the plane struck our building at 9:03 AM, Jonathan had just hung up the phone with his mom. He was getting ready to join Simon, Carl, and Florence in a deliberate 77-floor descent. Florence Jones had just asked the group to wait a moment, as she needed to go to her desk to exchange her "wedgy" shoes for her sneakers. She never got the chance. From where she was standing on the north side of the building, she had a clear view to the south, across the entire 77th floor. Florence could see all the windows on the distant south side when all of a sudden, she saw the plane's shadow just prior to impact. According to Florence, she didn't even have time to utter the words, "Hey, what's that dark thing?"[130]

Immediately, and without warning, the southeastern side of our floor was instantly crushed. Jonathan said, "I felt a violent jolt, and then a falling sensation." He remembers thinking the building was coming down and "this was the end!"[131] The impact caused the building to sway heavily.

I recall late nights working at the World Trade Center and hearing the building creak in the quietude of evening as it swayed in the wind. The noise was often greatest in the middle of the building where the bathrooms were located and torque was greatest. It was designed to sway to give it great flexibility. That engineering aspect likely helped the building stay intact from the impact, at first. Of course, the heat of the fires was another matter and would later determine the fate of both buildings.[132]

According to Jonathan, the South Tower swayed mightily and "was far beyond anything I'd ever felt before." Ceiling tiles rained down upon him, and he recalled "feeling the breeze from blown-out windows on the other side of the floor." Of course, that other side (the south side) was where my office had been. It's also the side from which Ron Perez, Nick Webb, and Henry D'Atri had already fled prior to impact. Fortunately, Carl Boudakian had just walked away from his office and across the floor to Simon Chen's office on the north side. Carl was with Simon, Jonathan Weinberg, and Florence Jones at the moment United 175 entered the building. Florence rightfully claims that she would have perished if she had been sitting at her desk switching shoes on the south side of the floor.

Around the corner on the west side of the 77th floor, and further from the impact zone, several members of Data Integrity were still on the floor. They included Alfredo Guzman, Eric Thompson, and James Magalong. Alfredo was chatting with fellow Data Integrity associate William Machuca just seconds ahead of impact. Alfredo was still replaying the unsettling vision of the man falling, again and again in his mind. "I'm still scratching my head trying to make heads or tails of this guy jumping. And, then all of a sudden…. VOOM!" As he glanced to the south side of the floor, he saw things falling down. "It's the [ceiling] tiles. They're all coming down. It's happening in slow motion like dominoes. And, I'm weaving back and forth." William immediately jumped under his own desk. Alfredo didn't jump or dive anywhere. He was trying to keep his balance. "Then it stops, and the air starts to fill with smoke. But very light smoke. Not dark, more like dust. It was getting cloudy on the floor."[133]

Nearby, Eric and James, along with product design specialist Allan Unger, were in mid-journey heading toward the escalator to take them up to 78. The impact caused Allan to dive under a desk. James paced furiously back and forth as the building rocked. Allan emerged after five seconds of violent gyrations in the building and described seeing James as a much older-looking man. His hair was covered in fine white dust.[134] Even closer to the southern impact location sat the very pregnant Jyoti Dave Vyas. She had just arrived back at her desk from her upstairs visit and was dialing her husband to give him an update. According to Jyoti, "The phone was ringing when the plane hit us."[135] Nearby, were Rob Rothman, Jyoti's manager, and a member of the administrative team, Aurora Fajardo.

At the moment of impact, there were twelve Baseline associates on the 77th floor. They were all disheveled, but still alive and well enough to collect themselves and begin to contemplate a harrowing downward journey. Our four colleagues on the 78th floor met a very different, and tragic fate. Prior to impact, Florence recalls seeing the 78th floor Sky Lobby outside our office entrance as a packed sardine can with people crammed in awaiting elevators to the ground floor. The entrance to our offices sat right off the Sky Lobby, and the wall separating us from that lobby was all glass. It would have been easy to witness the crowds. Florence was certain that Jill Campbell was in the Sky Lobby awaiting an elevator at that horrible moment. The tip of the plane's left wing entered our building at that very location.

Tragically, no one ever saw Jill again. She died that day leaving behind her husband, Steve, and a ten-month-old son, Jake. Ironically, and equally sad, Jill proactively sought the early shift that morning. Lorena Munoz-Udik originally had the 8:00 AM shift on 9/11. However, on the evening of September 10, Lorena received a call from Jill asking to take Lorena's early slot on the 11th. Jake's first birthday was approaching and, according to Lorena, Jill wanted to get an early start on party planning. To this day, Lorena carries a heavy burden of guilt for her acquiescence to Jill's request to switch time slots.[136] Of course, the corollary is that Lorena is still with us and has two beautiful young daughters. Fate can be both cruel and kind.

Jill and Steve Campbell with their infant son, Jake, on the occasion of his christening. Jill was Rob Patterson's executive assistant. This photo was taken just three days prior to the events of 9/11 that took Jill's life.

Also, up on the 78th floor were our financial leaders—Bob Levine and Steve Weinberg. They were our CFO and controller respectively. I had unsuccessfully tried reaching Bob by phone after the first plane hit the North Tower. According to Carl Boudakian, the two men had briefly come down to the 77th floor during that infamous 16½ minute span.

Florence shared that "I was talking to Bob and Steve, and Bob said 'you know, they're saying you can stay!' But I said 'these people can't get a fire drill straight!' They then asked Carl and me 'what are you guys gonna do?' And, we said 'we're leaving.'"[137]

Jonathan also acknowledged seeing Bob and Steve briefly on 77 outside his office, but they returned to their 78th floor offices right before the jet hit our tower. This was after the other finance department members, Myles Donnelly and Brian Branco, had elected to leave the building.

Steve Weinberg's wife, Laurie, shared that "Steve called from his cell phone and told me that he was looking outside at the other building that he could see debris, almost like confetti, and smoke. I told him 'you need to leave!' And he said 'they're telling us we're safe here, it's the other building.' And, I said 'I don't care!'"[138]

At the moment of impact Laurie Weinberg exclaimed, "My God, it went through the 80th floor. And, I just started screaming and felt that Steven is dead. Steven is dead!"[139] Regrettably, Laurie's premonition was correct. In a recent conversation, she described Steve as very dutiful. His boss, Bob Levine, had recently returned to the office after some surgery and a cancer scare that turned out to be a benign spot on his lung. Nonetheless, most of us were aware of Bob's good news and of his recent decision to quit smoking. It is quite conceivable that Bob didn't feel comfortable making a 78-floor descent. According to Laurie, "I always had the feeling that if Bob knew he couldn't make it down those stairs, Steven might have been saying 'well, I'm not leaving him here . . . I'll just stay with him.'"[140]

Another sad occurrence was that Bob Levine was on the phone with his son, Andrew, at the moment of impact. In a story that appeared in the *Las Vegas Sun* on September 11, 2009, Andrew horrifically recalled the moment. "I heard the roar of motors and windows shattering."[141] In the *Las Vegas Review-Journal*, he added, "I was watching it while talking to him, but television has that seven-second delay. I had already heard the sounds on the phone. I already knew what had happened before seeing it. I just fell to the ground in disbelief. I just rolled up in to a little ball and convulsed."[142] At that moment, Andrew, a Desert Storm veteran, began to call his friends and ask them to rescue him from his grief.[143]

Bob Levine and Steve Weinberg tragically lost their lives that morning. Bob left behind a loving wife, Roberta, and his son, Andrew. Steve left his adoring wife, Laurie, and three wonderful children all under the age of twelve.

Bob Levine (left) and Steve Weinberg in the summer of 2000 during Baseline's annual boat cruise. A year later, both men remained on the 78th floor during the fateful minutes of 9/11, and tragically lost their lives.

Facts surrounding Ruth Lapin's last moments are not known by Baseline's associates. Ruth had only recently joined Baseline, in the summer of 2001. She was a software developer and had been recruited for her systems analysis experience and her maturity. Ruth sat across from Allan Unger on the east side of the 77th floor overlooking the Brooklyn Bridge. Allan recalled saying "good morning" to the ever-pleasant lady around 8:15 AM but does not remember her last whereabouts. That time stamp awareness of Allan's unfortunately proved fateful for Ruth. Given her normal ninety-minute commute from East Windsor in central New Jersey, Ruth usually arrived at her desk around 9:00 AM. Her love for the New York Giants, and her husband David's consulting assignment for IBM in the city, placed Ruth in an unfortunate circumstance. On Monday September 10, instead of commuting home to New Jersey, she decided to join David at his Manhattan hotel room in order to watch the Giants on *Monday Night Football*. Being an early riser, Ruth was up and out of the hotel soon after 7 AM. Unfortunately, that enabled her early arrival at Baseline that morning.

It is thought that Ruth, like Jill, may have been among the crowd awaiting an elevator in the 78th floor Sky Lobby. Her husband, David Chazin, cited her caring personality as a likely reason for her death. At the age of 53, she was still an active Girl Scout leader. David described the trunk of her car as an example of her readiness to assist in a moment's notice. It contained blankets, flares, and water bottles just in case she might encounter a stalled traveler. David is certain that if Ruth had been on the staircase, and encountered someone in need, she would have stopped to administer love and support. He pronounced that "she was one of the Do-Gooders!"[144] Additionally, Ruth's daughter, Heather Daly, said that stopping to administer assistance would have been very understandable. According to Heather, her mom "was very helpful and caring. I couldn't make a conjecture as to why it took her longer than others to make it out. However, it wouldn't be out of character for her to be helping other people."[145] Just like Jill's story of switching shifts that morning, Ruth found herself unusually early to work that morning.[146] Her story became another sad and tragic loss. Ruth left behind her husband, David, her daughter Heather, and a son, Doug.

The loss of our four dear friends and the three Vestek colleagues will stay with us forever. They were victims of a heinous crime perpetrated on our country because of who we Americans are perceived to be. These individuals were innocent human beings caught in a storm of hate. They were simply in the wrong place at the wrong time.

In a short online story that Jonathan Weinberg published about his experience on 9/11 he wrote: "Seemingly insignificant decisions a person made that day determined whether they lived or died. It's still something that's a bit hard to fully come to terms with."[147]

CHAPTER 9

THE GREAT DESCENT

THE DEVASTATION ON the 77th floor ranged from utter destruction in the southeast corner to relatively unscathed in the opposite northwest corner of our one-acre floor. That northwest quadrant, described by Alfredo Guzman as filling up with white, dust-like smoke, was the least impacted of the four corners. Beyond the light smoke and downed ceiling tiles, the area remained fairly undisturbed. Those who stood with Jonathan Weinberg in the northeast corner of the floor saw a very different picture.

As previously mentioned, the plane hit our building at 9:03 AM at a speed of over 500 mph and on a slant, slamming into Two World Trade Center in the southeast corner from the 78th floor to the 84th floor. This was a big jet—a Boeing 767 loaded with fuel. According to Jonathan, "It went through our building right above our heads."[148] The South Tower literally exploded when the airliner came apart as it careened across the eastern half of the building, dropping its entire contents of fuel into a very combustible, friction-filled environment. The east side of the 77th floor was instantly inundated with thick black smoke.

At the moment of impact, all twelve people on the 77th floor became covered in ceiling debris. Their skin, eyes, and lungs immediately had to contest with flying glass, airborne fiberglass particles, small pieces of metal, and varying levels of white and black smoke. They were also soon coated in a layer of white ash.[149] In a matter of seconds, all of these associates gathered themselves and sprang into action. They were on a mission. Without any major injuries, they were going to find a way out. Fast. Most of them were aware of the building's three stairwells.

In describing the reaction to the explosion, Florence said, "Simon went one way. Jonathan went one way. Carl went one way, and I followed Carl!"[150] The four actually had the same thought which was to reach the largest stairwell in the building. The primary core stairwell in the middle of the building was known as Stairwell B, but it required them to advance southward, and into the black smoke. The four found themselves in difficult terrain. Visibility was low and the smoke was asphyxiating. Carl described wrapping his shirt around his nose and mouth. Jonathan recalls Simon Chen coughing and spitting out black soot.

Meanwhile, on the other (west) side of the floor Jyoti was still alone at her desk, increasingly in a state of shock. "I was just standing there not knowing what to do. I kind of felt my baby move."[151] She called out for help and decided to approach her boss's office, that of Rob Rothman. He occupied an internal office attached to the building's core. At the moment of the explosion, his office literally imploded. He was on the phone with a friend when he heard a loud bang over his head and the phone suddenly went dead. Ceiling tiles rained down upon him, the door to his office slammed shut, the rectangular glass window that overlooked the hallway exploded outward, and his bookcase and all its contents fell upon his desk. The tumultuous event sent Rob scrambling under that desk. "That's when I mentally went numb. I was just kind of checked out," exclaimed Rob. According to Rob, after what "seemed like an eternity, which was probably only a couple of minutes," he climbed out from under the desk, climbed over that debris-cluttered desk, and opened his door. He shared that "all I can remember is seeing Jyoti standing there like a little old woman. She was completely covered in dust."[152] Soon, Aurora Fajardo was at their side. Also, on that western half of the floor, Alfredo and William Machuca gathered themselves together and soon checked Stairwell A in their (northwest) corner of the building. It was filling with white smoke. They quickly passed on that option and soon joined with Jyoti, Rob, and Aurora in the center of the floor near the larger Stairwell B.

However, all sets of eyes from each side of the floor quickly drew the same conclusion about Stairwell B. It was inaccessible. According to Florence, viewing it from the east, it was just a massive black void.[153] At approximately the same moment, Alfredo and the others were examining the same void, but from the west. Alfredo commented:

> We looked towards where you would go to Stairwell B, but we didn't go down that way because it was pitch black. Normally, I could stop in the middle of the floor and see across the hallway and see the other side of the office, the daylight, the other windows. It wasn't like there was smoke. It was completely pitch black. So, either there was a void, or there was something there blocking (our view).[154]

As they would soon discover, much of the building's core had collapsed in on itself right below where the plane's fuselage had impacted the building's infrastructure. Florence admitted how traumatized she was at that very moment. "By this point I was really shaking because I had just come down the escalator from 78 to 77 less than two minutes earlier. And I knew the people that I had just talked to were all dead."[155]

Carl, who was with Florence, lamented about "all the people above us on the 78th floor waiting for elevators. To picture that in my mind is just an unbearable thought. To think they didn't have a chance."[156]

As this was transpiring, a third group of associates had more thoroughly pursued the dark void in the middle of the floor. Allan Unger, Eric Thompson, and James Magalong were literally facing the hallway to our middle core at the moment the world turned upside down. Through some circuitous route, they found Stairwell B. They opened the door and were greeted by the same dark, empty feeling. Something told them to go elsewhere. Simultaneously, the other groups that had just confronted the large, dark void near Stairwell B, now headed to Stairwell C about 70 feet from their respective locations. This was the same stairwell that Ron, Henry, and others had entered just a few minutes earlier up on 78, but prior to impact.

Carl and Florence approached the very smoky southeast corner. They knew that Stairwell C on our floor was behind the escalator and adjacent to the pantry where lunches were served daily. However, Carl described the area as utterly devastated and not approachable.

He recalls seeing that his office on the south face of the building had collapsed and that all the windows had been blown out on that side of the floor.[157] Jonathan confirmed feeling the breeze. Florence shared that our internal escalator had fallen through to the floor below. As the closest staircase to the plane's entry point, Stairwell C's usefulness had been altered by the impact.

Alfredo, approaching the pantry from the western side of the floor, drew a similar conclusion. "Whatever was above the pantry, was now where we were. Whatever was in the pantry, was now a floor below. But we could still get to the door [to Stairwell C]." As Alfredo eyed the situation, he realized that the pregnant Jyoti would have an impossible task trying to navigate through the fallen debris. There was also a metal beam lying across the path to the door. "I could slide through and get to the door," said Alfredo, "but not Jyoti. We were not going to risk a piece of metal sticking out slicing her. Not an option!" They never got to check the stairwell's viability. On their walk back from Stairwell C, Alfredo and company met up with Allan, James, and Eric. Alfredo shared the bad news surrounding Stairwell C, and they all concurred that the black void of Stairwell B was to be avoided.[158]

There was seemingly no way to escape. They had examined all three stairwells. At that very moment, Carl's thought was: *Oh, my God, we're in the same situation now ourselves as the people that we were just looking across at in the other building!*[159]

With a fatalistic outlook, Florence right then and there looked at the windows and thought: *If you have to jump, you have to jump. You just do it quick and you're done.*[160]

The evaluation of options facing the twelve remaining associates was dire. While conditions on the floor were not yet life threatening, they all knew they needed to get out quickly. Stairwell C wasn't an option given the collapsed floor and debris surrounding the pantry. Stairwell B was surrounded by an ominous, dark void in the exact center of the tower. And Stairwell A had already been examined and found to be dark and full of dense white smoke.

While not understanding the whys or wherefores, the larger group on the western side of the floor came to appreciate that Stairwell A was likely the best option they could realistically pursue. They were going to further investigate that thick white smoke. Alfredo returned to his desk and grabbed his fire warden-issued flashlight. At the same time, on the eastern side of the floor, Carl grabbed Florence and followed the cries of Jonathan who was hailing them. "Over here, over here, over here!"[161] Jonathan was calling them to that same Stairwell A in the northwest quadrant which was approximately 100 feet away. That was the same staircase that Alfredo's group was also about to re-explore. It had originally been found to be smoky. It still was. And pitch black.

All twelve remaining associates on the 77th floor had simultaneously found each other and this last potential way out. However, before the team entered the stairwell, they encountered a visitor from the 100th floor. Jaede Barg was with AON Insurance. He had walked down the stairs from up above and avoided injury by physically being in Stairwell A which happened to be shielded by the elevator machine room. According to Florence, soon after impact, he came into our space on 77 looking for some water. He quickly joined ranks with our group as they began their descent.[162]

In reflecting back on the moment that the group entered Stairwell A, Alfredo talked about everyone's focus on Jyoti, our pregnant associate. "We needed to make sure she got out. If we have to sacrifice ourselves we do so to make sure she got out. So, it was important. That's the whole thing about Baseline, we were all a family."[163]

Florence added to that communal feeling: "I just felt that we as a group were either all going to die together, or we were all going to get out of there together."[164]

Jonathan summed up the moment by adding that "The final image that I have is of my coworkers standing there banding together."[165]

Alfredo added: "At no point, did I hear any bickering, any indecisiveness, any objection to anything that we were doing. No one said, 'no, no, let's go here' or 'no, no, let's go there.' I didn't hear any of that. I didn't hear any indecisiveness or any contradiction. We just all stuck together. And when we started walking down, we did it together as a group."[166]

In reviewing the team's journey, Alfredo re-emphasized the notion of togetherness:

> We were family. The same way we handled any crisis or any issues at Baseline, we did it together. We trusted each other. I had trust in whatever the tech group was going to do, was going to solve my problem.

Client Support trusted that the nightly processing team would do whatever we needed to do to solve the problem. There was a level of trust. We trusted that Client Support would relay the correct message to the client. We didn't need to oversee anybody or double-check anyone's work. We had full confidence in the people that were doing their jobs knew what they were doing. My job that morning was to be co-fire warden with Simon. And that's what I did."[167]

At some point that morning, Simon Chen had amazingly donned his fire warden's baseball cap amongst all the chaos. Where he found the time or sense to put on that cap is beyond me, and yet very impressive. I know he wore the cap that day. A very famous photograph stands as proof.

The group entered the dark and smoky Stairwell A. Allan Unger, Eric Thompson, and James Magalong were the first in. Aurora Fajardo was directly helping Jyoti, our pregnant associate, each step of the way. The team inched along the first several steps of the staircase in total darkness, proceeding carefully by flashlight. Thick white smoke deterred their progress. No one could see more than a few feet in front of them, even with the flashlight.

At one point they felt what seemed to be water rushing past their feet. Rob Rothman recalled the moment: "My first thought was, *Oh my God, the sprinklers are going off!* It literally reminded me of a river running downstream, 'cause there's all this water pouring down the stairs. I'm probably ankle deep in it."[168] Some thought it might be a ruptured water main rather than sprinklers, but Jonathan Weinberg said it had a distinctive smell.

Having worked at JFK Airport in his teenage years as a baggage handler, Jonathan knew what jet fuel smelled like. But like most of the people in the World Trade Center that day, my colleagues were completely unaware as to what had actually just occurred. Jonathan said, "I could not put one and one together and make the connection that a jetliner had just crashed into the building only a few feet above my head and split open, spilling the contents of its fuel tanks into the building core."[169] It was decidedly jet fuel and not water. While Jonathan knew exactly what it was, others weren't so reminiscent.

Friends of Rob Rothman challenged him in the weeks following 9/11, saying "How could you not smell it?" Rob simply shared that "the minute I heard that bang over my head, I mentally checked out. So, you could have put whatever in front of my nose or face, and I never would have smelled it."[170]

After descending just one floor, their luck seemed to run out. Not only were their shoes becoming wet, but the bottom of their staircase also greeted them with a solid cinderblock wall. It felt like a dead end. Thankfully, the flashlight allowed them to canvass the area. Underneath the staircase and behind them they found another door. The light from underneath the door, and from an exit sign above, barely shone through the dark smoky air. The group found the door unlocked.

They opened the door and were greeted by lights. And an even wider staircase. This was different from Ron and Henry's experience: there was virtually no one in this stairwell. Allan, Eric, and James moved quickly and put some distance between themselves and the group moving more gingerly with Jyoti. When the advancing trio reached the 70th floor, Allan recalled encountering "an older woman in front of us dressed in a polo shirt." He added, "Her sleeve was dripping blood."[171] The woman was Mary Jos, who worked for the New York State Tax Department up on the 86th floor. She had come down to the Sky Lobby to switch elevators for her typical commute out of the building. She never got the chance to take the second elevator ride.

Because of its angled approach, the plane's left wing tore through our Sky Lobby, killing everyone on our side of the lobby. Another USA Today article by Cauchon and Moore, entitled "Life and Death on the 78th Floor," described the scene in the Sky Lobby based on eyewitness accounts: "The air turned black with smoke. Flames burst out of elevators. Walls and the ceiling crumbled into a foot of debris on the floor. Shards of glass flew like thrown knives. The blast threw people like dolls, tearing their bodies apart." [172]

Our dear Jill Campbell was likely right there, perhaps Ruth Lapin as well. We assume they chose to wait for an elevator in lieu of taking the stairs. Mary Jos, who was waiting on the north end of the lobby, was badly hurt in the ensuing explosion. "She could see people lying all around her, their eyes open, absolutely still. Her face was burned. The flesh on her left arm was ripped away. One shoe had been blown off, and her foot was bleeding."[173] She crawled into the nearby Stairwell.

That was Stairwell A—one flight above Alfredo's office. When Allan, Eric, and James came in contact with her, she had already gingerly descended eight floors.[174] [175] She was moving very slowly. She had suffered burns and had a severe laceration on her left arm from flying shrapnel. She was very bloody with her clothes in tatters and was missing a shoe. Allan, who was wearing an undershirt beneath his own polo shirt, quickly disrobed. He used his undershirt as a kind of tourniquet and wrapped Mary's left tricep. The Baseline trio decided to escort her all the way down.[176]

Mary was one of only a handful of survivors that came down from 78, or higher, that day.[177] Most of those survivors were waiting in the Sky Lobby to take an express elevator down to safety. As many as 200 people were crammed into that Sky Lobby awaiting elevators when the plane struck.[178] Mary Jos was fortunate that she had been standing on the north end of the lobby and adjacent to Stairwell A. I suspect that any survivors must have been standing on the north side of that Sky Lobby. Baseline, on the other hand, had its entrance off the south side of the Sky Lobby where the plane's left wing entered the building— nearer to Stairwell C.

To everyone's surprise, the group of fourteen individuals (Baseline's twelve plus Jaede Barg and Mary Jos) hardly encountered anyone else evacuating via Stairwell A that morning. They could, therefore, move at their desired pace down those 76 additional flights after locating the open, well-lit staircase. Of course, Jyoti and Mary were not able to move at a fast clip. According to Carl Boudakian, "we were only going as fast as Jyoti would go, because no one would go ahead. She had that mother's sense of 'I am going to get out of here because I'm going to protect my child.'"[179] According to Simon Chen, Jyoti "refused to take a break, put one hand on her belly, and leaned the other arm on the shoulder of Aurora who had been with her since the beginning."[180] Jyoti's recollection of the story was that, while she was exhausted and could have used a break, she couldn't feel her baby and wanted medical attention as soon as possible. Her focus was clearly on her baby. "I didn't really feel her moving, and not feeling her was a bit concerning." She shared that she "became like a focal point, sort of like a distraction. Everyone was focusing on me."[181] In retrospect, Alfredo ominously shared that "if Jyoti had asked to stop, we would have stopped. We probably would not be here today, but we would have stopped."[182]

By Simon's account "somewhere along the way, someone had left a half gallon of water on the ground. We wet our shirts, gargled, and later gave the remaining water to a couple we met."[183] About the same time, Florence's "wedgy" shoes were becoming a hindrance, and her asthma was kicking in. She was covered in ash and her eyes hurt as well. She was physically and emotionally distraught. Carl suggested she remove her shoes. The team's new friend, Jaede Barg from AON, offered his arm as an aid. Florence accepted his offer, then she continued the journey in her bare feet. Carl carried her shoes and handbag.[184]

Personally, I can't help but think of the countless souls that did not know about this open and lighted avenue to freedom. Inside our tower, Stairwell A was a godsend.

It was located in the northwest corner of the inner core of the building. The reason it was still an option was that the airliner hit the building in the exact opposite (southeast) corner of the skyscraper while also moving through and away from the building to the northeast. My colleagues were also aided by the design of the Twin Towers relative to the point of impact.

The World Trade Center's working areas were at the perimeter of the one-acre footprint of each floor. Elevator banks, lavatories, and staircases were all centrally located within the central core of the towers. A *New York Times* article from April 6, 2005, written by journalist Jim Dwyer, explained that "in the impact area of the North Tower, the three staircases were about 70 feet apart and were destroyed immediately. In the South Tower, the plane hit on floors where the three staircases were about 200 feet apart, and one of them survived at least partially intact."[185] That larger distance was due to an architectural relocation of Stairwell A to accommodate large elevator machines. Those machines also helped shield Stairwell A from the airliner's impact.

When United 175 exploded into the South Tower at 9:03 AM, it did so in proximity to an enormous elevator machine room located on the 81st floor. In a *USA Today* article entitled "Machinery saved people in WTC," which appeared on May 17, 2002 and was penned by journalists Cauchon and Moore, the machine room "contained a dozen 24-ton elevator hoists, which pulled high-speed express elevators from the lobby to the 78th floor. The Otis Elevator 339HT machines were the largest in the world when they were installed . . . during the towers' construction. Lined up like a room of soldiers in front of Stairway A, the machines helped protect the stairwell."[186] Additionally, the elevator machine room took up more than half the 81st floor, requiring the architects to route Stairwell A around the machines in the original design. In the same article, the authors further stipulated that "the detour moved Stairwell A from the center of the building toward the northwest corner—away from the path the hijacked jet would take."[187] My teammates on 77 had an available escape route thanks to the location of Stairwell A. While my colleagues were fortunately aided by Stairwell A, and the building's design, others who lost their lives that day at the World Trade Center were not helped by the design. Journalist Jim Dwyer, in the aforementioned *New York Times* article, entitled "Staircases in Twin Towers Are Faulted," went on to say that "neither building had enough staircases to meet any of the major building codes in the country, including New York City's."[188] Author Mitchell Zuckoff added to the hindsight concern:

> Exacerbating the potential fire risk was a quirk of timing in revisions to the New York City Building Code. As a public agency, the Port Authority wasn't required to comply with the code, but its top officials promised to meet or exceed the city's standards at the trade center. During initial planning, that meant applying strict rules adopted in 1938. But in the mid 1960s, as the towers took shape, a revised, less stringent code moved toward enactment. Even before it took effect, Port Authority bosses told the engineers to follow the new standards' more lenient, cost-saving rules. The old code would have mandated six emergency exit stairwells in each tower. The Port Authority interpreted the new rules as requiring only three stairwells per tower. However, even under the new code, each tower should have included at least a fourth stairwell, to accommodate visitors to public spaces on the higher floors. Also, fire safety experts generally urge that stairwells in tall buildings be spaced as far apart as possible. But in each of the Twin Towers, the three stairwells were bunched relatively

close to one another in the central core. That left them collectively more vulnerable to fire or other damage affecting the core and made them harder to reach for tenants and visitors working in desirable offices near the windows.[189]

This new revelation, discovered as part of my research for this book, was particularly hard to swallow.

When the team walking down with Jyoti arrived at the other Sky Lobby on the 44th floor, they were directed by building personnel into a larger staircase. That was likely the main core staircase known as Stairwell B in the center of the building. The trio escorting Mary Jos was slightly ahead of them but was never asked to switch stairwells. Mary, Allan, Eric, and James descended all 77 flights via that original northwest escape route—Stairwell A. While Jyoti did not stop, the same was not true for Mary Jos. According to Allan, somewhere around the 25th floor, Mary needed to stop and rest. Eric volunteered to stay with Mary, while Allan and James continued on their path out of the building.[190]

Somewhere around the 30th floor in their new stairwell, the group escorting Jyoti met two firefighters going up in search of victims to assist. They were encumbered with full gear. Rob Rothman described each of them as carrying two oxygen tanks and other equipment, while looking exhausted. Florence Jones recalls saying "God Speed" to these nameless heroes.[191] Their fate was probably already sealed as they rose with the greatest of intentions.

While the groups walking with Jyoti and Mary were making their way down, Ron and Henry were about twenty floors below them in another stairwell. Their stairway, Stairwell C, while intact at their location, had been utterly destroyed up above. When they got to the 44th floor, the location of the other Sky Lobby, they were also directed to Stairwell B. They, too, encountered firefighters ascending into a hellish environment. According to Ron, he saw several very young firemen.

There were three firemen. Kids really. No more than 22 or 23. The lead kid was a big handsome, good-looking kid. He asked, "Is everyone okay?" Yes, I told him. The kid said, "Okay, good. C'mon guys!" He was the first

guy up. The other two guys followed. I never forgot
that kid because I'm sure he never made it out.[192]

   The men my associates encountered were likely part of the initial
surge of firefighters. At 9:10 AM, the NYPD "declared an unprecedented
second Level 4 mobilization, summoning another 1,000 officers and
supervisors to the scene."[193] At 9:29 AM, as my friends were approaching
the end of their descent, the FDNY issued a full recall, bringing all its
employees back to work.[194] While the actions of the on-duty responders
were heroic, the actions of those off-duty were exemplary. In his book
The Only Plane in the Sky, author Garrett Graff said, "Even as the
massive NYPD and FDNY mobilizations activated additional units,
off-duty first responders and those who lived outside of Manhattan
realized the magnitude of the disaster and began to make their way
downtown. . . . Ultimately, 60 of the FDNY personnel killed on 9/11
were supposed to be off-duty that morning."[195]

   Ron and Henry exited Stairwell B at the mezzanine level (i.e.,
second floor) of the South Tower where visitors typically queued up
for TKTS[x] and for access to the Observation Deck. They were looking
north into the WTC Plaza where the bronze globe sculpture stood for
so many years marking the center of the entire World Trade Center
complex. Ron said a strange sight greeted him through the narrow
windows that were the Trade Center's hallmark façade. He saw what
he thought were clothes strewn about the plaza with a lot of other
debris. He came to the realization that the clothes were probably dead
bodies. But, still unaware of what had just transpired, Ron was at a
loss to understand what exactly was going on. At that point, a female
worker starting yelling at him. "Sir, you have to keep moving. You
must keep moving!" Ron admits being in a daze and not able to focus.
He acknowledges that he should have been focused on exacting a
quick exit. In his defense, however, he didn't know the danger he was
in. The building's collapse was imminent. They exited the concourse
on the northeast side near the Millennium Hotel on Church Street.
Ron described the scene as "total pandemonium; people, police cars,
fire engines." He recalls getting out to the street and looking up. The
Sky Lobbies on 44 and 78 had always been markedly different on the

x   TKTS. The kiosk for purchasing Broadway theatre tickets on the "day of the show." Of-
    ten up to 50% off the face value. Proceeds help support the Theatre Development Fund.

outside than other floors. There were contrasting bands of metal on the façade that made them easy to spot. He quickly located our floor and all he saw were flames shooting out of that Sky Lobby area. He shouted to Henry, "Those are our offices!"[196]

Just then a female police officer yelled at him. "Sir, what are you doing? Please get out of here. Keep moving!"

Ron said, "She actually seemed pissed off. I was still in a daze."

After a brief rest on the 25th floor, Eric Thompson and Mary Jos began their final descent. They were soon on the street where an ambulance whisked a badly-injured Mary to safety. According to Eric's friend and colleague, Igor Yampolsky, Eric immediately left the city and went hiking in the woods for two or three days. In a recent interview, Igor shared that Eric was a free spirit who loved to spend weekends driving to remote regions of the New York metro area on his motorcycle and then spending much of that time hiking. Eric looked for peace in such escapes. Igor also shared how he and Eric, practically every other workday on their lunch breaks, would condition themselves by jumping into the stairwell on 77 and descending the 77 floors on foot and then, immediately, turning about and climbing those same 77 floors. Igor exclaimed, "So, when Eric carried out that woman—when he saved that woman—it was not a surprise to me. He was very well conditioned to do that."[197]

The group accompanying Jyoti also soon made it to street level. Carl Boudakian described the scene outside as "mayhem." As this group emerged into the sunlight, Simon sought help for Jyoti. He was immediately assisted by a New York City police officer. They both grabbed Jyoti's arms, and whisked her away from the building as fast as possible. The officer's name was Ramon Suarez.[198]

Within a block of the Trade Center, a freelance photographer took the picture of Simon and Officer Suarez escorting Jyoti to safety. Months later, a Baseline associate by the name of Andrew Stellman was visiting a photography exhibition about 9/11 in the East Village of Manhattan when he recognized Simon in the photo with Jyoti.[199] He immediately informed Simon, who quickly went to see the exhibition. Because he was the person in the snapshot, Simon was graciously presented with a copy of the photograph. Wanting to extend a warm belated thank-you to the officer, Simon asked for the man's identity. He was instantly saddened to learn that Officer Suarez had lost his life that day. He had obviously gone back to rescue more people.

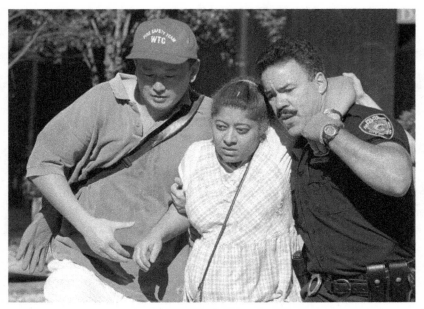

After an arduous 77-floor descent, Baseline's twelve surviving associates arrived at street level. Simon Chen and a NYPD officer, Ramon Suarez, helped the very-pregnant Jyoti Dave Vyas to a nearby ambulance. [Photo Credit: BRIGITTE STELZER]

As Simon and Officer Suarez carried Jyoti across Church Street to a makeshift triage center located at the Millennium Hotel, she was weak and very concerned about the safety of her unborn child. She told the EMT personnel that she could not feel her baby. Within seconds, she was in an ambulance and on her way to LIU Brooklyn Hospital. Alfredo witnessed the proceedings surrounding Jyoti, and recently recalled the moment of the ambulance's departure with a reflection of "mission accomplished."

At the hospital, an ultrasound scan provided immense comfort to Jyoti as it showed that the baby was fine. As Jyoti put it, "That was a terrifying moment for me. I guess [the baby] must have been feeling the stress I was going through, and she was just basically being quiet. For me that was very scary." Two months later, a healthy baby girl was born into this world. Jyoti and her husband, Jaldhar, named the baby "Shailaja" (pronounced shayla-JAH). Her name in Hindi literally means "Daughter of the Mountain." Jyoti made the point that "if you think about it, she came down from a mountain called the World Trade Center. So, she's a daughter of a mountain in that way. That's a fitting name for her!" Jyoti and Shailaja had indeed descended a mountain together. Today, Jyoti and her husband also have a son. Jyoti just recently departed the corporate lineage of Baseline. She worked for Thomson Reuters, and a subsequent spin-off, up until late 2019. As of this writing, she reports everyone in the family is healthy and doing well.[200]

Also injured that morning was Florence Jones. As she and Jaede Barg arrived outside, the sunshine had an impact on Florence's eyes. They were stinging, and it was difficult to keep them open. She was also terribly thirsty. Further, adding insult to injury, Florence and Jaede were separated from Carl. In the flurry of the exit, the police, security personnel, and the FBI were pushing evacuees to the north with great haste. It was easy to lose track of people. The separation from Carl meant that Florence was on the streets of New York without shoes. Within a block of the Towers, Jaede entered a convenience store to get her water. Florence leaned against a street lamp pole. Within seconds, her exhaustion had her sliding down the pole to the point where she ended up sitting on the sidewalk. Jaede returned with water but immediately knew Florence needed medical attention. A hospital, traditionally known to many New Yorkers as Beekman-Downtown, was only about a thousand feet from their location and quite literally under the shadow of the Brooklyn Bridge. Jaede's valor continued as he escorted Florence to the hospital where she was put on oxygen and had her eyes flushed. Jaede then began his journey home. Right above Florence on the bridge, Carl Boudakian was exiting Manhattan on foot . . . carrying her wedges.[201]

The 77-floor descent from the "mountain" had taken a lot of time. Only fifteen minutes after the survivors' arrival on the street, the building collapsed. It was 9:59 AM. While our building had been the second one hit, it was the first to fall. Simon, Alfredo, and the others were all in very similar locations north of Ground Zero at the time of the collapse. Police had been sending all the people northward from that exit point. That was fortunate for these folks because the collapsing building sent a horrible and asphyxiating debris cloud to the east. According to Alfredo, "We were several blocks north on Broadway and we began to hear this eerie sound. We looked back and saw the smoke and dust just shoot across the street. It went hurtling eastward."[202]

Ron Perez and Henry D'Atri had similarly made their way up

Broadway to City Hall, about six blocks north of the World Trade Center. There was a bank of pay phones there and many people were lined up to call loved ones. Henry and Ron got on the line, but were unable to complete a call. The phones were not working, likely the result of overused bandwidth that day. While at that spot they had a view of the tops of the Twin Towers above the smaller buildings in that area. Someone yelled. "Holy shit, one of the towers just disappeared!" Ron and Henry looked back up, and sure enough, only one tower was visible. "Oh, my God," said Ron. "One of the towers must have collapsed."[203] At the same time, Florence was receiving eye treatment at Beekman-Downtown. She and the medical staff heard a gigantic rumble. Our building had just come down, although that realization wouldn't occur to her for several more hours.

As Florence sat at the hospital, I had made it to Bergen County in northern New Jersey thanks to that crowded taxi. I jumped in my car parked at the Radburn train station, and drove further north up Route 208 towards my home in Franklin Lakes. It was just prior to our building's collapse. During that seven-mile drive I got a better sense of exactly what was happening across the country from listening to WCBS News Radio 880 in New York. I was in shock, and it got far worse as I exited the highway. I can still hear the words of the radio announcer. I recall that it went something like this:

> Okay, we're getting another newsflash. Let me ... um
> ... let me just read this. Can someone verify this for
> me? Okay, yes? Okay. Ladies and gentlemen, we are
> now being told, and it is confirmed, that the South
> Tower of the World Trade Center, that is Two World
> Trade, has just collapsed to the ground. I repeat, Two
> World Trade Center has fallen.

I hardly made it to the bottom of the exit ramp. I almost went off the road screaming, "What do you mean it has fallen? What the ___!" I began cursing again, but this time tears emerged. I couldn't come to grips with what I was hearing. What I had briefly witnessed in Hoboken across the water from Ground Zero had turned horribly for the worse. This was no dream. It wasn't even a cruel nightmare. This was a dose of hard-core reality that hit me across the face with such a blast.

Life as I knew it seemed over. Quickly. It just seemed over and done. Many thoughts filled my head. *That was my building. My company's building. Our building! Everything is gone?*

My first thoughts were just gut human emotions.

> *Oh, my Lord! Has anyone survived? What did they go through? Are they trapped? How many are hurt? My office with my pictures of my girls is gone? No more? The spanking new offices that we were all so proud of are gone? Could all the fine young people with so much promise who we employ be gone? The business that we just celebrated twenty years of perseverance and excellence is gone? The country must be at war, but with whom? Lord, what did we do to warrant this? Who did this to us, and why? Why?*

The onslaught of questions, emotions, and devastating possibilities was overwhelming. It easily stands as the most surreal moment of my life. Nothing else even comes close.

Having been right in the midst of the horror and chaos, Simon was less philosophical and more pragmatic about the surreal moment. Upon getting out of the building and escaping the collapsing tower, he said that it "dawned on me how close we were to death and how miraculous that the group of us escaped."[204]

Because the dust and debris cloud from our building blew eastward, many of the individuals who had descended the staircases were no longer in any imminent danger. The same could not be said about Rob Rothman or Nick Webb.

After descending 77 floors with Jyoti and that final group of Baseline associates, Rob Rothman decided to immediately head across Church Street on the eastern side of the towers. He held up at the Millennium Hotel right across from the World Trade Center. According to Rob, he didn't have the energy to go on. He recently stated that he was "out of breath, and my eyes were really bothering me. I needed to get some oxygen." At that very moment, the hotel staff was wheeling out a cart of towels, and a staff member was pouring water on them to distribute. Rob grabbed a towel and began to wipe his eyes. His back was to the Trade Center. Rob recently recalled the situation:

At this point, I'm not going anywhere. I'm kinda just standing there, and I'm cleaning myself off and getting myself together. And, then, I hear a rumble and I hear an explosion. I turn around and I see the tower we just got out of start to come down. I am completely paralyzed with fear. I can't move. I know I need to go, but I can't go. I'm standing next to the large planters outside the hotel, looking at the building coming down. Fulton Street is to my immediate right. There was a police officer in the street yelling "Run for your life, run for your life!" I guess that mentally must have set me off, and I began running up Fulton Street towards Broadway.[205]

Rob crossed Broadway. Incredibly, at that very moment, a photograph was taken of him as he furiously attempted to outrun the debris cloud. As he crossed Broadway and headed down Fulton Street, the cloud was moving faster than he. Rob felt utterly exhausted as the cloud came upon him. He said, "I was so out of breath, and thought I was literally going to have a heart attack." But Rob was determined to get through this experience. He thought to himself, *It's not going to end this way!* He found a doorway into a building as the cloud approached his position and he shared it with two strangers, a man and a woman, who to this day remain at-large strangers to Rob. He recently shared his sentiment at that very instant as having "an eerie feeling of 'you know something's coming, but you don't know what it is.'"[206] He braced for impact.

According to Rob, "Within a few seconds it was like the lights went out. I literally could hold my hand up to my face and not see it. That's how thick that smoke was. I wanted to protect my face, so I took the towel that I'd been given [at the hotel] to wrap around my head to protect my face. And, I kid you not, the dust was so thick that my cheeks were so thick I looked like a chipmunk. I had to keep opening up the towel to spit the dust out. That's how thick that stuff was. So, I kept spitting it out in order to breathe."[207]

After a brief moment, the three strangers went their own ways. Rob, still unable to see more than a few inches in front of him, walked cautiously along the walls of the Fulton Street buildings until he heard

As Two World Trade Center collapsed, Rob Rothman found himself directly beneath the descending debris cloud. He is seen here in a white shirt crossing Broadway in a mad dash for his life.[Photo Credit: DOUG KANTER/AFP via Getty Images]

voices. He narrowed in on them, and found himself inside a bar. It wasn't terribly crowded, but within a few minutes two unfortunate circumstances arose. The bar had begun to fill up with people, and with each door opening, more of that outside smoke and soot was making its way inside the establishment. The bar's management then ordered the bar doors locked and, according to Rob, "All you could see were these hand prints banging on the window wanting to be let in the door." Rob's next surprise occurred when he soon spied a house phone on the wall at the end of the bar. As he grabbed it to phone his wife, the bar owner barked at him, saying "What are you doing? You can't use that!" Because Rob didn't drink alcohol, and given the lousy disposition of the bar owner, Rob soon left the place—and literally shook the dust from his proverbial sandals. He then proceeded to walk over three miles to Penn Station in midtown.

As Rob Rothman walked northward on Broadway, he was in a daze. A kind shopkeeper hosed him off. He was appreciative of that gesture because he wasn't sure how toxic all that material was that lay on every inch of him. As he slowly trudged ahead on Broadway toward the train station that would help get him to New Jersey, he looked back toward the World Trade Center. A thought occurred to him: *The place where I work is gone!*

In a recent interview Rob reflected back on that moment, and said, "It's not damaged, you know, like a fire would damage it, where you'd look and see the smoke and you'd see the blackness from the fire. No . . . it's gone! I remember I kept saying to myself, *the place I work is gone.*" Upon getting to Penn Station, Rob would catch a train to Newark, New Jersey, and then find his way home via available, but sparsely occupied, trains.[208]

Another colleague caught up in the dust cloud was Nick Webb. He had been one of the earliest evacuees, but he stayed in the area due to both curiosity and a desire to assist wherever the need might have arisen. That desire to stay put below the towers allowed him to not only witness United Flight 175 hitting our building, but also become a victim of falling glass. After being bandaged up by that beneficent shop owner, Nick hung around trying to determine how he might intervene, but admittedly he was feeling pretty helpless. He had been able to call his wife to say he was okay and that he was down on the street. That was, until his building, our building, collapsed. Nick was standing near Broadway in Zuccotti Park. He heard a rumble and looked up. Like Rob Rothman about four blocks to his north, Nick saw the same major debris cloud descending furiously. The weight of the collapsing building was pulverizing everything in its downward path. Nick only had one thought. *Run!* He raced across Broadway and dashed down Cedar Street to the east, but the cloud was gaining on him.

The building at 120 Broadway has delivery doors on its north side along Cedar Street with recesses in them. Nick darted into one of the openings to take shelter from the advancing debris cloud. Unfortunately, the cloud overtook his position and was asphyxiating. Nick could feel himself choking, and he had the powerful sensation that *if I stay here I'm gonna die!* Blindly, he immediately reached out towards the street hoping to find an open vehicle into which he could dive for cover. Most fortunately, his extended arms soon found an unlocked van parked right next to him. He jumped in, and within seconds, a woman also climbed aboard. According to Nick, she was hysterical. Like the bar owner that Rob Rothman encountered, she immediately started to lock all the doors to prevent anyone else from getting into the vehicle. According to Nick, she was certain the van would soon be inundated with survivors. While appearing quite selfish, all reactions and emotions seem understandable given the circumstances.

By that time, the cloud had completely smothered the van in darkness. It looked pitch black outside. Initially, the noise from the collapse resembled rolling thunder. As the two refugees found themselves together, a cacophony of sounds included smaller, fine particles pummeling the vehicle. Then silence. Dead silence. The two waited patiently but were unaware of what would become their fate. After less than ten minutes, a twilight-type of light started to reveal their surroundings. The world outside was motionless, quiet, and covered in what looked like a recent snowfall. Unfortunately, it wasn't of the Currier & Ives variety.

Shortly, light re-emerged on the streets, and the owner of the van returned to the vehicle. Thanks to Nick's intervention, the doors had remained unlocked. To the owner's surprise, he found two strangers inside. He didn't seem to mind. In fact, he offered to drive them a distance. Both Nick and the unknown lady declined. They all hugged—complete strangers—and began their separate ways home. As the air cleared, Nick began a long walk towards Grand

Central Station more than three miles away. Soon after his departure from Ground Zero and the asphyxiating dust cloud, the other tower collapsed showering lower Manhattan with another deadly cloud of ash and debris. After an arduous journey on foot to Penn Station, Nick caught a train home to Connecticut and reaffirmed to his wife on another phone call that he was still okay.[209]

One group of victims not often talked about from the 9/11 ordeal are the significant others. Husbands, wives, partners, boyfriends, and girlfriends. The sheer dread they felt was horrific. The abject silence was deafening that day. It was easy for "no news" to be equated with "bad news." Cell phone networks were jammed well beyond their capacities, leaving most families in the dark for hours. I was very fortunate given my ability to reach my wife that morning to alert her that I was far from danger. But others like Jyoti's husband, Jaldhar, were left with a gut-wrenching ordeal that lasted for hours.

Jaldhar had neither seen nor heard from Jyoti since he dropped her off at the train station in New Jersey just prior to 8:00 AM. According to Jyoti, family and friends all knew she worked on a very high floor at the World Trade Center. She had tried twice from the office to contact Jaldhar, but was unsuccessful. Of course, if either of those calls had successfully connected, Jaldhar would have been given a false sense of security. Jyoti's second attempt had been actually cut off in mid-ring by the unexpected, and horrible, arrival of the hijacked jet. She was traumatized just thinking of her husband's thoughts as all this was transpiring. Soon after she received good news about her baby, she made a "collect" call from a pay phone inside the hospital. When she heard the operator ask Jaldhar if he would accept the charges from caller "Jyoti," Jaldhar screamed, "put her through, put her through, put her through!" The attending physician that performed and reviewed the ultrasound offered to speak to him and allayed any and all concerns, and both Jyoti and Jaldhar exhaled a big sigh of relief. By the time they spoke, both towers had already fallen, but up until then, Jaldhar had no idea how she was, or where she was.[210]

There was also Alfredo Guzman's wife, Mercedes. They had recently been married. Mercedes had visited us several times in the South Tower and was familiar to many of us. As the day unfolded, she sat at home with no knowledge of Alfredo's condition. Her thoughts included: *Is this really happening? This is crazy!* Soon after the initial impact to the North Tower she kept dialing and dialing Alfredo's number. There was no answer. Mercedes recalled the morning and all of its emotions for a video documentary on The History Channel entitled "Escape from the Towers."[211]

"And, then you see another plane. What the hell? My husband was in that building, and I still hadn't heard from him. It's horrible—you're seeing it—you're seeing it's on fire. It's unbelievable! These are innocent people! I was on the phone trying to reach Alfredo, not knowing where he was. It was devastating." She added, "Watching the [South] tower come down, that was it. I thought he died. I had tried calling and calling, and there was no service. You couldn't get anything. I wanted him to tell me that he was okay. That God did not take him from me and the kids. This is what I wanted. I wanted to hear him, to tell me, 'honey, I'm okay!'"[212]

Nick Webb's wife, Sue, was confronted with a similar sense of dread. She was drowning in the sensation of wondering if Nick's first phone call had prematurely given her hope. Sue recently recounted her memory of the morning:

> I remember distinctly that the house just filled up with people from everywhere. No one knew what to do or to say, but friends and relatives just started showing up with coffee and food to sit with me. There was no one to call, although I must have called Nick's cell and left dozens of hysterical messages before the service just stopped working. When I finally heard from Nick (relatively early in the day, on a borrowed cell phone), he told me he was going back to the buildings, that people needed help. I asked him if he couldn't please, please, please. Just come home. He said he was going back in. And after that phone call is when I heard that the buildings had collapsed. I was a mess and I remember saying to my dad, "Look. I'm going to be okay until about 5:00 PM, but if I don't hear from him before that, I'm going to lose it."[213]

Of course, most gut-wrenching of all are the accounts from the families of those who would never be heard from again. At the moment the second plane struck our building, Steve Weinberg's wife, Laurie, was struck with a terrible realization. "I went into the bedroom and sat down on his side of the bed praying for the phone to ring. I had maybe a very, very small glimmer of hope because Steve always used to say to me 'you always think the worst, don't think the worst!' And, so I thought, *well then, I'm going to try to think of a little bit of hope, maybe!*"[214]

When our building collapsed, Laurie was resigned to the worst of all news. "I knew there was no hope as soon as that building came down. Even if he had lived through the plane coming into the building, there wasn't enough time for him to get down from 78. And at that point, I said to myself 'I think we have to plan a funeral.'"[215]

CHAPTER 10

THE NEXT 24 HOURS

AS I DROVE up Peachtree Road in Franklin Lakes, after hearing about our building's collapse, I wasn't focused on what I was doing. I almost ran a neighbor walking her dog off the road. I literally believed that everyone I knew at Baseline in New York had just perished. In terms of what to do next, I only had one thought: *Family!* I pulled into my driveway honking my horn wildly. My wife greeted me and we hugged for a long time. I then drove directly to my daughters' elementary school. They were in the 5th and 3rd grades respectively.

I hadn't thought much about the process of entering High Mountain Road School. However, I knew word would be getting around that the Twin Towers had fallen during a terrorist attack, and I wanted to ensure that my girls knew I was fine. Upon entering the school, I quickly told the desk attendant of my association with the World Trade Center, and that I would like to see my daughters. Helen Attenello, the school's principal, was summoned. Apparently, I was one of the first parents to enter the building. I found Mrs. Attenello to be very supportive, but she had a plan that differed from mine. She had clearly thought it through. She acutely summarized for me that the school likely had several children whose parents worked at the WTC, and she frankly did not want me to introduce that very sensitive piece of news into her school. She also shared that it was unlikely that any of the kids were aware of the news. Remember, kids didn't carry cell phones, let alone smart phones, in 2001.

I fully understood her position. She then offered me the opportunity to be escorted to each of my girls' classrooms, where they would be asked to step into the hallway without any indication as to why they were being called. At that point, I had been given very strict instructions. I was to say "Hi, I thought I'd just come by to say hello!" The intent was simply to let them know I was clearly safe, knowing they would invariably learn the news later in the day. I spun a slightly different version by telling them that "I have cancelled my California trip and will be home tonight to play with you." I left the school knowing that they would later conclude that I was all right, based on my innocuous statement, but also knowing they would have said, "Dad's being weird again!"

Later that evening, I would learn that a few fathers from the school were, sadly, actually missing. One of them, my friend and father to a classmate of my older daughter, perished in the North Tower. He worked for Cantor Fitzgerald. Steve Schlag was an energetic, fun-loving dad. He left behind a wonderful family. In other personal circles, I would learn of the passing of Tom Cahill, a native of our town and the brother of a softball teammate of mine. He, too, worked at Cantor. And another local man, one of my brother's best friends, David Brady, lost his life due simply to attending a breakfast meeting at Windows on the World. He worked for Merrill Lynch and left behind a lovely wife and four small children. Finally, my town of Franklin Lakes additionally lost Frank Deming, a practice director for Oracle Corp who was working on a project at Marsh McLennan on the 99th floor of the North Tower. Frank sadly left behind his wife and five children.[216] While this book focuses on one company's journey, this infamous day was far more than a Baseline event. It was a New York tragedy. An American tragedy. A human tragedy.

At the moment my building fell, Baseline's evacuees from the South Tower had been seeking treatment or fighting to get home. Florence was still at the hospital. However, the collapse of the towers placed that medical center on ultra-alert for far more serious injuries to arrive. Florence knew it was time to leave. She departed the hospital and headed north. In her bare feet, she walked over three miles to a friend's office on 29th street. Once there, she again needed medical attention to flush more debris from her eyes. They were still stinging and she couldn't keep them open. A month later, she sought the attention of an ophthalmologist. Her eyes were not improving. After a quick evaluation, the doctor proceeded to grab a small tweezer-like instrument, and incredibly, extracted a tiny metal fragment from her cornea. It was a result of the explosion at Ground Zero which produced shrapnel and debris of all sizes.[217]

Also in retreat from Manhattan that morning was Barbara Tripp, our director of Data Integrity. Her day started exactly as mine had: with an ominous announcement from the PATH transit system. However, in her case, she made it all the way under the World Trade Center before hearing the same loudspeaker announcement indicating that "due to police action" PATH was suspending service. She had no idea what was going on right above her head. Despite her arrival at the WTC, her train's doors never opened. Immediately after the announcement, her train departed the WTC station and returned her to Hoboken. Once back across the Hudson, however, she took PATH's suggestion to go back to New York City via the midtown connection, and then take a city subway downtown. Unfortunately, when she got to Manhattan, and got out at 14th Street, both Trade Center towers were ablaze and in severe peril. She never got closer, and immediately needed to figure out an evacuation route. She headed north to the ferry terminal near the Jacob Javits Convention Center at 34th Street and the Hudson River on the west side of Manhattan.

Upon arriving at the ferry, Barbara found herself on a long line. She was bereft. Her world was turned upside down. Like me, she considered the horrible possibility that she was the sole survivor. All of a sudden, she heard a friendly voice yelling her name from behind. It was Deirdre Rock, one of Barbara's managers in Data Integrity. Barbara implored the people to let Deirdre through. According to Barbara, "New Yorkers are often known for being pretty tough, unyielding people, but that day everyone seemed to pull together like no other day. There was a sense of togetherness." The scene at the ferry terminal was refreshingly different than the one experienced by Rob Rothman at that Fulton Street bar. The people on the ferry line quickly understood the women's relationship and predicament, and let Deirdre come to Barbara's side. "We hugged so tightly," recalled Barbara. Deirdre was able to let Barbara know of several people who were still alive.[218] However, while they patiently stood on the line awaiting a ferry, the two ladies witnessed the collapse of our building.[219] Their comfort and joy in locating one another was short lived. Despair filled their hearts once again.

Brian Branco, our accounting consultant, after being forcibly pushed out of the World Trade Center just prior to the second plane's impact, had also headed north to the ferry in the West 30s. His walk was much farther than Barbara's—over three miles from the WTC. His arrival at the ferry was long after Barbara's, and the line seemed interminable. According to Brian, reports on the local news that night estimated the line to be over twenty city blocks long and involved 19,000 people.[220] There were so many people looking to flee Manhattan that other boating companies soon lent a hand. In fact, Brian's escape from New York that day was not via the ferry, but rather on a re-purposed Circle Line boat. On any other day, it serves as a tourist attraction that circumnavigates Manhattan several times a day. On 9/11, it facilitated Brian's homeward journey. His wife picked him up a mile or so inland on the New Jersey side of the river. His car, still parked many miles south in Jersey City, would have to wait for another day to be retrieved.

The exodus out of Manhattan was like a "modern day Dunkirk" according to author Mitchell Zuckoff. He described the evacuation below Canal Street, mandated by the Mayor of New York City, Rudy Giuliani, as "an evacuation that sent hundreds of thousands of people through dust-covered streets, uptown across bridges, or onto tugs, ferries, fire boats, Coast Guard vessels, and pleasure craft that sailed from the smoldering island."[221] This "makeshift unorganized armada" evacuated over 300,000 people from the island of Manhattan.[222]

By midday, Allan Unger and James Magalong, who had helped Eric Thompson get Mary Jos to the 25th floor, had travelled over five miles on foot to James's apartment on 71st Street on the upper east side of Manhattan. There, they would breathe a deep sigh of relief and gain some rest before catching a lift to their respective parents' homes in New Jersey the following day. Like Rob Rothman and Nick Webb, they too had been chased by the debris cloud and ran for their lives. Just a couple of miles north of Ground Zero, Allan and James observed fighter jets whizzing overhead at very low altitudes.[223] That added to the sense of dread and fear. Still, at that hour, those in retreat from the WTC had little knowledge of actual facts.

Minds raced in many directions.

By early afternoon on 9/11, Ron Perez and Henry D'Atri had reached the George Washington Bridge thanks to a couple of cab rides and thick shoe leather. They began their arduous journey when they proactively decided to walk down 78 floors prior to our building being struck. After being knocked down in the stairwell, they had travelled far. The bridge is about twelve miles north of Ground Zero. Crossing the bridge, however, proved problematic. The Port Authority had closed the pedestrian pathway. Perhaps officials were worried about gawkers congesting the semi-treacherous sidewalk that hangs 200 feet above the Hudson River in full view of Manhattan. Recognizing their predicament, Ron and Henry caught sight of a bread truck on a side street. Ron quickly surmised that it likely had made its rounds and was probably empty in the back. The guys approached the truck, but quickly noticed a line of people already waiting to enter the truck's rear door.

Fortuitously, the truck had indeed made its rounds and was empty. According to Henry's account, "We stood inside the back of this bread truck, in the dark, wall to wall, shoulder to shoulder, maybe fifteen people . . . as many as you can fit in the back of a bread truck." In recounting the moment, Ron said, "I can still smell the aroma of freshly baked bread." He was starving but was happy to be alive and heading into his home state. Within minutes they were in New Jersey. Upon arrival in the town of Fort Lee, the impromptu passengers offered the driver a fare that he summarily declined. Unfortunately, the roads were all closed in and around the bridge. Ron and Henry still had a three-mile hike ahead of them where a friend of Ron picked them up north of the bridge in Englewood Cliffs, New Jersey.[224]

Meanwhile, Simon Chen and Alfredo Guzman, who had endured the impact in our 77th floor office space, had made their way up to Alfredo's home on 102nd Street in Manhattan, to the delight of Alfredo's wife.[225] Mercedes received the gift of a lifetime when Alfredo came walking through their front door. "I'm still trying to reach him, and there's nothing. I feel like I'm gonna pass out. But he walked in the door and I was like 'everybody's been calling and crying!' And he said 'Did they start crying when they found out I was okay?'" That was classic Alfredo. At Baseline, we had come to know his humorous, dry wit all too well. And he made that statement because, as Mercedes said, "this is what he does!"[226]

Ironically, Mercedes actually played a role in ensuring her husband would arrive home safely. September 11 was her first day at a new job. Unlike her previous position, this one was walkable. To help her acclimate to the new walking route, Alfredo didn't drive to work that day. He accompanied Mercedes on foot early that morning to her new place of employment, and then hopped on a subway going downtown. It was the first day in his seven years at Baseline that he didn't drive to work and leave his car at the Battery Park Garage just south of the World Trade Center.

Later, when Alfredo saw Jyoti successfully placed in the ambulance, he began his route home. If he had driven to work that day, he would have proceeded south along the eastern edge of the Twin Towers before swinging west around Two World Trade (South Tower). According to Alfredo, given the timing of his departure from the ambulance scene, "The building would have collapsed on top of me."[227] Alfredo would have been directly below the South Tower when it came down. His wife's new job had saved him. It was another twist of fate.

While at Alfredo's home, the two men freshened up and then learned that the ferries were running to New Jersey from midtown. All of a sudden, Simon had a way home. Alfredo quickly offered his services, and the two jumped into Alfredo's car and headed back south, this time towards the west side of Manhattan on the Hudson River. This was the same ferry terminal behind the Jacob Javits Center that had provided Barbara, Deirdre, and Brian with an earlier escape route.

Simon's clothes were still covered in dirt and ash from his involvement at the point of impact. As a result, the ferry workers were hosing down all those in such a state. My guess is that there was fear that toxic chemicals were in that dust. They gave Simon a black plastic bag to protect his personal items and then hosed him down. As a result, his laptop remained dry. That would eventually prove to be an extremely fortuitous event for Baseline.

After Nick Webb had made his three-mile trek to Grand Central station, he was able to borrow another cell phone and placed his second phone call of the day to his wife. Recall that he first called Sue from the street below the South Tower just prior to its collapse when he ran for cover. According to Sue:

> Nick sounded robotic and emotionless. He was on
> a train home. Several of us went to meet the train.
> I didn't recognize him when he walked off the train.
> My sister said, "Sue, that's Nick!" He was dust covered.
> He had no phone, no briefcase, no jacket. He looked
> exhausted and dead inside. It looked to me like he
> had walked out of a war zone. I hugged him for a long
> time.[228]

It was mid-afternoon when Nick finally slumped off that train. He was exhausted. Sue was emotionally spent. Sue shared that throughout the day her feelings yo-yoed between being "scared, sad, angry, hopeless, confused, and devastated."[229]

As the day wore on, my associates were in various states of mental and physical health. I greatly welcomed the offer from Larry in San Francisco to keep a master spreadsheet of everyone's whereabouts. Larry was already giving me positive signals that a good number of my Baseline friends were alive. I communicated his involvement and phone number via email to whomever was tuned in. I was thankful that our Philadelphia-based mail server was still up and running. By mid-afternoon I had already been in contact with Rob Patterson and Simon Chen. Rob was thrilled to hear that so many of his associates had survived, yet was clearly saddened by the number of unaccounted-for individuals. He pledged to join us as soon as he could arrange transportation from Florida.

Some of the more fortunate employees, myself included, began to think long term. At about 3:00 PM, after visits from my parents and several friends, I sat in my living room contemplating what came next. I found myself at an emotional fork in the road as I saw two seemingly incongruent paths ahead of me. One path required me to stay focused on the WTC site, seek updates, and mourn for the families who were in dire straits waiting for any news. The other path involved seizing the moment, in the name of all survivors and clients, to resurrect Baseline so that good people would still have their careers and clients wouldn't be let down. While I didn't take my eye off the World Trade Center site and any news relating to our missing friends, I decided to attack the second option. That path was at least visible, and I felt an overwhelming obligation to do something.

Simon and I agreed to meet in our Philadelphia office the next
day. I then contacted Ron Perez and Barbara Tripp, and offered to
pick them up and drive to Philadelphia in the morning. If we were
going to survive as a business, it would only be from Philadelphia.

As an early sign that we would receive great support from our
associates, Simon informed me that he had heard from Peter Haller,
who managed our client server distribution and maintenance process.
Proactively, Peter had already been in touch with DELL Computer
to place an order for PCs and servers to be delivered to our Philly
office. According to Peter, once he received confirmation from Simon
that we likely still had a company, he arranged to have an emergency
conference call with DELL's management around 2:00 PM on the
afternoon of September 11. His request for expedited status within
DELL came with the urgent stipulation that "we are in desperate shape,
as victims of 9/11, and are going to need lots of computers . . . fast!"[230]

Within Baseline, Peter was the primary contact for DELL, and
had purchasing authority. During that 2:00 PM conference call,
DELL elevated our status. According to Peter, a DELL executive said,
"We have an allocation that we have to do for the government, but
you're next!" Peter recalls ordering twenty servers, with our standard
configuration for client machines, as well as numerous desktops.
They were all shipped to our office in Philadelphia. At the moment
that order was placed, we honestly did not know how, or if, we could
utilize them.[231]

As things quieted in lower Manhattan and much of the dust
cloud lifted, a bucket brigade commenced at Ground Zero. Brave
first responders from New York's fire, police, and rescue squads,
along with K-9 companions, descended upon the large, hellish pile of
debris. They had returned to the site from which they had just fled,
hoping to rescue survivors. What greeted them was a scene of death
and destruction. Dan Nigro, Chief of Operations for the FDNY on
9/11, said, "As you got back to the scene and saw what was left of it,
it looked like war."[232]

The debris from the collapse of the Trade Center's towers was
fourteen stories high in places. Luckily, the heaviest materials were not
spread much beyond the World Trade Center's sixteen-acre campus.
That was due to the pulverization of concrete and metal during the
collapse which more resembled a pancaking effect rather than an

angled toppling of the structures. Despite the hellish conditions, which included raging fires, extreme temperatures, and toxic gases, the responders began the arduous task of removing the debris, piece by piece, in order to listen for any signs of life. The heat from multiple fires remained an ongoing challenge to both rescue and recovery efforts. Astonishingly, it took more than three months to fully extinguish the various fires at Ground Zero. The smoldering ashes didn't give up their last burning ember until December 19 of that year.[233]

By early evening, the very-pregnant Jyoti was resigning herself to the fact that she was going to spend the night at LIU Brooklyn Hospital. It was not because the staff felt it necessary, it was because there was simply no way for her to get home. A slew of volunteers offered to drive her all the way to New Jersey, but many bridges and tunnels were closed. Reuniting with her husband would have to wait until Wednesday, September 12. As a courtesy, the hospital attempted to make her comfortable in the maternity ward. They gave her a room at no charge. However, Jyoti was all by herself. Outside, flashing lights and screeching sirens continued all night long. "I was terrified," said Jyoti. "To be honest, I felt alone. There was not much I could do. I had to stay there. I couldn't really go home. I was scared to even step outside on my own. Even though I was safe, I was still scared."[234]

As night fell, Larry in San Francisco was reporting that five individuals were missing. It was a very sad revelation. However, it was also very encouraging compared with my perspective at 10:00 AM when I first learned of our building's collapse. One of the missing turned out to be Eric Thompson who had escorted Mary Jos to safety. We soon learned that he was okay. For days, we held out hope for our other four missing colleagues. Our collective thoughts included: *Were they still alive? Were they trapped somewhere?*

Unfortunately, there wasn't any plausible way to even consider going to the site. Somehow participating in some kind of rescue was neither feasible nor realistic. Mayor Rudy Giuliani and New York Governor, George Pataki, counseled everyone against approaching the area. Their message was that between professional rescue personnel and the National Guard, all efforts to find survivors were well handled. Recall that Giuliani had also ordered the evacuation of the entire area below Canal Street, which was nearly a mile north of the World Trade Center site.

Hospitals, on the other hand, were easy to contact to ascertain the status of admitted individuals. Unfortunately, that ease was due to a dearth of patients from the tragedy. The medical community had prepared themselves for thousands and thousands of injuries soon after the first plane struck One World Trade Center. Author Garrett Graff stated: "Throughout the day, injured office workers, Manhattan residents, and first responders did seek treatment, but the arriving patients only ever amounted to a trickle, not a flood. Doctors and nurses were left with the sinking realization that no patients meant no survivors."[235] According to Francine Kelly, a registered nurse and manager at Saint Vincent's Catholic Medical Center:

> I think we saw 350 to 450 patients within the first eight hours of 9/11. We saw tremendous volumes of patients. We saw in those first couple hours some people who worked in the World Trade Center. We saw burns, shrapnel wounds, crush injuries, people in hypertensive crisis. Then as the day continued, we started to see rescue workers come in who were injured in their line of duty. Mid-afternoon, three or four o'clock, we were working nonstop. Then what happened, unfortunately, is all of a sudden, things slowed down. That was very difficult for us, because you kept wanting to hear that ambulance siren.[236]

The hospitals were practically devoid of patients. The terrorist acts were so destructive, so immediate, so complete that office workers and first responders in and around the WTC that day were either dead or relatively unharmed. There was very little middle ground. It was a definitive outcome.

While at home on the evening of 9/11, I received a call from Suresh Kavan, our group president within Thomson Financial. He was in London on a business trip. He nicely affirmed the organization's support for our employees and wanted to know how many people I thought we had lost. At the time, we had accounted for everyone but five people. He pledged his support, but also raised the obvious question. "Where are your people going to work?" His message was clear. Since we were without a home, we should consider an immediate move into Thomson Financial's new world headquarters at 195 Broadway in lower Manhattan. That prospect was too monumental an issue for me to tackle on that particular night. First, that building was immediately adjacent to Ground Zero. How was anyone going to get there? Second, how would my associates emotionally react to such an announcement (i.e., having to return to the area)? And, lastly, I knew such a move would fly in the face of Rob Patterson's ambitions. I politely dodged the question. In retrospect, it was a legitimate business question. On the other hand, given everything I had seen, heard, and felt that day, because my Baseline blood ran deep, Philadelphia was the only office I wanted to recognize that evening. Philadelphia also represented the fastest path to resurrect the business.

As midnight approached, I received another phone call. This one was more poignant. It came from Steve Campbell, the husband of our executive assistant, Jill, and father to ten-month-old Jake. It was heart wrenching. I had no news, and yet I felt very responsible for giving him accurate information. He was right to call, but I had nothing to offer him. I had received tough phone calls before in my career, but in each instance, I was aware of details and could provide an update or a status. Each of those instances were business related. That day's events were external acts of unprecedented terrorism. I felt completely helpless on that phone call. Steve was a New York City cop. I was incredibly impressed by how calm and collected he was. At that moment, I was holding out hope for all of my missing associates to eventually surface. I instructed him to reach out to Helen Byrne, Jill's supervisor, who was staying in close contact with her teammates. When I hung up the phone, I felt horribly inadequate. I tried to put myself in his shoes. It would have zapped the life out of me.

Bleary-eyed, angry, and depressed, I went to bed around 1:00 AM. I had to get some sleep as the next morning would represent the proverbial "first day of the rest of my life." And, what a different life it had become.

Wednesday, September 12 dawned with a thick, dark cloud of smoke and dust hovering over Manhattan. It was a sobering reminder of what had just occurred the day before. It hadn't been a dream; not even a horrible, but temporary, nightmare. It was a real-life, world-changing disaster that gravely affected the nation and, more specifically, the cities of New York and Washington.

As morning dawned on September 12, 2001, the only known facts were that a still-unknown number of friends were dead, and there was nowhere to report to work. Baseline's offices were gone, and the 170 Baseline-issued WTC IDs were suddenly useless.

Hundreds of thousands of people were directly impacted. They lost homes, businesses, jobs, and likely knew someone who had been killed. Tens of thousands lost a loving friend or family member. The citizens of two significant metropolitan areas suffered physical, emotional, and economic hardship at the hands of a real, and lasting, wartime surprise attack.

For the associates of Baseline in New York, just about everything was gone. Certainly, there was no home office in which to meet and decide next steps. There were no longer any servers to provide clean and efficient downloads of nightly data updates. There was no longer a sophisticated client support phone system to properly route calls to help customers sort through issues; nor was there any digital repository in which to log those customer chats or research prior account activity. Phone calls into once mighty Baseline were simply greeted with a fast busy signal. However, one important aspect was still alive at Baseline: its *esprit de corps*. Incredibly, many of my associates in the middle of their darkest hour were privately thinking along the same lines: *How can I help resurrect this wonderful business?*

Soon after dawn on September 12, I picked up Ron Perez at his home in Bergen County, New Jersey. Barbara Tripp was already waiting for us at the Sheraton Crossroads Hotel in the town of Mahwah. The three of us drove straight to 1601 Market Street in Philadelphia—about a two-hour drive. I knew Simon would be arriving that morning, and technologists Jonathan Weinberg and John Tabako were already en route together, along with John's wife, Darcy. Lines blurred those days between business and personal agendas. Life appeared so fleeting. So fragile. It was understandable, and acceptable, that my team wanted and needed familial support. Separately, Alfredo Guzman and his Pricing Team were also headed south.

Jonathan had only slept about four hours as he contemplated all the things he and his technology team would need to do in Philadelphia. As he sat as a passenger in Tabako's car on the Brooklyn Queens Expressway heading for Philadelphia early that morning, our vice president of Technology had a clear view of lower Manhattan across the East River as the sun began to rise. He saw smoke still rising from the site and was affected again by his emotions. He recently shared that "It was an eerie spectacle."[237]

John Tabako described the plume of smoke as a "long parallel across the top of New York City." John's mind was focused on his memories of visiting One World Trade Center—the North Tower. John kept reviewing over and over in his head how many times he had visited our client, Fred Alger Management, on the 103rd floor of Tower One. He was also recalling several of the Baseline management meetings we held just several floors above that client at Windows on the World restaurant. He couldn't escape the notion of "what if this had happened while he, or the wider group, had been in that building at that time." Adding to his despair were thoughts surrounding his primary tech contact at Fred Alger, Mike Howell. He enjoyed working with Mike. It was just a few days later that John learned that Mike Howell had lost his life on 9/11.[238]

As two of the key cogs in Baseline's technical wheel continued south towards Philadelphia, Jonathan received a phone call soon after getting on the New Jersey Turnpike. It was from Roberta Levine, the wife of our CFO Bob Levine. She, like Steve Campbell the night before, was searching for news. Any kind of news. She was understandably distraught and emotional. As Jonathan tells it, "it was one of the toughest phone calls I've ever had."[239]

At the same time, Jyoti was rising to a new day in her hospital room in Brooklyn. At first light on the 12th, she was asking to go home. Jyoti, being somewhat selective, waited until a police officer was available to drive her home. He took her all the way to the front door of her New Jersey home and remained until Jyoti, and her healthy *in utero* baby, were safely inside.[240]

In Philadelphia, Jonathan Weinberg and John Tabako were the first New Yorkers to arrive. According to Jonathan, "We then set about the task of trying to resurrect a business that was basically in tatters." Weinberg added, "I still hadn't had a chance to really process what had happened, but I realized that unless we immediately got to work, hundreds of people were going to lose their jobs."[241] Similarly, Alfredo Guzman had independently echoed Jonathan's sentiment. While at home on the evening of 9/11, Alfredo was trying to establish a path of action. He recently shared his thoughts from that moment:

> I figured I could stay home, and do nothing, and get paid. But, it wasn't about me. What about the people that work for me? What about the four people that work on the Pricing team? What about the four people on the Index team? What about the three people on the Nightly Processing team? What are they going to do if we don't rebuild?[242]

With that thought in mind, Alfredo quickly decided to pick up a few members of his own team on Wednesday morning. He met them at 6:00 AM at the 51st Street E-train subway station in Manhattan. Philadelphia was their destination. They, too, began a trip into the unknown. Questions abounded. What obstacles would they find? What level of cooperation from fellow associates would be required, or even materialize? Could they measure up to the highest standards that clients had come to expect? Only time would tell. But time needed effort. And effort was the first step.

As colleagues gathered in Philadelphia, Peter Haller brought his team together on that Wednesday in the New York City borough of Brooklyn to assess readiness. For the meeting, the home of his teammate, Robert Yu, was chosen because of its central location. Peter's team was responsible for customer fulfillment of servers, as well as internal desktop support. According to Peter, he had to "first and foremost, make sure the people were mentally ready to do this work." He knew the imminent workload would involve incredible deadlines, and require a "makeshift environment" housed within very close quarters and a long way from home. As the team gathered and watched CNN for updates, they began informally talking about the business. They started listing actions to be taken as a group. Peter shared that "it started to feel like it was a company because we were all there." He then took the group out for an early dinner. While seated at the table in that Brooklyn restaurant, the team started asking questions and making emphatic statements. According to Peter, they included, "So, what do we do now?" And, "shouldn't we get to work?" And, "we should do something!"[243]

With a newfound level of confidence, Peter then arranged for a caravan of cars to depart the next morning for our office in Philadelphia. He knew that the newly ordered DELL equipment would be waiting for him. Peter and his team would all arrive in Philly on Thursday, September 13.

As mentioned earlier, Philadelphia was our Software Development office. In the previous year we had duplicated our nightly update process on a bank of servers in order to make it a "hot site"—capable of instantly handling the nightly updates if for any reason New York was unavailable. The nightly update process would send a data packet to each and every (Baseline-supplied) client server. The file would contain the closing price for each of the 10,000 North American stocks we tracked, along with any stock split adjustments, as well as any updates from the previous day on reported revenues, dividends, earnings (including adjustments), earnings estimates, and publicly released financial statements. It would also update all the index constituents (e.g., S&P 500, Russell 2000, etc.) along with industry and sector files created by Baseline. The nightly update process was a critical aspect to our service, especially given that many customers ran morning routines with this data on their portfolios using the Baseline product.

While that hot site creation was at least a start in terms of full-scale back-up, none of the systems that created those data packets were in Philadelphia. The Philadelphia hot site assumed those files existed. It did not create the data packet files. The missing programs that created these packets represented a sizable problem. Given that Alfredo Guzman headed up our Securities Pricing, Indexes, and the Nightly Update process, his immediate focus on the business was essential. We were very thankful for his team's immediate response.

On that Wednesday, we realized that a plan for Baseline's survival would require several steps:

1. Inventory all the programs required to create the nightly update packet, and by Friday afternoon, design a plan to rehabilitate, or re-create, each one.

2. Determine which New York staff would be required in Philadelphia, and for how long, and how we would situate them during the day and where they would stay in the evenings.

3. Work closely with DELL to expedite the shipment of many new servers for client installs as well as to increase the capacity of the Philadelphia data center to be the primary nightly process facility. We also would need numerous desktop computers for the internal support of the imminently larger workforce.

4. Contact the insurance company and gain immediate involvement and agreement to our plan of action.

5. Find a replica of our end-user system in order to gain the most up-to-date Stock Lists that Baseline supplied (e.g., the S&P 500, or any one of 89 industry constituent lists). Other than being the back-up for the Nightly Process, Philadelphia was our primary software development site. It didn't house complete, working versions of our end-user application. (The complete, end-to-end back-up plan was in the midst of a multi-year process. In retrospect, I wish we had placed a higher priority on it.)

6. Locate a large, working Lotus Notes "client." By client I'm referring to an end-user installation with as large a database as possible. Lotus Notes was a replication tool. A laptop would "replicate" those records of interest to the end user. An experienced sales rep with a large territory and many clients, who overlapped with many account managers, would provide a healthy head start to getting our master client database back on track.

7. Establish where our new headquarters would be located.

Truth be told, we were aided greatly by the fact that the markets did not re-open until the following Monday. We had three full business days (and nights), plus a weekend to accomplish the above steps, or at least set them in motion. One thing was certain: for Baseline to survive, we had to update all 1,000 remote client servers by Monday evening, September 17, with updated pricing information. That would be no small task, and on 9/11 we had over 10,000 sophisticated users depending on us. If we didn't neatly append the closing price from September 10th with the closing price on September 17th, it would have serious financial consequences for Baseline. Additionally, given that the market fell nearly 12 percent in the subsequent week[y], requiring lots of analysis by all our clients, there would be little forgiveness for our lack of readiness. The question in Philadelphia on that Wednesday, September 12, was "will we make it?"

---

y   The S&P 500 index closed at 1092.54 on the last trading day (Monday, Sep 10) prior to the events of September 11. At the end of the first resumed trading week (Friday, Sep 21), the index closed at 965.80. That downturn represented a drop of 11.6%.

CHAPTER 11

NAVIGATING TRANSITIONS

AS BASELINE PREPARED to rebuild the business from our makeshift headquarters in Philadelphia, we were a little more than a year removed from our third corporate transition. At the time, we were a wholly-owned subsidiary of the Thomson Corporation. Bowne had been our initial investor in 1989, followed by total ownership by Primark in 1997, and Thomson in June of 2000. The results of these transitions added to the range of challenges facing us on September 12, 2001.

Having spent a good number of years in corporate America, Rob Patterson understood the intricacies of both venture-backed investments and corporate acquisitions. He often proclaimed how the respective agendas of buyers and sellers in such deals would not always mesh, and that conflicts often arose. That would be particularly true in the case of Baseline where advice, operational intrusion, or integration plans were rarely welcomed. Rather than being your typical corporate "yes man," Rob's non-conformant personality had him stiff-arm many edicts and intrusions from above. He was an entrepreneur with corporate moxie. He marched to the beat of his own drum. While Bowne was the only true acquisition/investment he ever sought or enjoyed, Rob was able to balance himself, time and again, as three different corporate transitions shuffled the sand beneath his feet.

Unlike many technology founders, Rob stayed the course through the transitions. That constancy proved invaluable to his clients and associates.

Early in its lifecycle, there's no question that Baseline benefitted from corporate ties. Bowne's infusion of capital in 1989 was of paramount importance to Baseline's successful rise to prominence within its market. Rob would have preferred an indefinite incubation period under the corporate umbrella of Bowne, but that all changed in 1995. Dick Koontz, Rob's longtime business friend and Chairman of Bowne at the time, sadly contracted thyroid cancer that year. He battled courageously, but lost his life in November 1996. Given his illness and the need to focus on his health, Dick stepped down from active management in October of 1995. While he remained chairman until July 1996, the management reins of Bowne were handed over to Robert (Bob) Johnson who was recruited from the Newsday organization. As a side note, the growth of Bowne while Dick was employed was impressive. His obituary in the *New York Times* on November 23, 1996 stated: "During his career, Bowne grew from a company with roughly $35 million in revenues to a $500 million company with 3200 employees and record earnings."[244]

I had the pleasure of meeting Dick several times, and of presenting Baseline's sales results and strategy to him at Baseline board meetings between 1993 and 1995. He was the consummate professional. He was a stickler for detail yet could see the big picture. A finance pro, he could talk facts and figures about his firm all day long, yet could give a clear and concise layman's overview of his business as well—shedding light on both current tactics and future strategy.

Dick's passing had a profound impact on Rob Patterson. It spelled the end of a period of friendly incubation. Rob felt totally in control of his business under the auspices of the Bowne Corporation, which more realistically translated to *under the friendly auspices of Richard H. Koontz.* There was mutual respect between Rob and Dick that went all the way back to their 345 Hudson Street days when they shared elevator rides while at S&P and Bowne respectively.

Rob immediately sensed that without his cheerleader we were in trouble, and he made me aware of his concerns. Soon after being dubbed the new CEO of Bowne, Bob Johnson announced that he was returning Bowne to its roots—to traditional financial printing.

Bowne planned to jettison non-printing assets. Rob Patterson seized the moment. Rather than being told that Baseline had been sold to some surprise suitor, Rob became proactive. "Ed, I've got to control where we go. Where we end up!" He considered the potential of a strategic purchase to be catastrophic. A strategic acquisition is one in which the acquirer sees strategic benefits in making the investment. Those benefits might include operational synergies, or acquiring a customer base to sell more product, or even obtaining the intellectual property (IP) rights to apply to other product lines. On the surface that might sound encouraging. To Rob, however, a strategic acquisition likely meant personally working for someone else. That was something Rob didn't want. In his mind, he hadn't spent fifteen years building a foundation for growth with his own sweat and blood to simply throw away his personal independence. Despite owning 90 percent of Baseline, Bowne had ostensibly left Rob alone. Rob wasn't interested in, once again, feeling like a corporate employee. Nor was he interested in a nice payoff. Baseline was firing on all cylinders, and he wanted to remain the driver of its success.

In Rob's mind, the ideal suitor for the 1996 transaction would be a financial partner; someone, or some entity, that would see the value accretion potential of Baseline as a standalone entity. So, on his own, and without approval from anyone at Bowne, Rob began a road show with large Venture Capital firms and a few Private Equity concerns. With 1995 year-end revenue at about $10 million, Baseline was a bit large for the traditional venture charters but not a big enough player for standard private equity agendas. However, Rob was resolute to control his own destiny. Simon Chen and I assisted him with his presentation and, from time to time, accompanied him on meetings. This process took place during calendar year 1996. When General Atlantic out of Stamford, Connecticut came through with a firm cash offer, Rob felt he had struck gold. My recollection is that the offer was for $28 million. General Atlantic was going to incubate us for about three years and then take us public. "Bob Johnson can't possibly turn this down, Ed. And the board, who knows me, will be both shocked and ecstatic!" To be sure, a $4 million investment in 1989 which would return $25.2 million (for 90 percent) just seven years later would be a magnificent return on investment. In fact, the math would suggest a pre-tax annual return of over 30 percent on Bowne's money.

Rob decided to go it alone on the day he would proudly share this opportunity with Bob Johnson. The reaction? According to Rob, Johnson was pleasantly surprised and saw this as aiding his agenda of purging non-strategic assets. However, as the new CEO, he felt it was his fiduciary obligation to put the business out for bid. Rob was devastated. He knew Dick would never have betrayed him in that way. But Johnson wasn't a friend—he was just being a businessman. He figured if a financial firm could come up with $28 million that quickly, a strategic buyer would likely pony up much more. Rob's nightmare scenario started to come into view.

Within days of putting Baseline up for public bid, I heard that Thomson Financial put forth a pre-emptive bid of $55 million. Rob knew it wasn't real. In his opinion, it was intended to stop all conversations with General Atlantic in their tracks while Thomson figured out their strategy. In the end, Thomson was not much of a factor in this particular round. While the General Atlantic bid initially looked terrific, two serious strategic bidders came into view: FactSet and Primark. FactSet, our primary competitor, was similar to Baseline in that both of us focused primarily on the buy-side of the capital markets community. While our own market focus was nearly identical to FactSet's, our strategies differed. However, that difference presented an interesting complementary variable in a potential merger. While Baseline provided an easy-to-use desktop tool aimed at portfolio managers, FactSet's system provided a deep utility for analysts that wished to dig further into the financial depths of public companies.

The concept of this marriage was not without merit. The Baseline management team participated in several discussions with key FactSet personnel as part of their due diligence efforts. FactSet chairman, Howard Wille, led the charge. In the end, I recall that they offered Bowne something like $39 million for the business. Rob's hope for General Atlantic and their IPO plans were suddenly dashed. Further, Rob knew that if the FactSet acquisition went through, his days as the designer of the Baseline user interface might be numbered. Recall that Rob was less about the money and more about his Baseline family of associates, and having control over his product. Merging with FactSet would have required a very carefully laid out plan for operational integration. There was also the possibility that FactSet might simply have eliminated the competitive obstacle by sunsetting the Baseline application and attempting a massive conversion effort.

To Rob's short-term delight, FactSet would be outbid. An entrepreneur and investor, Joe Kasputys, had successfully transformed a holding company for a gas utility into an information services conglomerate called Primark. In 1988, Primark officially separated itself from its Michigan Consolidated Gas Company by spinning off the utility. At the time, the energy subsidiary of Primark represented a sizable $1.4 billion of Primark's $1.5 billion in revenue.[245] This spinoff placed Kasputys at the helm of the smaller remnant, but the deal enabled Kasputys to focus on acquiring key assets in the emerging, fast-paced sector of information services under the brand of Primark. In building his own financial information empire, Joe Kasputys made several acquisitions in the early 1990s. He then seized upon the opportunity to add another arrow to his quiver by targeting Baseline. In late 1996, he offered a bid of $41 million, which was accepted by Bowne's board of directors. The deal closed in January of 1997, and represented an approximate pre-tax annual return to Bowne of 36 percent[z] as it "recorded a pre-tax gain of $35,273,000"[246] based on its 90 percent ownership stake in Baseline. The transaction also represented the end of personal ownership of the Baseline brand by Rob Patterson. Primark paid Rob at the time of closing for his 10 percent stake, but retained him as CEO.

In January of 1997, Baseline officially became part of the Primark organization, and was placed into what was known as PFAD—the Primark Financial Analytics Division. What Rob liked about this arrangement was that Primark seemed far less interested in mandating the types of operational integration for which Thomson was known, or that FactSet would possibly have engineered. Ostensibly, Primark was a holding company for assets with merit. In fact, Kasputys wanted to maximize the growth of his assets, and not threaten the status quo. His strategy seemed to be similar to private equity firms—to incubate, grow, and then liquidate. This meant that Rob could continue to operate his firm as a standalone entity. There were several meager attempts to create operational synergies, but not much came of those efforts. And, what Primark may or may not have realized was that

---

z   The value of Bowne's $4,000,000 investment in late 1989 became $35,273,000 in January of 1997. That represented a pre-tax annual return of about 36 percent based on an approximate seven year holding period.

Rob would have worked very hard to avoid, even thwart, anything that would have blurred the lines between his enterprise and others. Our PFAD division consisted of three separately run organizations: Baseline, I/B/E/S International, and Vestek. Baseline and Vestek, due to this acquisition, had cooperated in an office sharing arrangement in their respective New York and San Francisco headquarters. On 9/11, that simple business cooperative became yet another twist of fate in which innocent decisions had tragic consequences.

All three companies focused primarily on buy-side analytics, although each had very distinct approaches. The PFAD division was run by Joe Riccobono, the former chairman of I/B/E/S International, which itself had been acquired by Primark in 1995.[247] I/B/E/S was the largest of the three PFAD companies. They were a content provider, and amassed earnings estimates from sell-side analysts around the globe tracking the world's public companies. They sliced and diced the data, and were an excellent input for quantitative models. Their focus was aiding buy-side firms with research. Their data could be purchased directly, or accessed through several third parties including FactSet, our longtime rival. I/B/E/S was larger than Baseline, although that gap would shrink in the ensuing years due to Baseline's growth rate. I/B/E/S was originally founded by the sell-side brokerage firm of Lynch, Jones & Ryan and began collecting data in 1976.

The final piece of the PFAD triumvirate was Vestek. They focused less on equity research, and more on portfolio analytics, including portfolio construction and optimization. Vestek's product was quantitatively oriented and focused on optimizing industry and sector weightings as well as risk factors, and also helping to analyze portfolio composition and performance attribution (i.e., "Where do my gains and losses stem from—stock selection or sector weightings?").[248] Vestek was smaller than Baseline. Its revenues relied upon direct, and involved, support from a team of PhDs on staff. Baseline, on the other hand, chose not to focus too heavily on statistical analyses nor be a product designed for a small, quantitative segment of the market. Baseline was a workflow tool for the mainstream buy-side community.

One might conclude that Rob's days would have been numbered under Primark given that he no longer owned any shares of Baseline and was known as occasionally being the proverbial "fly in the ointment." However, Rob's genius went beyond product design. He knew how to keep a business growing and yet remain discreet. Rob was very adept at communicating only the bare minimum. During an off-site meeting in 1999 with top Primark managers, I was walking a few feet behind Rob and Joe Kasputys. Joe was heaping praise upon Rob for the growth of both the top and bottom line. Then, Joe said something along the lines of, "But, Rob, I still don't get it. I've seen your product. It's very attractive, but it seems very simple. It doesn't delve deep into financial analysis, yet the industry is clamoring to sign up. I really don't get it!"

Rob's response was a bellowing laugh and a quick "You don't need to, Joe. Just leave it to us!" Rob then gave me a glancing look over his shoulder with a quick smile. And, that's exactly how Rob liked it. He figured the more he explained his strategy, the more questions would ensue. He had zero interest in helping Kasputys know what made us tick, nor was he insulted by the "simple" comment or driven to dissuade the thought. From Rob's vantage point, the less a parent company knew about us, the better off we were. His security was lodged in our success and their ignorance of how we marched. Of course, it goes without saying, that strategy only works if you're killing the numbers. And we were. During the Primark years (1997–2000), Baseline would enjoy a tremendous growth spurt, rising from $13 million in annual revenue in 1996 to $39 million in 2000.

In my opinion, Joe Kasputys had a keen eye for macro opportunity. He knew that the market for financial data was growing. Global data, derived data, and new data ideas (e.g., trade tracking data, insider trading data, and short interest) were making the market expand in the 1990s at attractive rates. New ways to deliver information were also gaining traction (e.g., optical disk). Additionally, as desktop PCs became more commonplace, the potential user audience was growing in numbers. Acquiring companies like Baseline, I/B/E/S, and Vestek made good sense. However, from a micro perspective, many senior executives in the financial information industry didn't have the same knowledge as the entrepreneurs in the trenches. Founders of information services had a keen awareness of individual users and what drove their workflow.

As the founder of Baseline, Rob Patterson intimately understood the buy-side portfolio manager. According to Chris Tresse, the sales executive whom I followed to Baseline:

Rob's whole magic was building something where he just knew what the user's process was. He built a product that enabled the portfolio manager to be more efficient and to make decisions with greater confidence and greater clarity. Back in the day, you had FactSet, but they were coming from the perspective of the research analyst, or the director of research, with the interface and technology to crunch numbers and do modeling. But it wasn't a portfolio manager's tool. Baseline was always a portfolio manager's tool. There was nothing like it. The usability was amazing.[249]

Chris added:

Rob had a Steve Jobs sort of intuition as to what would really excite the end user. He intuited what it would take to simplify a process and make it obvious. Rob toiled with every little thing . . . from the color choice, and the font, to the way PE bar charts faded in the background. It made it sexy. It made data analysis fun in the sense that you could get something done quickly. Rob had launched an entirely new idea. Kind of like the iPad. You didn't need an iPad until you had one. Now, I use it all day long. Rob built a whole new market aimed at the portfolio manager.[250]

Unlike other Primark subsidiaries, Baseline's success was not about data quantity. Other Primark companies had more data. Our success wasn't about having "value-added" data like the I/B/E/S earnings estimates, nor was our success based on newfangled technology like Primark's Disclosure subsidiary, which was compiling and offering public filings on CD-ROM.[aa] Rather, our success was all about being a value-added workflow application. In other words, it was about providing a tool that easily helped portfolio managers receive insight into their portfolios, the sectors they followed, and the individual stocks they owned or might own. Content was important, but we

aa   CD-ROM (Compact disk—Read only memory). Optical disk technology.

never became a slave to any specific source. We collected our own data and scrubbed it, while adding key pieces of ancillary content from institutional-quality data providers. A client didn't need to subscribe to any specific database. Just Baseline. We were a turnkey solution. Our client-driven stock picking application was king. Not the content.

Mark Van Faussien, a portfolio manager with Azimuth Capital Management and formerly of Wilson Kemp & Associates, recently commented on his view of Baseline. "For us, it was just a great tool. It was simple. It was consistent. But it was elegantly consistent and simple. And it was good for us. It was also the way things were done. A lot of things that were in [Baseline], the way they came out, could easily be put in front of a client and explained to them."[251]

Joe Kasputys of Primark was right in one key aspect. Baseline was indeed simple. Simple to use. Simple to gain insight. And, per Van Faussien, simple in its elegance. But, beneath all the beauty and simplicity was an incredibly powerful tool. According to Ron Perez, "portfolio managers told me many a time how Baseline helped them 'see' opportunities and risks that otherwise weren't so apparent. Baseline delivered 'insight' into the data so that the data could give the portfolio manager a 'signal'—a path through the noise of too much data—a 'signal' to make better buy/sell decisions."[252]

In 2000, Joe Kasputys understood Baseline well enough to consider spinning us off as a standalone entity. With the dot-com explosion seemingly making every garage-incubated idea a success, Kasputys asked Rob to prepare a plan for Baseline to be spun off as its own entity and to prepare for an IPO as *Baseline.com*. I even drafted the S-1 in preparation.[ab] But three problems quickly arose.

First and foremost, Baseline was not an online, dot-com application. It was a Windows-based, local area networked product. There was nothing dot-com about it. Further, the Primark executive team either didn't understand the complexity of making ourselves a dot-com product or didn't care. We were not happy about being the management team of a potential public company having to defend what surely looked like false advertising. On the other hand, Rob was giddy about freeing himself and his team from the clutches of any superiors.

---

ab   Form S-1. The initial registration form for new securities required by the Securities and Exchange Commission for public companies that are based in the United States.

Second, the other PFAD executives were not pleased with the idea. Perhaps envy better describes their reaction. Joe Riccobono, who led the PFAD division and was Rob's boss, quickly suggested we spin off the whole PFAD division including I/B/E/S and Vestek as one public company. His argument was that a $100 million entity, like PFAD, was more interesting than, at the time, a $40 million item like Baseline. However, the Baseline team failed to see size as a compelling argument. However, Riccobono also felt there was great synergy in that we all serviced the buy-side. That was a palpable explanation, but only if the three entities somehow benefitted from synergies. It also appeared to me that Joe Kasputys may not have first cleared the idea with Riccobono, our own division head, because we had first been contacted directly by Kasputys and had time to investigate the possibility and draft the S-1.

From my vantage point, I did not see a lot of synergies regarding the spinoff of the entire division. I/B/E/S was your classic data organization which felt that "content was king" and that most applications to get at data were simply a means to an end. Their data fed multiple applications/platforms. In truth, they did an outstanding job of creating a database of global earnings estimates and slicing that data in myriad ways to create additional value-added insight. The equity markets have always been said to trade on expectations as opposed to historical results. The I/B/E/S data highlighted what top analysts on Wall Street thought about tomorrow's performance. But as a value-added ingredient in an analyst's or portfolio manager's daily routine, I/B/E/S was often one piece of a larger puzzle that was often assembled on an end user platform. And, FactSet, our primary competitor, was the platform of choice for most I/B/E/S subscribers. Baseline, as a platform, also utilized earnings estimates, but from *First Call*—a Thomson product.

The notion of creating a new public company that was actually three firms (Baseline, I/B/E/S, and Vestek) made little sense to Baseline's management team. We were our own fully integrated platform. We competed with FactSet who carried the I/B/E/S data. Conversely, we had fully integrated the First Call Earnings Estimates, which was a direct I/B/E/S competitor and owned by Thomson. The three PFAD companies made for strange bedfellows given all the cross relationships. It made far more sense to me to enrich Primark shareholders by vetting Baseline alone and avoiding the strange bedfellow arrangement that would have been PFAD.com, or whatever name we might have more creatively adopted. It also seemed quite logical to select the firm with the handsome growth rate to pitch as an attractive IPO.

As a side note, way back in 1990, as New Baseline was being designed and implemented, Rob Patterson's choice for earnings estimates was Thomson's First Call. The First Call partner model made more sense than I/B/E/S. Baseline could utilize select First Call data elements and pay them a flat rate based on the number of Baseline clients. The I/B/E/S model, on the other hand, required us to grant access only to I/B/E/S subscribers, therefore requiring Baseline clients to also sign I/B/E/S contracts if our users had wanted earnings estimates. The differing models made it a no-brainer to choose First Call—both in the early years and also later as a Primark subsidiary. We knew our users would need earnings estimates, and further, did not want to have any third party (e.g., I/B/E/S) involved in client sign-up. Nor did we want users to over-think, or over-prioritize, earnings estimates as part of the overall workflow solution of Baseline. Earnings estimates are only one piece of a portfolio manager's workflow puzzle.

Regarding Baseline.com, we never learned whether the "public" PFAD concept (taking the whole division public) was just a bluff, or if it actually had been endorsed by Primark's chief executive, Joe Kasputys. The reason we never found out was that all conversations surrounding Baseline.com, and even PFAD.com, quickly became moot due to an external force. The market itself was the third and final problem with Baseline going public. The dot-com bubble exploded into what is now known as the dot-bomb phenomenon.[253] The tech sector had ridden an unrealistic growth curve buoyed by too many fantasies. Kasputys was right to salivate over what was happening with nearly every tech IPO, and to potentially tie Baseline's growth story with that market enthusiasm. However, the dot-com bubble burst loudly, and quickly, due to out-of-control expectations without fundamental footings. Many of the IPOs at the time attracted money with strategic plans that were either ill-defined or nonexistent. My S-1 draft efforts were rendered moot by all three factors.

When the opportunity for a Baseline IPO became untenable, Joe Kasputys turned his attention to monetizing the whole lot of Primark's assets. On a Sunday afternoon in June of 2000, Rob called me at home. He wanted to give me the heads up that we were no

longer part of the Primark organization. I stood silently waiting
for his next few words. "We're part of Thomson Financial now."
Kasputys had sold all of Primark to the Thomson Corporation. After
everything Rob had told me over the years, I did not have to ask him
how he felt. Rob knew that Thomson's financial services division was
known for integrating businesses.

Thomson's financial services division, known in the industry as
simply Thomson Financial, was aggressively accumulating businesses.
It wanted to rival the better-known behemoths of the global financial
information services market, Reuters and Bloomberg. The tough part
about the Primark sale announcement was that Baseline appeared
to be a tag-along asset—an afterthought. A primary reason behind
the acquisition of Primark seemed to be Thomson Financial's desire
to grab a larger foothold in Europe. Primark's assets of I/B/E/S and
DataStream, a global econometric company, each possessed global
data, as well as significant client footprints on the European continent.
On June 6, 2000, an article appeared in *The Guardian*, a British daily
newspaper, that bolstered that sentiment.

> Primark's global presence—it operates in 61
> countries—was a key part of its attraction for
> Thomson. Following the acquisition, 20% of revenues
> at Thomson Financial, the group's second largest
> business unit, will come from outside North America,
> compared with 9% today... Primark is particularly
> strong in Europe.[254]

Baseline found itself part of this deal having been purchased
by Primark from Bowne in early 1997. As of June 2000, we became
a subsidiary of Thomson's financial services division. Unlike
our first two parent companies, Thomson Financial was wholly
focused on becoming one operating company. As such, they were
integrating acquisitions along functional lines. In 2000, the good
news operationally for Baseline was that Thomson Financial needed
to devote their attention to the larger, more-European focused
assets, as well as on the operational efficiencies from merging those
enterprises. That, in and of itself, provided us a respite of sorts from
any immediate assimilation into Thomson Financial. At the time

of the acquisition, our exceptional growth curve allowed for the application of an old cliché—"if it ain't broke, don't fix it!"

And so we continued to function "quietly" from our offices in the World Trade Center, and without too much intrusion, until the events of September 11, 2001 turned us upside down.

CHAPTER 12

RECONSTRUCTION

THE FIRST DAY of a "post 9/11" world drew to a close on September 12, 2001, and emotions were raw among my colleagues. Reactions to the events of 9/11 ranged from abject anger and deep despair to utter bewilderment. Some were simply numb. We were mourning the loss of friends, dealing with the deprivation of a streamlined business environment, and facing an uncertain future in a country that had, surprisingly, proven to be entirely vulnerable. Simultaneously, we were facing an exasperating list of tasks to complete in order to pull off a miracle.

The distant city of Philadelphia suddenly became the center of our universe. In the first few days of a new world that felt post-apocalyptic, several managers had descended upon the City of Brotherly Love to chart a path forward. To me, the city's moniker was an appropriate nickname for what we needed at that time: brotherly love and sisterly support. To have any chance of rebounding, we were going to need a very high level of cooperation. While a handful of our associates chose not to return to work, the overwhelming majority wanted to enthusiastically pitch in. Maybe some of it reflected a national pride not seen since post-Pearl Harbor enlistments. On the other hand, having witnessed the growth and maturation of our company culture, I believe the majority of enthusiasm stemmed from what was an absolute love of Baseline. The dividends of having a great company culture were about to pay off.

By Friday of that first week we had a plan. The critical path item became the integrity of the data, and that put much of the burden squarely on the shoulders of Barbara Tripp and her teams. It would, therefore, become essential to have key members of the Data Integrity department present in Philadelphia to oversee the restoration of our full database. Data Integrity was the largest group we employed at Baseline, and its multiple teams responded with incredible dedication. The Pricing & Index Team led by Alfredo Guzman, the Earnings Team headed by Bernadette Ross, the Business Overview Team run by Deirdre Rock, and the Valuation Team would all find their way to 1601 Market Street. Orna Lalehzari, who ran our Valuation Team, was pregnant at the time and she expertly guided her team remotely from her New York residence. Our Due Diligence Team, managed by Tony Mei, would report daily to his house in New Jersey to help restore the quality of financial statements data. During this intense period, security prices, earnings per share results, and earnings estimates were the most critical data items to be restored and quality assured. As mentioned earlier in the book, we called these items our Primary Data. It was what Rob first anchored his business to—namely, the data that most readily drives investment decisions.

In addition to a sizable representation from Data Integrity, we decided that Client Support should be co-located to reduce the delays between client feedback and needed remedial action. Carl Boudakian, and manager Brian Noody, would soon be in Philadelphia with their team. We would also have Operations programmers with us. No job was beneath anyone's pay grade. I recall Simon Chen brushing up on his FoxPro[ac] skills in those first few days. He jumped in to ensure resurrection of the nightly process programs.

One of the more fortuitous events on 9/11 from a business continuity standpoint was Simon's decision, at the time of impact on the 77th floor, to grab his laptop before descending. That laptop housed a fully functional client copy of Baseline. It updated nightly along with approximately 1,000 client servers. It purposely mimicked the entire

---

ac   FoxPro. A popular text-based programming language and database management system of the 1990s. Developed by Fox Software and later sold to Microsoft. Many of Baseline's internal support programs were FoxPro based.

nightly update process and contained every piece of data that all client servers housed. According to Simon, having this laptop "enabled us to create copies of the database for all post-9/11 new clients of Baseline."[255] New clients could be installed as easily as prior to the catastrophe. Sales efforts, therefore, could continue unimpeded. Thank goodness for the men on that ferry who gave Simon that plastic bag before dousing him. More importantly, we were all thankful for Simon's own presence of mind to grab that laptop after being thrown to the floor from the impact of United Flight 175.

From a customer service standpoint, another laptop proved critical. It was discovered early that the laptop of Ogden White contained a major chunk of our master Lotus Notes database. Oggie had been selling Baseline since 1986 (in the Old Baseline days) and had amassed many clients through his personal efforts. He was one of the more senior sales executives at Baseline, and had contributed handsomely to our success. Given his large number of clients, he had the opportunity to work with many account managers who also had clients that transcended other sales executives. The result was a superset of data. Nearly 60 percent of all client data sat on his laptop. We used Oggie's local copy of the Lotus Notes database to re-populate a new master server, and then subsequent replications from others on the sales team filled in most of the gaps. All of a sudden, we could research many past issues for follow-up, and log all new challenges and opportunities. Quickly re-establishing the Lotus Notes database was a major boost to the Client Support team, which was well represented in Philadelphia during reconstruction.

Another important aspect of outstanding customer service was order fulfillment. As you may recall, Peter Haller had proactively phoned DELL to grab the attention of their executives on the afternoon of 9/11. That momentous telephone conversation put us on the map to receive expedited service. When Peter and his team arrived in Philadelphia on Thursday, September 13, they had new equipment with which to work. They dove right in. A small room, described by Peter as not much more than a walk-in-closet, would be their home for the next two weeks, before they gained access to a larger room. In that initial space, the team was only able to fit ten servers on a shelf for the required "burn-in" QA testing period. Previously, at the WTC, as many as eighty servers could be tested simultaneously with additional storage for components, and work bays for repair work. It was tight in that closet of a room, but the team made the most of the situation. They superbly installed and serviced all the new desktops that arrived in Philly for the larger workforce, and deftly tested and shipped quality-assured servers for new customers who began to be signed up again that very month. In testament to the team's resilience, the Systems Distribution Lab was relocated four times after 9/11, including two eventual spots in Manhattan, as they awaited the final office decision.

On Friday of that week, September 14, we received a surprise visitor in the form of Joe Riccobono. Joe was a senior executive with Thomson. Recall that he had previously been Rob Patterson's boss under the previous Primark umbrella. Joe had run the three-company effort called PFAD, after originally being the Chairman of I/B/E/S. While nearly retired and out of the day-to-day management of the business, Joe had stayed with Thomson to help with various acquisition projects but had turned over operational management to Suresh Kavan, also of I/B/E/S lineage. Thomson Financial had placed us within what they termed the "Investment Management Group" and had appointed Suresh as its president. Baseline reported into Suresh.

I considered Joe's visit to be a magnanimous gesture. It was well intended, and heartfelt. He offered his assistance with whatever we might need from Thomson. The challenge with his visit was that, frankly, we didn't need anything. We were still an independently run, well-oiled machine that had just suffered a major disruption. We knew that only we could ferret through the issues surrounding our proprietary systems. I thanked Joe profusely and let him know we would follow up with him (if necessary). The worst part about his visit was his discovery of our August employee newsletter which was lying in plain view on the coffee table in our Philadelphia reception area. It touted our 20th anniversary celebration on July 24. Recall that we had invited no one from Thomson. That discovery hit Joe hard. I could tell he took it personally. He visibly demonstrated both sadness and anger over being left off the invitation list, and for Thomson being unaware of the event. That piece of news learned by Riccobono might have been the first inkling at Thomson that we were still stubbornly marching to our own tune.

In the meantime, on that Friday, our entire management team was preparing for the arrival of many associates on the ensuing Monday. Rob Patterson would be there as well. He had already provided his entire Baseline team with an uplifting and heartfelt memo, scheduled a Town Hall for the following Thursday, and finally made it back from Florida. Spirits were high.

On Monday, September 17, we began two major shifts of personnel that would commute to Philadelphia from the New York area. One group would arrive Monday mornings and work through Thursday evenings, while the second shift would arrive Tuesday mornings and depart Friday afternoons. Just about everyone travelled via Amtrak. The majority of our staff stayed at the Sofitel with overflow at the Crown Plaza. I estimate that approximately seventy people made that weekly trek between New York and Philadelphia. Insurance monies paid for the entirety of this process.

Early that Monday morning, I picked up Rob Patterson at his home in Madison, New Jersey. It would be his first trip to our new makeshift headquarters in Philadelphia. We drove to the Amtrak Metropark station in Edison, New Jersey and grabbed a southbound train to Philly. I hadn't seen Rob since before 9/11. He was visibly nervous. He knew he was facing his associates for the first time and didn't know what to expect. Were they angry? Sad? Depressed? Energized to rebuild? The reason I picked him up was to review everything that had transpired in the previous six days. I was able to assure him that the feeling was mostly positive, and that the teams of people now beginning to commute to Philadelphia had great resolve to keep this business moving. Still, Rob seemed edgy and apprehensive.

Rob enjoyed spaciousness, and he often purchased a first class train ticket on his many trips down to our office in Philadelphia. While he often railed against demonstrations of grandeur, first class on Amtrak was not particularly posh, but seats were roomy. That enabled papers to be spread out. Rob often worked on his way to and from our software development office. He had a first class ticket in hand on that Monday, while I had grabbed a coach ticket by default. That dichotomy didn't seem to faze Rob. "Well Ed, just come up into first class and sit across from me. I'll cover for you. I need you with me to prepare for today." Rob hadn't lost his non-conformist swagger. A confrontation soon ensued between Rob and the conductor.

"Tickets, please!"

Rob quickly showed his credentials, and I felt like some thief in the night.

"Ticket?" The conductor looked at me sternly.

"Umm. I'm with him," I murmured as I deflected responsibility.

"That's nice, but where's your ticket?" the self-assured train employee asked.

Rob then entered the fray. "Oh, he's with me, sir!"

"Do you have a ticket for him?"

"No," said Rob, "but I need him here to discuss business."

I then thought I could help somehow. "Yes, sir, here's my ticket."

The conductor's voice hit a new decibel level. "That's a coach ticket! You can't sit here. You need to leave. Now."

Rob then shouted, "How dare you! We are 9/11 victims from the World Trade Center going to Philadelphia to rebuild, and we have to talk!"

I showed the man my business card to verify Rob's statement, still feeling that what I was doing was plain wrong. The conductor hesitated, then left.

I said to Rob, "Let me just upgrade and we can continue our talk."

"Nonsense!" Rob retorted. "You have a ticket already, and they need to acknowledge our situation from 9/11." However, no more than thirty seconds elapsed when the conductor was back.

"Look, if you want to sit here you need to upgrade. I can sell you an upgraded fare right now." He was focused only on me.

Rob then interjected. "Hey conductor, you're out of line. You mean to tell me you're going to kick my son out of this car?"

Dead silence. I didn't know whether to laugh or cry. The conductor seemed to exhale a long sigh, and then quietly slinked away. My "dad" and I never heard from him again. Our business conversation continued.

Rob's arrival in Philadelphia was like an emperor's triumphant return into Rome. Hugs and tears were everywhere. His appearance was all the more meaningful given that the first shift of associates (Monday–Thursday) had just arrived. The entire environment was very tight quartered. We asked the Philly team to share their cubicles and offices. Alfredo Guzman recalled the environment with his typical dry wit. "It was crowded. Three to four people per cubicle. I never felt closer to three or four people in my life. I could smell what they had for lunch," he said with a laugh.[256]

While reconstruction was logistically challenging, it was far more demanding from an emotional standpoint. Less than a week after being ripped from a well-scripted daily routine—in a comfortable corporate culture with plenty of amenities, by a murderous act that destroyed our building and killed several friends—our associates found themselves away from home and their families. It would be four days per week for an as-yet-undefined period of time. They were grieving and, in many respects, in need of family love and support to help them through it all. From my vantage point, this made the overall resolve by a great number of Baseline associates all the more astounding.

For Barbara Tripp, our director of Data Integrity, it was especially hard. She had recently been married and being away so often from her husband, Bill, was difficult. She recently recalled the situation. "It was hard on Bill. It was hard for everyone. It was an emotional time. Not only had we lost friends, but there were also time pressures for getting critical data up and running. And, not having our normal procedures, we had to find ways of getting it done. Additionally, the amount of exception reporting we had to do was huge. There were many extra audits we had to do." Barbara also recounted that "what was challenging was not only having to correct data and have it accurate, but also rebuilding what we had lost. We also had new initiatives going on, like supporting system enhancements to the end user customer application. It never let up!" And, keep in mind, she and her team did all this from a distant office crammed three or four to a cubicle.[257]

Regarding the sales department, Nick Webb wasted no time in setting up shop for his team. While they weren't critically required to be in Philadelphia, the need for revenue growth didn't disappear. As long as the nightly process was set back up in Philly, they could sell as they had before. Simon's protected laptop on the day of his escape from the towers proved to be invaluable. To maintain momentum, Nick turned his family's Connecticut home into "sales central." During the next couple of months, as many as ten members of the sales team worked from Nick's home, with several of them there each day. His daughter Molly's bedroom became the cold calling room, but the team found respite wherever a quiet corner could be found. One day, soon after the home office period began, Nick's wife immediately recognized how different the world had become. An article by the Associated Press on October 1, 2001, entitled "Families attempt to Cope," captured her sentiment:

> Susan Webb entered her 3-year-old daughter's bedroom to put away laundry and had to laugh at the businessman on the purple and pink bed. "There was a gentleman sitting on her Powerpuff Girls bedsheet," Webb said. "He was on a conference call. I thought it was cute."[258]

More recently, Sue mentioned how the sales team contributed to the sanity of the family at that difficult time. For example, she claims that sales rep Devin MacDonald kept her youngest daughter amused with a great Scooby Doo impersonation. He apparently also bestowed a fantastic asparagus recipe upon the Webbs which they still enjoy today. From a more philosophical perspective, Sue shared her thoughts on the weeks following the events of 9/11:

> I know that my overarching feeling during that entire time was pure gratitude. Gratitude that people were alive and coming to the house, gratitude that we had wireless Wifi (very new and unusual in a home setting in 2001), gratitude that every person who came to our home to work was happy to be there and became family. Gratitude for the two employees of Thomson who showed up at our doorstep with boxes of office supplies (everything you could imagine), and told us they would bring whatever we needed. Gratitude for something to do—some way to help—some way to feel like we could rise above the hatred, death, and awfulness to try to get back on our feet.[259]

During the time the Webb family was sacrificing in the name of Baseline, the San Francisco sales office was still functioning at a high level. That provided an important sense of normalcy to the entire national sales team.

Another group that needed interim office space was our Finance & Accounting team. They were the ones most devastated. They had lost their leader, our CFO, Bob Levine. Additionally, they had lost their friend, our controller, Steve Weinberg. Through our relationship with Soft Dollar[ad] broker, Autranet, we were able to secure complimentary space in their headquarters in Jersey City. I greatly appreciated the efforts of Autranet's president, Vic Fontana, and our sales contact, Steve Volk, for rolling out the red carpet. Because of Rob's financial background, he became the acting CFO and controller, and set up shop in Jersey City with the remaining members of Finance & Accounting. He also served as the project leader, and primary contact, for all insurance claim issues. I also maintained an occasional presence in that Jersey City location to be near both New York clients and Thomson.

One of the greatest pulls on our emotional strings were the funerals of our colleagues. Rightly, the business came to a dead stop on the day or two leading up to the services. Nothing reminded us so fervently of the thin line between life and death, and the fleeting luxury of what had been our standard of living, than these farewell services. We went, we listened, we cried, we hugged. We naturally played the "what if" game and imagined ourselves in their places. And then we went back to work, until the next one.

The first funeral was that of our CFO, Bob Levine. It was held in a Manhattan synagogue on a rainy Saturday afternoon in late September. Then, in early October, Steve Weinberg's family held a service at the Nanuet Hebrew Center in Rockland County, New York. Steve had been our controller. Each of the services was overflowing with friends, relatives and colleagues. Ruth Lapin's family held a service in her honor on September 30, at the American Hotel in Freehold, New Jersey, which was attended by hundreds. The family of Jill Campbell celebrated her life on June 8, 2002 at Our Lady of Hope Catholic Church in her hometown of Middle Village, Queens. Rob Patterson delivered a eulogy. Despite our rebuilding efforts, we were never far from the hardcore reality of that horrific day.

---

ad   Soft Dollar Broker. A broker/dealer firm (sell-side) engaged in offering trading and
     clearance services in exchange for the provision of third-party research services,
     which might include analyst reports or electronic research services.

Baseline's four lost colleagues are forever enshrined in a beautiful memorial
erected at Ground Zero. [Photo Credit: BRIAN BRANCO]

The difficulty of attending funerals was never more pronounced
than with Kellie Kenny's own journey. She lost dozens of friends on
9/11 when the two hijacked flights impacted both Cantor Fitzgerald
and Baseline. According to Kellie, "We had so many funerals to attend
that we [she and her husband] had to plan our days out by the tactical
way we could get to as many funerals as possible by location."[260]
While the funerals were taking place, Kellie incredibly maintained her
strict training regimen for the upcoming New York City Marathon.
Not only was she focused on the race, but she also turned it into a
mission of remembrance. Kellie identified 26 friends and colleagues
who had lost their lives on 9/11, and had 26 flags embroidered with
their names—one for each mile marker. She pinned them to her
shirt during the race. At various points she attempted to give some
flags to bystanders, but most did not accept the flags. "As I ran and
would go to give a flag to someone, many would say 'no, that's your
flag!'"[261] Joining Kellie that day, and wearing the same 26 flags, was
her dearest friend at Baseline, Caroline Darmarajah. With the same
dedication that fueled their marathon mission, the two ladies also

re-engaged their Baseline clients as we all focused on the resurrection of the business.

During the six months following the 9/11 tragedy, Rob Patterson's own persona took center stage. His particular approach to caring for his associates was still very evident. He instructed his management team to put people's recovery first. He walked the halls preaching "take care of yourself." Brian Branco, our friendly accounting software consultant, put it plainly:

> After 9/11, you couldn't have asked for anyone else but Rob to go through this with. Anything you wanted in terms of support, you got. If you couldn't deal with stuff, you were given leeway. You wanted to come in late, or go home early? No problem. You needed to go out for lunch? Whatever you needed to take care of yourself, you got. Rob said to the Accounting team: "Take care of yourself first. The business will always be here."[262]

This need for comfort and solidarity was particularly germane to the accounting and finance folks who had holed up in the Autranet offices in Jersey City. They had been severely impacted. They had lost both their leaders. According to Brian, Rob's words helped immensely during what Brian called the "Dark Days." From an accounting continuity standpoint, it was actually Brian who saved the day. When he left the building on 9/11, he and his consulting firm were in possession (off-premises) of the only copy of our accounting system. That copy was only two to three weeks removed from the live system, and it contained all of Baseline's financial data. The fact that we were in mid-stride with an upgrade to our SBT system became most fortuitous. At the time, the remote copy enabled Brian to test things quickly on his own. Because of this remote copy, the only data missing after 9/11 were just three or four invoices.[263]

Within two weeks of 9/11 it was clear that we would successfully rebound. Our clients never went without a nightly update, and we slowly filled voids of historical data that were likely not apparent to the average user. Our work shifts in Philadelphia continued through early December when we decided to allow the staff to return to their homes for the holiday season. We had bridged many of the difficulties and set ourselves up to allow for a lot of virtual work. John Sharp, who ran our Philadelphia development office, said it best: "A river of confidence flowed beneath our feet. Not once did we think we weren't going to succeed."[264]

Another key decision was to locate contiguous office space in New York for when these commutes to Philadelphia would subside. As mentioned in an earlier chapter, the process of locating new space was anything but ordinary. It was also extremely stressful. Thomson Financial wanted us to neatly take our place in their newly established headquarters at 195 Broadway in lower Manhattan. Recall the phone call I received the night of 9/11 from the president of our division. While the call represented an appropriate gesture of support, it also brought our physical location front and center.

As September and then October rolled by, what started as a nice gesture to get us up and working again—namely, to move right into Thomson Financial's headquarters at 195 Broadway in lower Manhattan—started to appear more like an edict. While Thomson quickly accepted the expediency of our temporary Philadelphia measures, they pushed for us to join them upon the conclusion of our reconstruction. The non-conformant in Rob Patterson took this as a personal affront. He saw it as a strong-arm attempt to gain operational control of his company. In no way, shape, or form was Rob going to allow his business to fold into some floor-map schematic of a larger corporation, which Rob personally considered bureaucratic and ineffectual. Of course, let it be reiterated that Rob no longer owned any shares of Baseline. While his control had waned, his passion had never been as high. There was also the more germane issue to Baseline's management team of coming back to work in the same exact neighborhood where four Baseline friends had just lost their lives, and where everyone else had narrowly escaped a similar fate. While many of Thomson Financial's top executives had similarly witnessed the same day's events close at hand, they had not endured the additional experiences of fleeing from a building struck by an aircraft, barely escaping the collapse of that building, or losing four close and dear colleagues.

Despite our stubborn resistance due to continuing recollections of independence, the likelihood of joining them at their headquarters was, in reality, a *fait accompli*. Thomson acquisitions got absorbed. Period. Starting in the late 1980s with quality services like ILX, First Call (the competitor to I/B/E/S estimates), and Autex[ae], and continuing earnestly throughout the 1990s, Thomson Financial acquired many small to mid-sized businesses. Early on, its operating strategy mimicked Primark's—allowing brand names to flourish as separate entities. However, by the turn of the century and upon its large acquisition of Primark, Thomson Financial had developed the mindset that it had sufficient mass to directly combat Reuters and Bloomberg with a multi-purposed end-user platform. Theoretically, it would do so by systematically integrating these acquired businesses and products into a singular emphasis known as *Thomson ONE*. It was a noble, yet very ambitious, concept.

Beyond the obvious challenges of rebuilding the business, the interjection of 9/11 brought additional psychological hurdles front and center for my colleagues at Baseline. From associates to managers, the feedback was clear: "Please don't make us go to work right there overlooking the World Trade Center site." The back of Thomson's building at 195 Broadway faced Church Street which was immediately adjacent to the pit of Ground Zero. One could hardly find another building closer to the site than Thomson Financial's headquarters. Through the efforts of the same real estate broker who found us the World Trade Center space, and without any Thomson knowledge or approval, Rob quickly located space on Fifth Avenue in midtown. It was late October. Documents were prepared for signatures. He knew his associates wanted out of the downtown financial district. At the time, most office workers in lower Manhattan didn't relish the return to the area known as Ground Zero. It literally looked like a war zone. I witnessed this first-hand as my brother and I made a visit to the area within a couple weeks of the disaster. On top of the horrifying physical appearance of Ground Zero was the numbing fact that we had lost four good friends on that very spot. That realization made it impossible to return to the area.

As stated, Rob made it his mission to find us space, and the Fifth Avenue option was a good alternative. When we held a Town Hall

---

ae   Autex. An electronic trading platform that allows potential buyers or sellers of a large block of shares to identify other large traders of a particular stock through what is known as "indications of interest" (or IOI's).

meeting at the Union Club on the Upper East Side in early November, Rob was positioned at the podium to begin his "update" on the business. Present that day was Thomson Financial president, Sharon Rowlands. She was there to show support, but before Rob could get a word in she made a beeline for the podium. I thought she might speak, but Rob later revealed that she asked him not to say a word about finding space. The Fifth Avenue lease had not yet been signed, and Sharon was very aware of Rob's desire regarding office space. Rob's execution of the lease would have flown in the face of everything Thomson Financial was trying to accomplish regarding unification. Further, it would have set a dangerous precedent for Thomson Financial management regarding the ability of an acquired asset to determine its own path, regarding real estate or otherwise. Rob acceded to Sharon's request and did not mention the office space issue at the Town Hall.

As part of the decision process regarding office location, the Baseline Ops Team was brought together with Sharon, Suresh Kavan, and a psychologist hired by Thomson Financial to assess our sentiments. The group met at a smaller Thomson office on 56th Street in Manhattan. Rob Patterson was not present. To my surprise, tears flowed freely from a few of my Baseline executive teammates. No acting. No agenda. Just real-life stress, tension, and sadness over what had happened to us. Sharon seemed moved by the honest emotions. There was no discussion about 195 Broadway after that session. In the end, a compromise was reached where we would forego our own midtown office efforts, and relocate to a Thomson-held floor at 395 Hudson Street in the West Village neighborhood of Manhattan. It was an unoccupied space leased by another Thomson division—Thomson Legal & Regulatory. This was a compromise that sat well with Baseline's associates. We moved into our new home on Hudson Street in late January 2002.

While we successfully overcame the emotional hurdle regarding office location, there were additional Thomson challenges. None of them were explicitly aimed at Baseline, but were simply a result of our association with the overall corporate entity. For example, in asking our Baseline associates to sacrifice time and energy to make those weekly journeys to Philadelphia, we requested that they carry any and all vacation days into 2002. We strongly encouraged them to postpone vacation plans while we rebuilt, although we did not make it mandatory.

At some point in the fall, and I think it was November, every employee of Thomson Financial received a form letter email citing a new policy that "no vacation could be carried forward." That sent our rank and file into a tizzy, as many of our associates had indeed delayed their vacations and planned to carry those unused days forward into 2002. All of a sudden, we had damage control to perform when we were the group least able at Thomson to handle such an edict. As Barbara Tripp recalled, "It put a damper on people's enthusiasm. We had to manage morale at that point."[265] We settled everyone down by simply saying, "Ignore that email. We are Baseline and we are in a special situation." Neither Rob nor I sought permission. We simply knew it was the right thing to do, and our managers could quietly police the 2002 time-off schedule to be fair and accurate.

We were also thrown a technological curve ball. Baseline was a DELL shop. From a procurement perspective, Thomson had begun to consolidate corporate-wide purchasing power around IBM systems. According to John Tabako, who ran our computer room, Thomson insisted that we begin an immediate conversion process from DELL to IBM. Tabako, who purchased our in-house servers for internal support and client access to nightly update packets, didn't budge. We were not inextricably tied to DELL, but during our reconstruction period it was critical to work with known partners and known technical issues. An extracurricular conversion effort was not an option. The issue became more germane when we agreed to move into Thomson space at 395 Hudson Street in early 2002. Technology procurement managers with Thomson demanded that we comply as we planned our new computer room. The question before us at that point was whether to begin an extensive conversion process, with unknown issues and consequences for clients, or "let sleeping dogs lie" as the proverbial statement goes. We did not want to monkey around with anything while still in the final throes of reconstruction. According to Tabako, when he approached Baseline's Ops Team about how to handle the sensitive issue, Rob Patterson quickly interjected with, "as you build the operations center here at 395, put it back the way it was. Make it great."[266] The decision was made by Rob Patterson to ignore the edict. From my perspective, Rob probably relished in the nonconformance. However, it was one stressful issue that Baseline could avoid during reconstruction. The issue was never brought up again.

Additional challenges came in the forms of a hiring freeze, a limit on raises, and a statement from Thomson executives that bonuses would be cut back. Thomson Financial was in the midst of an austerity program as it consolidated several acquisitions, but the timing of those restrictions added to the challenges confronting Baseline's management team. Despite our 9/11 setback, revenues at Baseline still achieved double-digit growth in 2001. The same was not true for Thomson Financial overall. Our salary raises, which had averaged 5–7 percent across Baseline annually, were now subject to the same restrictions that affected all Thomson Financial personnel: a cap on raises within teams to an average of 3 percent. Those unilateral decisions made it hard to manage through such a difficult period. The employees of Baseline were confused over why their exemplary conduct was not being rewarded.

In the end, the Ops Team members went without raises so that those dollars could at least be spread across all our teams. We successfully argued for no change to our year-end bonus pool, and we muddled as best we could through the hiring freeze. The latter became a bigger challenge in early 2002. After hiring 20 to 30 temporary employees with insurance money to further assist us with data issues, we attempted to hire several of the individuals as full-time employees as reconstruction waned. That proved to be yet another extracurricular activity, as it flew in the face of the hiring freeze. In my opinion, none of these operational challenges occurred due to any intended malice toward Baseline. They were all due to Baseline being a tiny part of a much larger organization that was trying to act like a single operating unit.

The austerity program that we found ourselves under was mostly the result of Thomson Financial's aggressive acquisitions of larger assets. In 2000, Thomson had acquired both Primark and The Carson Group[af] with thousands of employees between them, and revenues approaching $1 billion. That appetite for growth placed Thomson in the necessary position to aggressively seek operational synergies in order to make the mergers worthwhile. Thomson Financial was clearly concentrating on eliminating redundant operations, but that took time. As such, an austerity program was ushered in across the

---

af   The Carson Group. A company focused on solutions for Investor Relations departments at publicly traded corporations. While Thomson had solutions for both the buy-side and sell-side of the financial services industry, it was lacking tools for the issuers—the final leg of the Capital Markets triangle.

board. For the first time, we knew we were part of something larger. We were being affected by the performance of other Thomson assets.

The gravest difficulty surrounding our reconstruction efforts was the uncertain future that awaited us at the other end. Rob and I, and a few other managers, knew that Thomson acquisitions got absorbed. We also understood that there was momentum afoot to merge assets for the purpose of creating an all-encompassing end user application. The question before us was whether our teams would simply be integrated into their functional equivalents at Thomson, or whether the Baseline product itself might be impacted. John Sharp, our head of software development in Philadelphia, would often quote with tongue-in-cheek from *Star Trek, the Next Generation*, by saying "resistance is futile."[ag] Regardless of what the future held, it was our responsibility to ensure that revenue continued to flow, and to do that required getting our systems back on line quickly. To that end, we were full steam ahead. We were determined to bring back the business as it was, albeit not in our favored location at the World Trade Center. And, we would do it without fully understanding our fate.

Ron Perez nicely summed up the overall sentiment:

> It was loyalty to Rob and to one another that got us through it. People were willing to accept personal sacrifice. Those were wild and hectic times. Stress levels were so high, but everyone had a vested stake in our comeback. Our people identified with Baseline— what it meant to them personally and professionally. I've never seen that type of commitment across the board like that. It manifested itself after 9/11.[267]

The loyalty Ron speaks about was directly connected with the overall corporate culture that had been engendered over the years. I firmly believe this culture aided in the evacuation of many associates on 9/11, and in the subsequent reconstruction efforts of Baseline. People cared. According to Peter Haller, "We did not forge the close ties we had because of 9/11. We survived through 9/11 the way we did on the backs of the relationships we had already forged."[268]

---

ag   In the science fiction television series, it was a statement made by an alien race, known as "The Borg," during their attempts to "assimilate" planetary cultures.

The anger, sadness, and bewilderment experienced by my associates in the days and weeks following 9/11 slowly gave way to a great resolve. The proverbial "light at the end of the tunnel" seemed closer as we approached year end in 2001. Despite being literally blown out of our headquarters, enduring the frenetic evacuation of a doomed structure, suffering the loss of four friends and having to immediately regroup in Philadelphia some ninety miles from our families, this team of Baseline associates miraculously stood firm and quickly rebuilt the business. The nightly process programs were all restored, gaps in historical data were filled, and new business contracts renewed their furious pace.

Up until September 11, 2001, Thomson left us to our own devices, and that enabled another year of superb growth. Revenue at the end of 2001 was $47.6 million, which represented a year-over-year growth rate of 22 percent. We were extremely proud of that figure, given that we had just waded through a very challenging and emotional time. In late February 2002, we released a new version of Baseline. It was only four months behind schedule. It was easy to come to grips with that delay given the alternatives that not only included losing the business, but also losing our lives as the result of a horrible terrorist attack.

CHAPTER 13

REBOUNDING WITH FERVOR

THERE WAS A palpable buzz among our associates as we exited the period of reconstruction. As a team, we had accomplished the near impossible. We had overcome huge odds. By late January 2002, the associates of Baseline had a new headquarters and the business was back on track and growing. While 9/11 slowed us down, never before did Baseline have so many clients, so many users, and so many tools to offer the asset management community. As we moved into 395 Hudson Street, the business was poised to experience the greatest momentum in its history.

In 2002, Baseline would again achieve record levels in revenue and numbers of users. The product was a true workflow tool used by portfolio managers from coast to coast at over a thousand institutional firms. In just ten years, Baseline's sophistication and flexibility had made leaps and bounds. Its market presence was aided by daily references to our charts in the *Wall Street Journal,* and in television commercials by E-trade which was offering their customers access to a tiny sample of Baseline's high-quality price charts. I recall watching a World Series broadcast where ads for E-Trade continually flashed views of our graphics across the television screen. I was incredibly proud. We had smartly diversified our product offering by making a static "one pager" of key fundamental data available to retail investment web sites. Fidelity, E*TRADE, TD Ameritrade, Scottrade and others were our clients, and the revenue for that offshoot business had already topped $2 million. More importantly, brand awareness for Baseline soared.

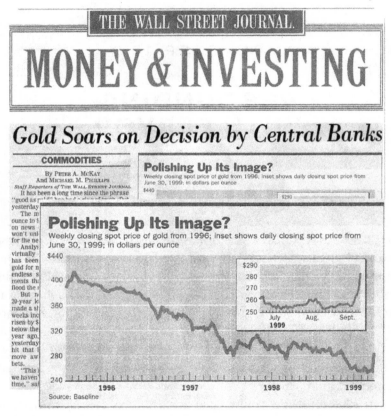

A clipping from the Wall Street Journal dated Tuesday, September 28, 1999. Baseline was the Journal's go-to source for data and charts. The lower left corner of the chart cites Baseline as the Source. [Republished with permission of Dow Jones & Co., Inc., Copyright © 1999 Dow Jones & Company, Inc. All Rights Reserved Worldwide. License number: 1126163-1]

Our mainline product, however, remained the growth engine. It was fueled by a constant flow of new features, a commitment to visually revealing graphics, and timely analysis of earnings figures. Additionally, a strong commercial orientation in our Sales and Client Support teams had us constantly in front of buy-side professionals.

Stunningly, despite a major upheaval, 9/11 barely made a dent on the business. In 2002, we kept up our onslaught on the market by releasing one of the most insightful new tools to come out of our enterprise. We called it "Earnings Purity," and it received wide acclaim.

Earnings Purity was so impactful that we patented the process and registered the trademark. Truth be told, it was Thomson that applied for the patent on our behalf, since Baseline was no longer a legal entity. Nonetheless, it received great fanfare. *Fortune Magazine*, on September 16, 2002, published a story entitled "Sweet Purity . . . Companies that Abstain from Earnings Write-offs Outperform those that Partake." According to author, Nashua Watson:

> . . . the idea behind the new "earnings purity" feature created by financial software company Thomson/Baseline . . . [is that it] calculates the percentage of a company's earnings per share that doesn't include write-offs in the trailing 12 quarters. If the total amount of its write-offs is greater than its earnings in that three-year period, the company is judged to be 0% pure. Likewise, companies with no write-offs are ranked as 100% pure. So far this year the corresponding performance has been remarkable. Take the S&P 500, for instance. According to Baseline, 52 companies in the index scored a zero for earnings purity through the second quarter. On average those stocks are down 31% this year-to-date, while the overall index is down 17%. Meanwhile, the 57 companies in the index with earnings that were as pure as Ivory soap dropped only 7%—24 percentage points better than their impure peers.[269]

Additionally, in an article in the *Wall Street Journal*, on December 16, 2002, entitled "Exit Sign? Pattern of Exclusions, One-Time Charges Hurts Stocks," authors Bryan-Low and Sidel quoted Ron Perez that a pattern of recurring and substantial exclusions (to operating earnings) "is often a symptom off more serious issues" and a good exit signal to investors."[270]

The ability to track the purity of earnings was made easier by a decision made a dozen years earlier. One of Rob Patterson's earliest, and smartest, decisions was to bring EPS (earnings per share) collection in-house. From 1991, Baseline's Data Integrity team had collected quarterly earnings numbers from the thousands of public companies we tracked. It wasn't just reported earnings—it was true operating earnings. We scrubbed the data. Non-recurring and extraordinary items were removed and duly footnoted. Many data services were simply capturing whatever was articulated in company press releases, namely *pro forma* earnings.[ah] Our team, on the other hand, would scour the announcements, sometimes calling the companies for clarification. Items such as restructuring charges, tax adjustments, and non-core items (e.g., gains or losses from investments) would systematically be removed and footnoted.

This scrutiny of earnings numbers over time put Baseline in the unique position to highlight the "purity" of earnings, or lack thereof. As Earnings Purity was released in 2002, there was a lot of excitement among salespeople and customers alike. It was yet another example of Baseline extending its value proposition to customers. Because it simply applied an additional algorithm to an existing data set, we made the decision not to charge for it. It was visually revealing, and it added significant value. Classic Baseline!

While Rob's original valuation model had been surpassed by the functionality of New Baseline in 1991, the sophistication of the "evolved Baseline" in 2002 similarly dwarfed what was New Baseline in 1991. The product management process had become extremely disciplined, and the enhancements to Baseline in that eleven-year period were significant. Baseline's product strategy, which enabled our revenue growth, was based on a 3x3 matrix. To be considered appropriate as a new feature of Baseline, an enhancement had to focus on one of three core workflow areas for clients: stock selection, portfolio analysis, or marketing. Additionally, the potential feature needed to add value, be unique, or advance ease-of-use. All proposed

---

ah   Pro forma earnings. Companies use their own discretion in calculating pro forma earnings, including or excluding items depending on what they feel accurately represents the company's true performance. Pro forma earnings are not in compliance with standard GAAP methods and are usually higher than those that comply with GAAP.

additions to the product needed to check one of the nine boxes in the matrix. Earnings Purity, for example, not only focused on stock selection, but was also very unique.

BASELINE PRODUCT STRATEGY MATRIX

	Adds Value	Unique	Ease-of-Use
Stock Selection			
Portfolio Analysis			
Marketing			

Every new feature of Baseline had to first check one of the nine boxes before entering the design phase of software development.

From 1991 through 2002, every addition to the product focused on some aspect of a user's workflow—researching stocks, evaluating portfolios or marketing themselves to their clientele. Our Best Practices Handbook and end user training were designed to instruct daily routines along the lines of these workflows. So much could change day-to-day within a fund or portfolio that the "story" a portfolio manager may have used to communicate a buy/sell/hold decision might, on any given day, start trending in a different direction. We encouraged morning routines by our clients to capture those trends, and we knew quite well that daily routines created "sticky" applications. A sticky application would be one that was hard to extricate from a daily routine. From a business standpoint, that meant the client relationship would be hard to cancel. In 2002, our annual renewal rate among clients remained at our historical level of 95 percent.

John Lee, the aforementioned portfolio manager for Midlantic Bank in 1991, stayed a user of Baseline for many years and in 2002 was with the Bank of New York. According to John, Baseline was a product that helped him build a story. In a recent interview, he recalled his daily routine with Baseline:

The intuitive ease of use was very important. It (Baseline) enabled me to quickly provide a macroeconomic overview, or story, as to why someone should be invested in equities, fixed income, cash, or real estate. The ease of use of the product allowed putting together something that tells a story as to where the economy is going, starting with commodities or inflation. Why invest? To beat the rate of inflation. Show me those great oil charts, show me the price of oil over time, natural gas, and the CPI index. In other words, where is inflation going? And then let's look at four or five fixed income components together— Fed Funds, 90-day T-bill, 2-year Treasury, 10-year Treasury, 30-year Treasury. Then look at Equities.[271]

Lee then added:

It's basically a macroeconomic story that Baseline helps paint before one dives into equities. That's something I'd do almost on a daily basis, and in the afternoon, I would do the screening. Let's say I needed a growth (stock) idea. I need (a company) that's got a great growth rate, but I want the relative valuation to be at least 1x. I want a P/E less than its growth rate (i.e., a PEG less than 1.0). I'd look at the results. I'd want to know: what is going to propel this company or that one?[272]

In addition to researching macroeconomic conditions in the market, and searching for specific equity investment ideas, Lee also acknowledged that he would have all his client portfolios automatically uploaded to Baseline on a daily basis. Each account would be a Queue, the name given within Baseline to the ubiquitous lists of stocks. In the early years of Baseline, client portfolios would be uploaded manually. However, the process became exponentially easier with the advent of Baseline's Portfolio Link in the late 1990s. By 2002, Baseline was technically interfacing with over fifteen top portfolio accounting systems to automate the nightly update of customer holdings. The advancement of this handshake with third-party systems, coupled with our creation of sector and industry composites, gave portfolio managers the ability to perform "top down" analysis. According to Ron Perez, "this would enable (portfolio managers) to compare weighted characteristics of a portfolio with the corresponding benchmark (e.g., S&P 500, Russell 2000, S&P Midcap, etc.)." He added that "Baseline was the first front office application to bring the number of shares held into a product. Portfolio Link allowed portfolio managers to analyze portfolios on a daily basis to spot outliers both at the stock level as well as possible style drift at the sector/industry level."[273] With this process in hand, bank trust officers and portfolio managers, like Lee, were instantly prepared for analysis or presentation. John Lee commented, "so if I had a meeting with Mr. and Mrs. Smith, I'd pull up the account . . . XYZ. Here are your holdings, here are your weightings (by sector), here is the performance, and what the income is. It was very easy to do."[274] These several comments from John Lee articulate the workflow that was Baseline.

Our corporate ability to grab the attention of portfolio managers came down to communicating our understanding of buy-side "workflow routines." We worked diligently in-house to advance these skills in our client-facing professionals. One of the best salespeople at Baseline for understanding and communicating client workflows was Ogden White. Recall that "Oggie" was our Lotus Notes savior, post 9/11. Thanks to his laptop and a local copy of the Lotus Notes database, our entire customer database was reconstructed quickly. Oggie was one of Rob Patterson's earliest sales executives. As previously mentioned, he was also a classmate of Rob's and had spent 27 years with the Bank of Boston in an asset management capacity. His experience was a big help to Rob in the late 1980s as the early Valuation booklet service needed more clients. Whether the service involved only Valuation, or the full complement of workflow tools in 2002, Oggie knew how to grab attention and drill right to the heart of his client's workflow.

He would start many sales presentations with an exclamation: "Question!" For example, he would likely use a recent market event to highlight his grasp on current market conditions to establish credibility. From my own witness of his style, he might make a factual statement like: *Question! A major downturn occurred yesterday in Consumer Cyclicals, what was its impact?* The actual event would be irrelevant, other than to create a discussion point. According to Oggie, "the question would vary based upon the client. It was really to draw the client out so that they would express what was on their mind. I would then want to ask 'How do you go about determining what you want to be looking at, on any given day, based on what happened in that previous market session?'"[275] With that question, Oggie was looking to understand the client's process. Their routine. Their workflow. He could then demonstrate how the product's flexibility could match the client's workflow. Our sales presentations never led with a product demo. Any demonstrations that occurred, only came after meaningful dialogue.

Speaking of Ogden grabbing attention, one of the greatest acts of comedic bravado by any sales executive at any sponsored conference occurred in May 1999. We exhibited at the AIMR Annual Conference at the Hyatt Regency in Orlando. Along with Bloomberg, we were one of two "anchor" exhibitors at the conference. As such, both our booths were directly below the escalator that offered access to the Exhibition Hall where investment and technology solutions were on display for the investment firms in attendance. While traffic at the booth was typically good, it soared one afternoon when Oggie descended the escalator with a tall, multi-colored parrot on his shoulder. Up on the main floor, the hotel proudly displayed three tropical birds on their perches for guests to admire. The act of borrowing one of the birds was probably not on the hotel's list of expected interactions. Upon arrival at the booth, Oggie began to give personal demonstrations of our system with the talkative bird clutching his suit jacket. Immediately, there were over fifty people watching Ogden in his element. As a result, and as the highest-ranking Baseline manager in attendance, I received a major tongue-lashing from both the hotel and the AIMR (known today as the CFA Institute). I apologized, but knew I'd invite the spontaneous, attention-grabbing gesture again in a heartbeat. As Ogden recently recalled, "like most conferences, you had to do something different to get a crowd."[276] To this day, I have no idea how Oggie coaxed the bird onto his sleeve.

One very important outcome from that conference was the off-chance meeting between our Aimee Kenniff and a Bloomberg sales rep, Will Day. Aimee was one of our top producing sales executives. With the co-location of our respective booths, it was impossible not to mingle with the Bloomberg team. Whether it was the appearance of the parrot, or a proper alignment of the stars above Orlando, the two young sales representatives met that week. They began dating, and, today, Will and Aimee are married with two lovely children.

In 2002, Baseline was every bit as impactful to the buy-side as the Bloomberg Terminal or a FactSet ID. The Baseline service specifically acknowledged a customer's particular situation. For example, mutual funds have charters. Our tools would help a fund determine if their actions and results were befitting their charter. Trust Banks, another sector of the asset management community, needed to ensure that their approved stock lists were adequately researched and then made available to all remote trust personnel. Our Queues provided seamless distribution. Independent money managers were faced with rebalancing client portfolios, and the research of individual stocks within Baseline could help ferret out which investments or divestitures should be made. In all cases, Portfolio Link gave each user access to his/her client portfolios (as Queues), updated daily, to show customized portfolio analysis. Thanks to our tight grasp on the workflows of various asset management firms, Baseline was embedded into the daily routines of over 13,000 users by year end 2002.

Baseline had become a complete tool, but it hadn't lost its elegant design or its ease-of-use. Mark Van Faussien was a client for nearly twenty-five years. He was one of the early adopters of Rob's "New Baseline," and stayed with the platform through our corporate transitions and his own journey from Wilson Kemp to Azimuth Capital Management. In a recent interview, Mark commented on his use of Baseline. "It was a perfect package. It was comprehensive. It was easy to use. It had great historical information in it. And, you could bring that all together in a report or a graph so easily, it was ridiculous. Our support staff could easily pull things together for us. You didn't have to be a PhD."[277]

The national War on Terror unofficially began on 9/11, yet that day did not derail us. We rebuilt what we had lost as if we were indeed at war. Passion, drive, and commitment were extra-evident every single day from September 12, 2001 through the end of that year and into 2002. Sacrifices were made by associates and families alike. Sleep became an overrated luxury. The entire Baseline family gave every inch of themselves. Rob Patterson, despite owning no shares in the company, took on the establishment of Thomson Financial to ensure his associates were handled properly post 9/11. He also walked the hallways of multiple makeshift offices, figuratively holding the hand of any employee who needed encouragement or support.

As mentioned, 2002 saw us achieve record revenues and an all-time high in number of users. Given everything that had transpired, and everything we had lost, it was a miracle we were even still in business. Thanks to the solid foundation of its corporate culture, and an undaunted determination, Baseline came out of 9/11 stronger than ever.

CHAPTER 14

THE ULTIMATE IRONY

GIVEN BASELINE'S REMARKABLE rebound from the obliteration of its offices on 9/11, it was reasonable to believe that nothing could stand in its way. The sense of accomplishment among my associates was overwhelming. Having bravely overcome an unprecedented disaster in the annals of corporate America, the company should have been able to maintain its record-setting momentum. However, after all we had been through, and after everything that had been successfully reinstated, and after bringing forth a new version of Baseline with Earnings Purity and other exciting features, Baseline would suffer an ironic fate.

As we entered 2002, Thomson Financial was deep into its mission to rival Reuters and Bloomberg, the two main players in the financial information space. Throughout the 1990s, Reuters had built a trading and information workstation, the Reuters 3000 terminal, around its best-in-class global news service. During the same period, Michael Bloomberg had leveraged his deep domain knowledge of fixed income, and a $30 million investment from Merrill Lynch, to build the Bloomberg Terminal business.[278] In my opinion, both large players were ostensibly built organically—internally, from the ground up. That was certainly true with Bloomberg. Reuters, while it did acquire the assets of Quotron and Bridge Information Systems which helped add users and some capabilities, was already in the real-time terminal space primarily due to its world-class news bureau. Thomson Financial, on the other hand, had taken a different approach than those of the industry's two biggest players. It had purchased most of its businesses. In 2002, its management team was very focused on the vision of integrating most of their acquired content and end user applications into one super-smart desktop tool to rival Reuters and Bloomberg. The product was known as Thomson ONE. This ambition for the integration of Thomson Financial's assets, coupled with the loss of our independent headquarters, presented a real challenge to the continuation of business as usual for Baseline.

In 2002, as Thomson continued on its path toward a Thomson ONE reality, it placed its flagship product, ILX, at the forefront of this effort. As highlighted earlier in the book, ILX was a real-time quote, charting, and news service primarily used by securities traders and retail wealth advisors (stockbrokers). It concentrated on the sell-side of the market, as opposed to Baseline's buy-side focus. ILX was easily Thomson Financial's most utilized platform with more than 180,000 users.[279] ILX would become the application "container"[ai] into which most of Thomson's content and tools would, hopefully, be placed. Soon after the rebranding of ILX to Thomson ONE, a major contract was signed between Thomson and Merrill Lynch. The 2002 agreement cemented the existing provision of ILX/Thomson ONE on the desktops of 27,500 Merrill Lynch professionals. While ILX had independently acquired the Merrill business in the mid 1990s, this particular deal provided for the bundling of additional, separately delivered services under the Thomson ONE branding.

The Merrill contract represented a coup for Thomson Financial as its breadth of services enabled a victory over both Reuters and Bloomberg. The highly publicized contract with Merrill Lynch gave buoyancy to the notion of Thomson ONE—if not yet as a technological platform, then certainly as a bundling ability by Thomson across all its products and services. All of a sudden, the notion of Thomson ONE had legs, and internal pressure mounted for all content and applications to get onboard for a technological integration. The challenge facing

---

ai   In 2002, the term "container" was a loosely-defined euphemism for an end user application that was (hopefully) extendable to incorporate a wide set of features and data sets.

Thomson Financial was that there were many different businesses under their corporate umbrella. My recollection puts that number at over three dozen. The big question was whether or not a majority of the respective product functionalities would make it into a Thomson ONE platform without the loss of particular capabilities or, worse, revenue. Intent was one thing. Execution was another.

It is my conjecture that when Baseline initially arrived on the doorstep of Thomson in June of 2000 by virtue of the Primark acquisition, Thomson Financial had no preconceived notion of just how Baseline would be utilized, leveraged, or integrated. As we continued on a temporary path of independence soon after the sale of Primark, we held out hope that our ongoing success would preclude such assimilation. However, 9/11 immediately forced everyone's hand. We instantly became more visible due to our lack of a home, and soon found ourselves inside a Thomson building.

All of a sudden, our historically strong results no longer insulated us from the impending integration of our functional departments. Organizational integration was a foregone conclusion. Whether or not our product would remain independent or be assimilated into Thomson ONE was still to be determined. However, unlike our prior parents (Bowne and Primark), Thomson Financial was quite clear about its plans to merge its assets into one overarching operating company. It was also touting its intention to integrate its wide array of content and applications into a market-leading desktop tool. As for Baseline, our management team understood the value proposition of our product and how it brought specific value to the desktops of portfolio managers. However, it was not entirely clear to us how Baseline would fit into the concept of Thomson ONE.

At the time, and in my opinion, Baseline, ILX, and SDC[aj] were the only successful front-office workflow solutions under the Thomson Financial umbrella. While Baseline focused on the buy-side, ILX was a leading desktop tool for sell-side wealth advisors, and SDC was dedicated to the workflow of investment bankers. In this context, I

---

aj   SDC—Securities Data Corporation—An investment banking application and database providing access to key insights on initial public offerings, mergers and acquisitions, private equity and venture capital deals, as well as corporate governance proxy fights. The group was formed primarily through Thomson's acquisitions of Securities Data Publishing and IDD Enterprises in the 1990s.

am defining a workflow solution to be one that aggregates multiple content sets together in one end-user application, but also integrates those various pieces of data/information to mirror the typical decision-making process of the targeted end user. At Baseline, we clearly understood that our days as an independent company were dwindling, but we also hoped that our platform (our workflow solution) would help drive Thomson's overall buy-side strategy.

In terms of being the buy-side catalyst, Baseline had two things going for it. First, our growth rate was annually north of 20 percent and showed no signs of abatement. That was a very positive anomaly among many of Thomson Financial's mature businesses. Second, we were a thriving workflow solution. We were already an integrated platform which had incorporated several disparate information sources under one end user experience. However, it was not the mere act of bringing various sources of information together in one application that set us apart. Anyone could do that. What set Baseline apart was that its end user application was built organically based on the requests of its users, i.e., portfolio managers. Baseline was unique in that it was content agnostic. It cared only about the workflow of portfolio managers and what drove their decisions. Based on that acquired market intelligence, we continually located the right pieces of content to be woven into the fabric of the platform. We were, in my opinion, the very definition of what Thomson Financial wanted to achieve—at least as far as buy-side strategy was concerned. Since the earliest days of New Baseline in 1991, we had integrated one of Thomson's own pieces of content—First Call earnings estimates—into our workflow solution. When independence as an operating company was clearly no longer an option for us, we continued to perceive ourselves to be the right solution for Thomson Financial to "own" the buy-side—whether joined at the hip with ILX inside of Thomson ONE, or as a separate offering.

As integration became more than a talking point, Baseline's management team soon recognized a lack of awareness within Thomson Financial surrounding our strong value proposition. After years of our insolent independence with little effort to share our strategies, the fact that very few people knew much about our "special sauce" became an instant liability. In retrospect, it appears that our own self-reliance and insular attitudes were coming home to roost. Baseline's standard operating procedure regarding parental interaction—of deflect and ignore—suddenly became a hindrance. As previously mentioned, Rob Patterson consistently stiff-armed requests for deeper involvement with respect to any and all parent companies. His opinion was that he needed no one to assist, or even understand, his efforts. However, as we took up more and more space in the annual reviews of our corporate parents, it became increasingly important to nimbly navigate the politics of these larger players. While Rob's style helped drive ideas from vision to execution, it did not facilitate cross divisional relationships, nor did it educate those around us. Rob was simply not interested in such, yet the environment we found ourselves in at Thomson Financial required it. According to Ron Perez, Baseline's vice president of Product Management:

> Corporate politics was, and still is today, a blood sport played with cunning by its practitioners, something Rob wanted no part of. By failing to "play the game," he let others dictate the rules . . . rules that were totally stacked against Baseline, its product and the organization, once we were folded into Thomson Financial.[280]

While Rob might be admonished for not playing the political game, he stayed true to his values over the years. Internally at Baseline, he railed against any attempts at political games or fiefdoms. Perez continued by saying:

> It was his total disregard and disdain for corporate politics that equipped Rob to make Baseline as successful as it was—an organization which placed teamwork and talent first. An organization which reflected who he was. And to be part of it, you needed to buy into that culture where factions and petty loyalties were never given entrance or tolerated. Instead, we all worked to do what was right for our clients, the business, and our associates.[281]

Whether or not this apolitical appetite led to a general ignorance of Baseline within Thomson, our relatively small size was certainly problematic. It provided us with little leverage. At the end of 2001, with annual revenue exceeding $47 million, we barely made the Thomson radar screens. It was a lot of revenue to those of us who had pioneered the Baseline wilderness, but to the $2 billion[282] financial services division of the Thomson Corporation we represented only 2.5 percent of their top line. Further, Thomson Financial's acquisition of our former parent, Primark, was primarily aimed at other assets. It was difficult for us to be thrust into a plan of integration when the primary intent behind the acquisition didn't involve us. As previously highlighted, it was arguably the European-focused assets of Primark that drove that merger. Practically speaking, we were a tag-along asset in that global transaction. While we had a lot of runway left in the market to build a much larger business, especially with additional Thomson content, a snapshot of Baseline on a P&L statement at the time probably looked small to those above us. Our growth potential and buy-side leverage were probably not fully apparent to our new owner. In 2003, three years after the acquisition, when the aforementioned Thomson market research study portrayed Baseline so favorably, the integration plans were already well underway. However, from a product perspective, it gave credence to placing Baseline components into Thomson ONE.

Baseline's ability to actually lead the buy-side effort, however, was additionally affected by a crowded in-house landscape of varied end user applications within Thomson Financial. In contrast to the three workflow-oriented applications of Baseline, ILX and SDC, many of Thomson Financial's separate businesses were content providers. In other words, they were not aggregators of useful, and insightful, data points to create a workflow for a particular end user. Rather, they *were* the various data points that aggregating platforms like Baseline might utilize. Examples of those Thomson content providers included First Call, I/B/E/S, Disclosure, Nelson's, and Worldscope global fundamentals, to name just a few. They were deep and highly specialized databases that commanded premium subscriptions for access to their particular strengths. While they occasionally sold the data directly to clients, most access was done through third-party platforms (e.g., FactSet).

With the advent of the internet, many content companies began writing their own end-user applications. The hope was to lessen the reliance on third-party platforms. Thomson's own content companies were no exception. One traditional barrier to entry to become such an application had always been electronic delivery. However, that barrier was greatly reduced with the sudden emergence of a widely available public network and an easy way to present content on the world wide web using HTML.[ak]

Applications driven by content started popping up overnight. These content companies argued, smartly, that they did not want to be slaves to the sales efforts, or technical capabilities, of third-party platforms. They wanted to offer their customers another channel to access their proprietary information—a direct channel. This made perfect sense—as it does today. However, such efforts muddied the waters within Thomson Financial. Prior to integration, several subsidiaries had created end user applications around their proprietary data. When these firms realized that wasn't enough to sway large bands of users, they began adding other pieces of content as well. For example, I/B/E/S added financial statements and securities pricing to their new platform, *I/B/E/S Express*. Disclosure created *Piranha* with other data beyond their SEC filings. First Call had created *First Call Analyst*. These actions resulted in many end user applications under Thomson Financial's roof. It became difficult to separate the wheat from the chaff, that is, the exceptional workflow solutions from the ordinary data delivery applications.

On the surface, many of these products from various corners of Thomson Financial looked eerily similar. They all contained like data. However, many of the content-driven applications stagnated. The reason, in my opinion, was that the firms placed their proprietary information at the center of their solar system, so to speak. Baseline, however, viewed key pieces of content more like planetary bodies that orbited the primary piece of value—the end user experience. Nonetheless, Thomson Financial's nighttime sky became dotted with many points of light—some exceptional, some ordinary. It was a crowded field, and Baseline's historically insolent behavior didn't help to differentiate us.

Thomson's hope was that key components of Baseline, and dozens of other independent products, would fit neatly into a wider

---

ak   HTML. Hyper Text Markup Language is the standard language for content to be structured and displayed in a web browser.

Thomson offering that all clients of those independent products would migrate towards. An all-encompassing Thomson ONE became the unmitigated goal. The plan would give clients a one-stop-shop opportunity, simplify Thomson's customer service issues, and reduce internal infrastructure costs. Baseline, like others, was asked to begin the process of integrating its most important components into the newer Thomson ONE (i.e., the expanded ILX) platform. This grand plan was facilitated by the realignment of subsidiary departments into the Thomson Financial mothership. For example, sales forces from firms like Baseline, Vestek, First Call, I/B/E/S, Datastream, and Nelson's were merged into one team focused on all of Thomson's products. At the time, while many of Baseline's associates missed the familial camaraderie of Baseline's organization and culture, many held out hope that all this effort and juxta-positioning could lead to a world-class, market-leading product.

As product integration began, Baseline's PE analysis component was dropped "as is" into Thomson ONE—with Baseline's colors, fonts, and symbology requirements. That entry into Thomson ONE attempted to add diversity and sophistication to the new platform. With time-to-market as a key consideration, many existing components from across Thomson were quickly added into the platform. This certainly added diverse functionality, but in my opinion, it also served to make the user experience a patchwork of differing solutions with varied presentation styles.

More germane to the end user were the data concordance issues. For some, symbology differences became a problem. Not all the backend data repositories were equivalent sets of data. For example, the Baseline ticker symbol for a microcap stock might not be the same as ILX's ticker symbol. This presented a challenge to a Thomson ONE user who might have moved from an ILX screen to a Baseline PE analysis. The ticker symbol she used seconds earlier would no longer be valid. The original screens were still looking back at their respective databases.

Speaking of PE ratios, Baseline's Ron Perez, who became a VP of product management for Thomson ONE, was chastised by a user during a visit to Toronto in the 2005/06 timeframe. According to Ron, the user said, "I'm confused. On this page the PE for Stock X is 28. Over here it's 32, and in the PE bar chart it's 25.5. Which one's right?"[283] The answer was that they all were right—in a way. The pages were reading from different databases based on the page being visited by the user. According to Perez, "Baseline's PE would be updated overnight, while the First Call PE was based on something like a weekly price point, while ILX might have utilized a real time price quote."[284] The numerator was potentially different in all three scenarios.

Further, in the early stages of Thomson ONE, not all of the respective Thomson components calculated earnings per share in the same manner, yet those earnings figures were being read from their respective, and original, Thomson products. The result was three screens and three different PEs—each acceptably calculated in their own right. However, users justifiably wanted consistency to bolster their confidence in their own decision-making process. From my perspective, front end design differences, coupled with symbology and data inconsistencies, proved problematic for Thomson ONE. According to Perez, the components of several products were "technically combined, but not harmonized."[285]

These issues did not constitute a death knell for Thomson ONE, but were natural fallouts from attempting a merger of systems vs. a complete rebuilding effort. To be fair, a total rebuild would have been very expensive and taken far longer. Thomson Financial chose the integration path. Time-to-market was a critical determinant. In the end, however, I would argue that Thomson ONE did not turn out to be the successful competitor to Bloomberg and Reuters as envisioned.

As a result of the Thomson ONE initiative, Baseline would find itself caught in the middle of two acceptable possibilities. Sadly, neither would ever materialize. First, the majority of Baseline's functions, the ones that replicated its famous workflow, would not make it into the Thomson ONE application. In my view, this was primarily due to the sheer magnitude of the Thomson ONE endeavor squeezed into a short timeframe. Second, the existing Baseline product would not receive enough attention to enable it to flourish independently. Ironically, Baseline was on a collision course with obsolescence at the exact moment it had reached its own summit of influence within the investment management community.

The new version of Baseline software released in early 2002 would constitute the last multi-feature enhancement to Baseline. Later that year, Earnings Purity hit the Street. Thereafter, bug fixes and maintenance releases were all that surfaced. No longer left to its own devices, Baseline could not set its own course. Tired and marginalized, Rob Patterson departed the scene in June of 2002. His exit certainly pulled the plug on the creative and intelligent ideas he proffered, and Baseline had no board to allow him to remain as an advisor. Further, there would no longer be a dedicated Product Management team, nor a dedicated Sales force.

In addition to overseeing the vestiges of Baseline, I was tasked to lead and integrate several Thomson Financial sales forces into a cohesive team focused on Thomson ONE. The die was cast. The chart below clearly shows the drop-off in Baseline's revenue growth in 2002, when revenue grew year-over-year by only 8.4 percent to $51.6 million. This was partly due to the residual effects of 9/11, but was also the result of sales attention being diverted elsewhere. While the depleted Data Integrity and Software Development teams continued to support an existing base of business, Baseline was in severe jeopardy. Due to existing momentum, revenue still grew in 2003, topping off at $55 million, but then deteriorated annually from that point forward.

BASELINE ANNUAL REVENUE

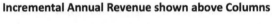

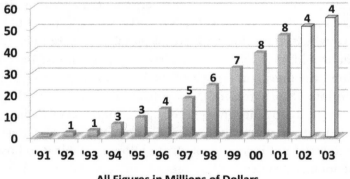

All Figures in Millions of Dollars

Baseline's revenue soared from 1991 through 2001, but growth rates tailed off as the organization was integrated into Thomson Financial in 2002.

Meanwhile, the Thomson Corporation, which had desired to compete head-on with Reuters in the financial sector via Thomson Financial, eventually acquired the news giant in 2008. In that transaction, Thomson bequeathed leadership of its financial segment business to Reuters' executives. The combined financial businesses became known as the Markets Division of the newly formed corporate entity. It joined the other traditional businesses of the Thomson Corporation to become the new global entity known as Thomson Reuters. This acquisition immediately placed the effort known as Thomson ONE under the magnifying glass. While there were several historical "wins" like the Merrill Lynch deal, Thomson ONE was an ambitious plan. In my opinion, to compete head-on with established, enterprise-wide applications by way of integrating acquisitions and applications is a bold attempt in any industry, in any decade. In the information services industry, vastly different database structures, end user interfaces, and corporate cultures are not easy to discern or resolve.

The new Markets Division of Thomson Reuters understood the value of Thomson ONE as an effective workflow tool for the wealth management industry. From my point of view, it was still mostly ILX at its core, and thus had a long-standing reputation for excellence with wealth managers.[al] As a result, it continued on as a key offering from Thomson Reuters in that space. However, to broaden penetration in other sectors of the financial community, the Markets division soon produced a new tool called EIKON utilizing the historical Reuters data feed.[286]

While I have offered some general facts and sentiments surrounding Thomson's journey over time relative to the financial community, I acknowledge that there is far more to the story than I can relate in a simple chapter in a book about Baseline and 9/11. Thomson did efficiently eliminate redundant operations at many levels due to its larger acquisitions. It also created teams of sales specialists that focused on the wealth management industry, investment banking, and institutional investors. Given Thomson Financial's size and diversity

---

al Wealth Managers—For purposes of this book, the term "wealth manager" is synony-
    mous with the terms "financial advisor" or "stockbroker." They are primarily focused
    on managing money for individual investors and are most often employed by the larg-
    er, sell-side firms that are members of stock exchanges. This contrasts with the term
    of "institutional investor" who manages money for institutions and employs portfolio
    managers. Baseline was primarily focused on institutional investors.

due to acquisitions, and the need for profitability and organizational focus, it was not an improper decision to attempt integration from a top-down perspective. According to Nick Webb, who spent nearly nineteen cumulative years with Baseline, Thomson Financial, and subsequently Thomson Reuters, "a single platform did make sense because otherwise you were training people on 10's of platforms or you were running 10's of separate sales forces. Neither was appetizing."[287] At the same time, however, technological hurdles challenged the perfection of Thomson ONE, and many Thomson Financial businesses were not leveraged as well as they might have been.

History will show that some functionality of Baseline was ported into larger Thomson/Reuters tools, but the Baseline workflow that was designed for portfolio managers never saw the light of day in those all-encompassing products. The original Baseline product was finally sunset by Thomson Reuters in 2017 as revenue became too small to profitably support. A year later, Thomson Reuters made the decision to spin off its risk and financial businesses. The resultant firm was called *Refinitiv*.[am] [288]

From 1991 to 2003, Baseline was an exceptional tool for portfolio managers and it realized strong year-over-year revenue gains. It rode a growth curve as an entrepreneurial success. During that time span, Baseline grew its annual revenues from $1 million to over $55 million, grew its employee base from 12 to 225, and raised its customer ranks from 40 firms and 100 users, to over 1,000 and more than 13,000 respectively. Year after year it kept pace with its chief competitor, FactSet. In that most fateful of years, 2001, Baseline continued to appear in that five-year shadow of its larger competitor, just as Rob Patterson had opined. That year, as Baseline successfully rebuilt itself while withstanding the challenging effects of 9/11, it reported year end revenues of $47.6 million on December 31, 2001. That represented a growth rate year-over-year of 22 percent and another record achievement. Five years earlier, on August 31, 1996, FactSet, in its 10-K filing, reported annual revenues of $44.3 million.[289] Adjusting for the difference of four months in the two fiscal year-end dates, the numbers are practically identical. FactSet, however, would continue

---

am   In a 2018 leveraged buy-out, Thomson Reuters spun off its Risk and Financial business as a separate entity known as Refinitiv. The private equity firm, Blackstone, took a 55 percent stake. In 2019, Refinitiv was then sold to the London Stock Exchange.

on its independent mission with unabated acceleration well past 2001. Today, FactSet remains an independent company. On August 31, 2020, its fiscal year-end revenues were reported to be $1.494 billion.[290] Its stock, which is traded on the New York Stock Exchange, had an impressive market capitalization on that date of over $13 billion.[291] FactSet went public back in 1996. Coincidentally, that was the same year it unsuccessfully attempted to acquire Baseline, when it lost out to Primark. Ironically, if Joe Kasputys of Primark had eventually brought Baseline forth as an IPO, that, too, would have been approximately five years after the FactSet IPO. But I digress.

Speaking of FactSet, as an example of their impressive rise as a leading financial information service, they obtained that lucrative Merrill Lynch contract in 2018 which Thomson ONE celebrated in 2002. FactSet captured the contract to provide services to all Merrill's wealth management desktops.[292] Back in 2002, no one would have dreamed that FactSet would have been a future candidate for such an agreement. In another stroke of irony, it was ILX that first provided FactSet with an intraday price feed in the late 1990s as FactSet decided to dabble in the real-time space.[293] Goran Skoko, who led the ILX product effort for years and was a major technological spearhead for Thomson ONE, joined FactSet in 2004. Goran's arrival at FactSet coincided with their commitment to develop their own ticker plant[an] with direct links to exchanges. He was brought on board to drive a comprehensive real-time solution into their platform. As an aside, in the late 1990s Baseline had also recognized that there was a need among portfolio managers and analysts to have a better handle on intraday activity. At Baseline, we called that service Market Action. Regardless, given Goran's arrival at FactSet, it was highly likely that they would eventually advance intraday capabilities, seek a much wider audience of users, and eventually compete for the Merrill Lynch business.

As of this writing, Goran Skoko is executive vice president in charge of Global Wealth Management for FactSet based in London. Goran recently recalled working with my Baseline colleagues during the period of organizational integration at Thomson Financial. According to Goran, "everyone [at Baseline] was very competent, laser focused on

---

an   Ticker Plant. A specially formatted software and hardware system that delivers massive data streams of highly time-critical securities prices from exchanges to both end user platforms and computerized trading systems which take actions based on sophisticated algorithms.

delivering fantastic service, and employees were treated with respect . . . a bunch of people that acted like a family."[294] As for the Baseline product itself, Goran was a big fan. As separate products, ILX and Baseline focused on very different segments of the market. However, the integration of organizations and products placed Goran in close contact with many of Thomson Financial's products. Regarding the Baseline product, he was struck by "how easy to use and elegant it was. It was the design, and company level analysis that I always admired."[295] He admired it so much that he eventually persuaded two key Baseline managers to join FactSet in the subsequent years. Sharon Dipre and Simon Chen were brought on board to help advance company-level analysis and charting respectively. Sharon Dipre was the first person on Baseline's original product design team when the business became too large for Rob Patterson to be the sole designer. Sharon, of course, benefitted greatly by being mentored directly by Rob Patterson. FactSet instantly became the beneficiary of such wisdom when Sharon joined their ranks. As for Simon, who ran all of Baseline's product and technology teams, his most recent role was directing FactSet's product strategy in the Asia/Pacific region.

While the story of Baseline represents a terrific tale of accomplishment, its downturn sadly occurred during its greatest growth spurt. The ultimate irony is that it wasn't the death and destruction of 9/11 that derailed Baseline, but rather something far more mundane. Baseline became collateral damage in an ambitious strategic plan that occurred right on the heels of our amazing rebuilding effort.

From my vantage point, there were several factors that acted in concert to effectively curtail Baseline's momentum. These items included Thomson's integration mandate, our historical insular attitude which affected Thomson's awareness of our solution, their motivation for acquiring Primark, and a plethora of in-house end-user applications. Even in late 2002, as our departments were aligning themselves within Thomson's organizational structure, my associates and I were still planning to further Baseline's growth curve as a product. Efforts to alter the symbology of ticker symbols to allow inclusion of global equities were underway. So, too, was our adoption of Microsoft's .NET capability in which we would utilize the internet's large bandwidth to free us from the major expense of dedicated servers in the field. Those blueprints, however, never became a reality.

Three loyal Baseline clients that remained to the very end were John Lee, Tom Maurath, and Mark Van Faussien. According to John Lee:

> The [Baseline] product was one of the greatest of all time. They [Thomson Financial] tried to introduce their version of Baseline [Thomson ONE], then tried to introduce the Reuters version of doing business [Eikon]. If we wanted to do business with Reuters we would have. But we didn't. We wanted to do business with Baseline. Then we got the ultimatum (in late 2015). It's going away in a year and a half.[296]

At the time of this writing, Mr. Lee is a Senior Managing Director of PGB Trust, a division of Peapack-Gladstone Bank, in New Jersey. He used Baseline for over twenty-five years from Midlantic Bank, to Fort Washington Advisors, to Bank of New York, to PGB Trust. He was the quintessential user of Baseline—one of 13,000 at the height of Baseline's market position in 2002. Similarly, Tom Maurath, a Senior VP and Portfolio Manager with Goelzer Investment Management in Indianapolis, said:

> We stopped using Baseline when Reuters told us they weren't going to support the business any longer. Baseline was a good product when we started using it back in the '90s. It was easy to use and fit our needs. In the end, we tried upgrading to the new Thomson Reuters product, but we felt it was not ready to be rolled out.[297]

After an extensive search for a replacement research tool, Maurath concluded that "Baseline was far more intuitive than any of the other products I saw or tested."[298] In the end, Goelzer selected Baseline's longtime rival, FactSet, over Thomson Reuters and other services, to fill the void left by Baseline's disappearance. In 2018, Maurath shared that "we have been using FactSet for a couple of years and I still need to get help to do supposedly easy tasks in FactSet. Particularly in the screening area."[299]

Likewise, Mark Van Faussien at Azimuth Capital Management in Michigan was left without his favorite tool. Today, he and two of his partners use Bloomberg, while the rest of the team uses FactSet. According to Mark, Bloomberg "is difficult to use, and it's hard to get at good things that you can put in front of clients. There's a ton of information in there, but getting it out sometimes is a little difficult." He lamented that the removal of Baseline from the market "has left a void for all of us in terms of doing research."[300]

Baseline, arguably the most user-friendly and intuitive product in the industry, was unfortunately no longer available. The death of this fantastic enterprise happened without fanfare and without much of a plan. The mere fact that users still existed in 2017 with no enhancements (other than bug fixes) since 2002, and without a dedicated support team, spoke volumes about the value of the Baseline workflow. Clients found it addictive. Ideally, the Baseline product would have seen either the continuation of its evolution or the transport of its workflow capabilities into a larger container. Neither happened. Instead, the most loyal of Baseline customers hung on for years, refusing to switch to competitive offerings, or even migrate to a Thomson Reuters platform that, in my opinion, only included a few snippets of Baseline functionality without bringing along its very sticky workflow experience. Baseline, in whatever bare-bones existence, saw its last nightly update in 2017. Thomson Reuters finally sunset the product. Ironically and perhaps most fittingly, it was the same year that Rob Patterson took his final breath.

Upon Rob's passing, another client of Baseline paid tribute to his vision and effort. Mark Weiss, chief investment officer of Virtonos Capital in Massachusetts, and a former user at Loomis Sayles, said, "I don't think I have ever met one investment professional who didn't marvel at the brilliant and elegant simplicity of Baseline. It was one of the first investment applications I ever learned and I have always judged other applications against it for ease of use. He truly was a pioneer."[301]

George Maniscalco, who worked closely alongside Rob at both Standard & Poor's and Baseline, recently remarked about Rob and the Baseline journey:

> In all of my career, nothing even comes close to my
> experiences at Baseline. I [still] speak of it today. My

> heart is full when I talk of the people there. My heart
> is sad when I think what a wonderful company led by
> such a wonderful person suffered such devastation
> based on 9/11. It's just staggering. To think of all the
> things that Rob had accomplished at Baseline, and all
> of the good that he did, almost vanished overnight.
> And, in my opinion, his experience under the rule of
> Thomson was like sending him to prison. So sad to see
> such a wonderful experience turn into such a mess.[302]

To be fair, Thomson Financial was similar to other large divisions of public corporations. Their methods of creating structure, eliminating redundancies, and looking for synergies were not unlike many large firms with diverse product lines in a global economy. Ongoing demands for quarter-over-quarter improvements in earnings certainly impacted their courses of action. However, Maniscalco's use of the world "prison" is a realistic portrayal of Rob's perspective. Rob Patterson was an entrepreneur who reveled in his ability to implement a vision with a handpicked group of talented team-oriented individuals. In Rob's mind, corporate structure and rules stifled creativity. And, while he could leave his ego at the door while collecting product feedback, his ego was never more visible when being told how he should organize his team or integrate his product's primary capabilities.

The Thomson Corporation, which lost a total of eleven employees on 9/11, including our four associates and Vestek's three, did play a positive role in several areas. First, in Baseline's darkest moment, the team of Sharon Rowlands and Suresh Kavan were gracious as they acceded to our request not to be immediately located near Ground Zero in the aftermath of 9/11. Second, Thomson made good on their promise to continue paying the salaries of the fallen for a period of one year. Third, they held true to their word when they agreed to pay the college tuition of the living children of their fallen employees. According to Steve Weinberg's wife, Laurie, Thomson "set up a 529 College Fund, and I don't remember how much money was in there. But, through the years it grew. And obviously we used it for college and even for [my daughter's] graduate school."[303] Jill Campbell's son, Jake, who is currently a student at the University of Michigan, recently shared that Thomson came through "big time" in that area. Fourth, in regard to insurance coverage, Laurie Weinberg commented that Thomson "gave us health insurance for the first five years, which was really the best thing we ever could have had. They really were wonderful with that because that would have been the end of it all if we had no health insurance."[304] Finally, while the Baseline organization was disbanded as an independent enterprise in 2002, Thomson Financial's executives ultimately recognized and appreciated the level of talent that existed at Baseline. A good number of Baseline associates enjoyed many fruitful years of employment at Thomson (and subsequently Thomson Reuters), including several who attained relatively senior management positions.

Perhaps, if 9/11 had not impacted the World Trade Center, Baseline's independence might have been maintained. It is conceivable that Baseline would have continued to achieve record growth, and that our status and recognition within Thomson might have been different. However, given the destruction of our headquarters and an aggressive strategic plan, that was not meant to be. Although Baseline impressively rebounded from 9/11, it was quickly assimilated into Thomson Financial in the 2002–2003 timeframe as the Thomson ONE initiative got underway. Baseline's fate was met with an incredible stroke of irony as it began its decline in the midst of its greatest growth period.

CHAPTER 15

REFLECTIONS

FOR THE ASSOCIATES of Baseline, there were many aspects of the infamous day that left an indelible mark. All of us "vividly recall" 9/11 with all its horrors and ramifications. In the blink of an eye, our place of work was destroyed and our long-time independence as an operating unit was put on notice. We also experienced the loss of four good friends. The names of Jill Campbell, Ruth Lapin, Bob Levine, and Steve Weinberg will stay with us forever. Despite the strongly emotional time, we successfully brought the business back from the brink of oblivion, and were incredibly proud of that achievement—regardless of what followed. Of course, the events of 9/11 went far beyond the confines of our two floors.

Baseline was a small part of the World Trade Center campus where 50,000 individuals reported to work each day. Their destinations included corporate offices, retail shops, transportation hubs, and law enforcement stations that continually monitored the sixteen-acre site. September 11, 2001 was a devastating day; it eclipsed Pearl Harbor in terms of human loss. While we lost four friends, other organizations that occupied materially more space in the Twin Towers suffered significantly more losses.

In One World Trade Center, the first tower to be hit, all paths to safety were destroyed by the impact of American Airlines Flight

11. According to author Garrett Graff, "the fate of everyone above the 91st floor in the North Tower was already sealed" by virtue of the impact.[305] At 8:30 AM they were happily going about their day. Just twenty minutes later, they had all received a death sentence due to the elimination of all exit routes. Cantor Fitzgerald, a fixed income trading company, which was headquartered on floors 101 through 105, sadly and incredulously lost 658 colleagues that day.[306] Dozens of those individuals were good friends of Baseline's Kellie Kenny. At Marsh McLennan, which occupied floors 93–100, 295 employees along with 63 consultants were tragically lost.[307] The Windows on the World restaurant facility at the zenith of the North Tower suffered 72 casualties, while Carr Futures situated on the 92nd floor lost 69 souls.[308] [309] Additionally, the Port Authority lost 37 police officers while Fred Alger Management lost 35 employees.[310] [311] The firm of Fred Alger was a Baseline client, and the one that John Tabako lamented about so grievously on the morning of September 12th. He had visited them a dozen times.

Overall, there were far more fatalities in the North Tower, since those in Two World Trade (the South Tower) at least had a chance to weigh options prior to the impact of United Airlines Flight 175. In that South Tower, where Baseline was situated, Morgan Stanley employed over 2,700 people, and they occupied many floors. Their vice president of Security, Rick Rescorla, purposely ignored the building's announcement that it was safe to remain inside the structure. He wasted no time. The former British paratrooper and Vietnam veteran sprang into action to ensure the evacuation of his employees. In the end, due to Rick's quick assessment and heroic actions, only 11 of his 2,700 colleagues lost their lives. Unfortunately, that included Rick and two of his security officers.[312]

Suffering the most losses in the South Tower that day was AON Insurance which experienced the murder of 176 employees.[313] They occupied floors 92 and 93, along with floors 98 through 105. Fiduciary Trust International, another Baseline client, which occupied space on the 90th floor, as well as floors 94 through 97, lost 87 coworkers at the hands of the terrorists.[314] Other substantial losses in terms of numbers were experienced by Keefe, Bruyette & Woods (67),[315] Sandler O'Neill (66),[316] and Euro Brokers (61).[317] All three firms were above the impact zone. Mary Jos, who was escorted down 70 flights by several

Baseline associates, lost 39 colleagues that day at the New York State Department of Tax and Finance on the 86th and 87th floors.[318] Fuji Bank, which shared the 78th floor with Baseline and also occupied floors 79 through 83, lost 23 souls.[319] In the South Tower, only 18 individuals would escape from the impact zone or above, via that protected Stairwell A.[320] According to Florence Jones, while being filmed for The History Channel's documentary "Escape from the Towers," she learned that Baseline's 12 evacuees are counted among them.[321]

It is fitting and proper that a Memorial and Museum now stand solemnly at Ground Zero to pay tribute to the individuals who lost their lives that day. Even though new buildings have impressively risen on the WTC campus as signs of American pride and resolve, none of them touch the original footprints of the Twin Towers. Today, two lovely pools with cascading waterfalls adorn the exact locations of the two perfectly square one-acre spots. They are surrounded by a belt-high "Wall of Remembrance" that lists the names of the 2,977 innocent people from around the nation who lost their lives that day, as well as the six killed in the February 1993 attack on the same buildings. Inside the museum, there is a wall with a photograph of each victim. For the benefit of visitors and family members, the museum rotates the pictures so that all can eventually be seen at eye level. On September 11, 2018, Ruth Lapin's memorial photo was situated at a viewable angle. Her daughter, Heather Daly, made sure that three of Ruth's grandchildren, whom she never knew, made the journey into the museum that day. Additionally, the museum recognizes the tragedy of more than 3,000 children who lost a parent on 9/11, including approximately 100 who were born after 9/11 and would never know their fathers.[322] Finally, the museum pays tribute to the efforts of the many first responders who made the ultimate sacrifice in the line of duty that day.

On 9/11, several thousand on- and off-duty police and rescue personnel responded to the calls for assistance. As thousands of office workers fled the towers, these heroes ran in the opposite direction. They did not hesitate. They sprinted into the buildings and up the stairs with heavy packs upon their backs to rescue the injured, and to prevent the spread of fire. Tragically, the day saw over 400 of these brave men and women lose their lives. The totals included 343 New York City firefighters, 37 members of the Port Authority Police Department, 23 members of the New York Police Department, and a dozen other

Three of Ruth Lapin's grandchildren visited the WTC Memorial & Museum on September 11, 2018. The museum's standard practice of rotating the photographs of the fallen enabled Ruth's picture to be at eye level that day. [Photo Credit: HEATHER DALY]

government agents and EMT workers.[323] Tragically, the total number of casualties from 9/11 keeps rising. According to Garrett Graff, "In New York, 9/11-related ailments bedevil the first responders who spent days, weeks, and months cleaning up the wreckage at Ground Zero. All told, more than 7,000 firefighters and EMTs in New York were treated for 9/11-related injuries. New York estimates that 20 percent of those first responders also suffer from PTSD.[ao][324] As a member of the FDNY, Jill Campbell's father, Joe Maurer, was among those additional casualties due to his spending many hours at Ground Zero in the wake of the attacks. Joe succumbed to cancer in 2014.

While I earlier shared the accounts of the day from those who were fortunate to be alive when the ordeal was over, most of the victims had no escape path. It's hard to imagine the horrific experiences suffered by the souls who are unable to tell their stories. I cannot fathom the emotions of those who consciously observed and endured the impact, weathered the deteriorating conditions from extreme heat and smoke, and then perished with the ultimate collapse of the buildings. They

ao   PTSD. Post-Traumatic Stress Disorder.

experienced it all in real-time. Other than a few final phone calls from those dear souls, the devastating stories of those victims of this murderous act will remain silent. We can only contemplate their panic, dread, pain, and resignation. God bless them.

Clearly, the world changed greatly on September 11, 2001. In retrospect, there were both macro and micro implications of the infamous day. From a macro perspective, the world became a different place overnight. All of a sudden, enemies were no longer easily located on a map, bank accounts came under greater scrutiny, immigration laws and processes were enhanced, travel restrictions and screenings increased, and many people developed a new outlook about life itself. Jyoti Dave Vyas, the pregnant software engineer at Baseline who descended 77 stories on 9/11, recently stated:

> This was something that changed a lot of people's lives. For me, it's now about looking at things differently. I take one day at a time, and don't take things for granted. And when I see my kids, I see the positive attitude that Shailaja has, and that keeps me moving. I also try to see the good in people, not the bad in people. Yes, bad things happen, but how many people were there that day to make sure I was okay, and Shailaja was okay. So, I try to look more at that—there are a lot of good people out there in the world.[325]

Jyoti's colleague, Lorena Munoz-Udik, added that "for any of us who survived 9/11, it's like we got a second chance, and so we have to make the most of life."[326]

There were also those who recognized that changes in the world might go subtly unnoticed. In researching for his book, Garrett Graff talked with Rosemary Dillard, an American Airlines manager in Washington, DC. Her husband, Eddie, was aboard one of the hijacked flights. Dillard reflected more directly on the world's changes when she said, "I still think that we all walk on eggshells. I don't think that the young people who will be reading this will know the same freedom I knew growing up."[327]

Today, in the United States, we still find ourselves challenged by unfair bias, economic imbalance, and sociological differences. In most

A 2021 photograph of Jyoti Dave Vyas and the product of her courageous descent on 9/11—her daughter Shailaja.

cases, we do an acceptable job of allowing free speech and peaceful protests, while seeking legislative reforms. The individuals who attacked us on 9/11 wanted to make their own statement about their perception of America, but were not interested in anything peaceful. Their statement was lodged in a mission of hate. It is essential that we not forget the day nor the people we lost, for 9/11 should remind us of how much we actually have in common here in this country, and across much of the free world. Nor can we, as a species, allow ourselves to digress to earlier histories of human warfare based on hate and mistrust, as such acts are an unacceptable stain on our evolutionary progress. As the Spanish philosopher, George Santayana, stated in *The Life of Reason*, "Those who cannot remember the past, are condemned to repeat it."[328]

Regarding the events of September 11, 2001, there may never be total closure. Perhaps that's acceptable, as we never want to forget the victims or let our guard down again. However, some act of finality was gained on May 2, 2011 when US Navy SEALs raided a compound in Abbottabad, Pakistan and killed the Al Qaeda leader, Osama bin Laden. Another came as the new One World Trade Center was opened on November 3, 2014. It employs life safety systems that far exceed NYC building code.[329] It also stands at exactly 1776 feet tall—a clear indication of the might and resolve of a nation.

Twenty years after the infamous day, the world finds itself embroiled with another disaster—one of a biological nature. The pandemic from the Covid-19 virus that unleashed itself on the world in late 2019, and which continues into 2021, has killed over 3.1 million people (as of April 28, 2021).[330] A grave reality. The entire planet has been undeterred

Opened in 2014, the "new" One World Trade Center towers over the same sixteen-acre site that was devastated on 9/11. Its height measures exactly 1,776 feet in honor of the founding of the United States. The two pools mark the exact footprints of the original twin towers. [Photo Credit: iStock.com/ferrantraite]

in its fight against this pathogen. Masks, social distancing, and limitations on travel, entertainment, and education have likely done an effective job to curtail far more casualties. In the United States, despite the competitive nature between back-to-back White House administrations, the government has achieved a record number of vaccinations in record time. On Saturday, April 10, 2021, citizens of the United States received over four million Covid vaccinations in one day. It set a record.[331] From the "warp speed" creation of vaccines to an effective rollout, consecutive White House administrations have, thus far, worked commendably with the CDC in an all-out attempt to conquer this latest foe. It was another example, in a long line of national responses to tragedies, of an undeterred populous. In a macro sense, it was not dissimilar to the collective response and will of the American people regarding the September 11 terrorist attacks.

From a micro perspective, 9/11 was a defining moment for Baseline. During our period of greatest growth, the actions of the terrorists affected us significantly. They not only destroyed our headquarters and removed any semblance of independence within Thomson Financial, but they also sent us on an arduous rebuilding journey. The emotional toll on our associates not only included the loss of our colleagues, but most of us also had connections to others lost that day including friends and neighbors. Funerals were frequent occurrences.

As mentioned earlier, Kellie Kenny, a member of our sales team, lost scores of friends at Cantor Fitzgerald. While she had the wherewithal to run the marathon and honor twenty-six fallen friends with individual flags during the race, she wasn't immune to the effects of what happened on 9/11. A tragic and surreal photo from Kellie and Brian Kenny's wedding in 1999 is on display at the 9/11 Museum. It depicts many of her Cantor friends in attendance. Sadly, half those people in the photograph lost their lives on 9/11. According to Kellie, she and her husband "not only lost our very best friends that day, but we actually lost more than that. The people who survived didn't want to be around us anymore. We were the living reminder to a lot of people." She also shared how her roommate and fellow Cantor trainee, who was her best friend, left New York soon after 9/11 and rarely communicates with her. Kellie added that "we not only lost the people that actually passed, we lost all of it." She described Cantor as a fraternity of people that looked out for each other. "And, when it came apart, it came apart completely."[332]

While most of Baseline's associates were bounding enthusiastically into 2002, Kellie felt the effects of a void in her life. She was unique given her additional ties to Cantor Fitzgerald and the devastation that occurred there. In an honest appraisal, she recently shared with me that "when we went into the new location on Hudson Street was when it started getting hard. I struggled coming back into the city, and I struggled to find the work important."[333] This was quite germane given that Kellie had left Cantor, and spent a year with Paine Webber to gain the right experience to land a sales position with a technology company that serviced asset managers. Baseline had been a perfect fit. Kellie left Baseline in early 2002 after locating a not-for-profit opportunity that involved both technology and wealth management. She could work from home, and more poignantly, she felt she was contributing to the "greater good." I completely understood her motivations. Clearly, 9/11 affected people more than just a temporary disruption in lifestyle. Among survivors, stories abound related to bouts of panic attacks and ongoing cases of PTSD.

Beyond the human toll and emotional strains, 9/11 certainly brought forth a challenge to the independence of Baseline. At the time, Baseline was 100 percent owned by the Thomson Corporation. While Baseline remained intact as an operating unit up until and through 9/11, Thomson likely considered Baseline to simply be a product of theirs with useful human talent to help them advance their objective of being a real competitive threat to both Bloomberg and Reuters. Their goal was to incorporate all meaningful products and capabilities into one massive end user tool. That ambition, which received mixed reviews, instantly halted the advancement of the user experience known as Baseline.

The once industry-leading product created by Rob Patterson, and enhanced by his associates, lost its swagger soon after the business was integrated into Thomson Financial in 2002. As part of the Thomson ONE project, all of Baseline's departments were folded into functionally similar corporate groups at Thomson Financial. An attempt then followed to incorporate Baseline functionality into Thomson ONE, while the Baseline product was put on life support. Baseline's revenue, which hit a high of $55 million in 2003, steadily dropped off over time. In July of 2002, at the age of 65, Rob Patterson retired. He had the energy to continue, but his beloved Baseline was no longer an independent entity nor his to direct.

While Rob Patterson tended to be a private man, he was no less a sophisticated man. He was a student of world history, a frequent globetrotter, a fan of Shakespeare, and an ardent supporter of service dogs. During my nine years of a direct reporting relationship with Rob, he would often speak of "the thin red line." He was referring to the expanse of the British Empire around the globe in the 18th and 19th centuries. He was impressed with Great Britain's ability to impact world commerce from a tiny island in the North Atlantic. On the other hand, he often drew parallels between their expansion and eventual contraction, and corporations that spread themselves too thin. It was but one example, among several that he would use to dissuade overly aggressive ideas for Baseline's expansion. He was happy with steady, measured growth without taking on risky ventures. He also used this metaphor to privately chastise our parent's overzealous ambition to merge so many corporate cultures, databases, and end user applications into one marginally successful platform.

Regardless of the outcome, in its heyday and even while it went through the horrors of 9/11, Baseline was a significant player in the investment management industry. Baseline's growth story is undeniable. Its leadership was legendary. Its corporate culture tied beautifully with the founder's vision of both product strategy and organizational behavior, and clients found the product's workflow to be very compelling. The associates of Baseline should feel very proud of what they all accomplished. They took a product, conceived and developed by their founder, and built an exceptional infrastructure to enable accurate data, outstanding customer service, a well-oiled sales engine, and an efficient software development cycle. Further, they did it in a well-groomed familial culture where challenges felt like fun. Finally, and perhaps most impressively, my associates rose to the occasion with the events of 9/11 to rebuild an enterprise and carry on when faced with incredible odds. In my opinion, albeit a biased one, it is one of the most amazing rebuilding stories in the history of corporate America.

From the founding of the original Baseline in 1981 until his retirement from Thomson in 2002, Rob Patterson remained thoroughly committed to his mission. His undeterred passion took on many shapes and sizes. Early in his Baseline journey, Rob persevered through several years of mediocre performance, knowing a broader market awaited a solution. He steadfastly pursued different product angles and fervently sought funding. The resultant workflow solution revealed his unwavering pursuit of perfection while the process for acquiring team-oriented, human talent to help manage growth was never compromised. Perhaps the greatest symbol of Rob's untiring dedication to his vision was the constant protectionism he placed around his company and its culture. That constancy enabled a clear path for his associates to understand the overall mission, and it engrained a loyalty to Rob that was quite special. It was this culture, in my opinion, that enabled the teamwork and fortitude displayed on 9/11 and explains the undaunted commitment to rebuilding despite grave sacrifices and very emotional conditions.

In his farewell letter to the Baseline associates back in the Summer of 2002, Rob Patterson used a slightly modified quote from Shakespeare to say goodbye:

> "Love looks not with the eyes but with the heart." I have not hidden it. For a significant portion of my life, my beloved has been "Baseline." I've loved building a product that is the marvel of our industry. More importantly, I've loved helping to bring together all those that work at Baseline so that we could commit to one another and focus on helping our clients. I've said it a hundred times—success in this business requires only two things: commitment to one another and client focus. It's true. It's easy. And it works![334]

Thank you, Rob. For the journey, the leadership, and the lessons. But, more importantly, for a lifetime of memories with lifelong friends. Your associates will never forget Baseline, nor will we ever forget 9/11 and our four wonderful colleagues.

* * * * *

As a former member of Baseline's management team, it is my sincere wish that my colleagues will never forget the special environment we called home—how we built an amazing company, suffered through 9/11 and the loss of friends, and had the collective resolve to rebuild with astonishing speed. As the author of this book, I hope I have provided all readers with a useful glimpse into the workings of an entrepreneurial success while sharing stories of incredible bravery and determination.

A TRIBUTE TO
FOUR WONDERFUL SOULS

THE STORY OF a company, regardless of how interesting, pales in comparison to the loss of innocent human life. As I write this narrative nearly twenty years after that fateful day, my sentiments are that it was *the people* of Baseline that made its corporate journey so wonderful. Rob Patterson possessed a keen vision and deftly set the corporate culture in motion. However, it was the carefully selected human resources that successfully implemented that vision, while advancing an amenity-rich place of employment into a familial culture. It was the "associates" of Baseline that made it a unique family.

I've been fortunate to maintain contact with many of my colleagues who survived the terror of 9/11. For the four dear souls we lost, they are equally cherished and remain beloved members of the Baseline family. They were not only innocent victims of a heinous act of mass murder, but they were also exceptional human beings. Not a day goes by that the Baseline family doesn't think about them in one way or another. While the surviving associates can share and discuss Baseline as an experience, it's also important to shed light on the accomplishments and grace of our lost friends. The phrase "never forget" is often used to describe the need for future generations to never lose sight of the horrible events in human history, lest they run the risk of repeating them. In order that we never forget our four friends as equal and wonderful members of our team, I offer the following tributes to them.

JILL MAURER CAMPBELL
June 2, 1970–September 11, 2001

JILL CAMPBELL was an energetic, fun-loving, adventurous young woman. She was also bright, capable, and a very pleasant co-worker. I rarely saw her without a smile. Her adventurous side saw her successfully parachute from an airplane. Her fun-loving side enjoyed being a lifelong New York Mets fan. Her intelligence manifested itself in her Magna Cum Laude degree from Adelphi University, and in her exemplary work at Baseline. She also excelled at being a loving and supportive mother. Jill left behind quite a legacy.

On the morning of September 11, 2001, Jill Campbell arrived at work enthusiastically contemplating all the planning she would put forth for "her precious Jake."[335] Her son had been born ten months prior on November 4, 2000. She was determined that his first birthday would be a memorable one, and she was looking forward to a late afternoon of shopping for Jake's upcoming celebration. Jill had married Steve Campbell in 1999. They were incredibly proud parents, and from office conversations we all knew that Jill cherished Jake. Upon Jake's birth, Jill often played the Etta James hit single, *At Last, [My Love Has Come Along]*.[336]

While Jake was arguably Jill's greatest contribution to this world, she left her mark on many. Her unique talents, both innate and learned, came not only from her education, but from her upbringing as well. Jill was the daughter of Jeanne and Joe Maurer. Her dad enjoyed a lifelong career as one of "New York's Bravest," a New York City firefighter in the Red Hook section of Brooklyn. Before retiring with the rank of Captain, Joe spent many hours in the rubble of Ground Zero searching for signs of his daughter. Given her service orientation, passed on from her father, it is more than likely that after the initial explosion in the North Tower, Jill remained on the 78th floor in our South Tower due to her conscientious desire to help others.

Jill joined Baseline in 1997 in our 61 Broadway location. It wasn't long before her impact was felt by everyone. Our office manager, Helen Byrne, described Jill as "quick, efficient, and extremely productive." Helen added that "she was young, beautiful (inside as well as out), and very intelligent." . . . . and "her work never contained any errors; it never failed to amaze me!"[337]

As a key member of the Administrative team, Jill was tasked with being the primary executive assistant to Rob Patterson. Her attention to detail was admired, and greatly appreciated, by Rob. Her pleasant demeanor and sharp skills also led to her being a frequent occupant of our reception area, greeting visitors and handling the incoming phone calls. Soon after Jill started with us, Helen exclaimed, "I knew I had hit the jackpot with Jill."[338]

As for her work with Rob Patterson, she was a godsend. To his closest associates, Rob was a self-described dyslexic. While he was a brilliant man, he did occasionally suffer from the misinterpretation of letters or numbers strung together. That fact, to me, made his success even more impressive. At Jill's funeral, Rob offered a eulogy. Among his remarks in his typical self-deprecating fashion, he said, "For somebody like me, who can't spell and whose written grammar is often confusing, Jill was a blessing." Rob also commented on her personality. "There was more to Jill than perfection. Jill was gracious. She embodied the word. She made a lot of friends at Baseline. She will always be remembered for her willing and friendly demeanor, her easy acceptance of others, and for her inherent kindness."[339] He added:

> I was always going up to her with a draft of a letter that I had written, or an announcement that I was going to issue. I would give her the draft and say, "Here, fix it up." When she gave it back to me, the spelling would be perfect. The grammar would be impeccable. And even more important, my confused syntax would be corrected and now the recipients of my letter or announcement would understand what I was trying to say.[340]

In addition to being gracious, Jill was extremely confident. She didn't have any qualms about disagreeing with Rob Patterson about changes to documents, or communication strategies with employees. In fact, Jill's cousin, Lisa Bowden, summed it up by remembering Jill as "being free-spirited, self-confident, and independent." Her friends knew she was not afraid of what people thought of her. Lisa added that Jill "didn't let anyone put her down or make her feel insecure. She never hid anything, including the fact that she smoked or had a tattoo of a shamrock on her leg. That's what made Jill, Jill."[341]

One of Jill's best friends at Baseline was Lorena Munoz-Udik. As mentioned earlier, Lorena switched shifts with Jill on that infamous morning. In an online tribute to Jill soon after 9/11, Lorena wrote: ". . . there will always be a part of me that will feel a little bit of guilt. It should have been me, not you, Jill. I will never forget you." Lorena went on to describe Jill as "one of the most honest, wonderful, funniest, caring, generous, and loving people I have ever met in my life." Jill was a mentor to Lorena. According to Lorena, "Jill taught me a lot of things. She taught me how to be personable. How to pick up the phones. How to talk to people as they came into the office. What kind of questions to ask if someone calls."[342]

Another friend of Jill's was Myles Donnelly, the always affable Irishman who ran Baseline's Accounts Receivable effort. Myles said he enjoyed their friendship, because "Jill and I were at a similar point in life. Jill was pregnant with Jake, as my wife Kirsten was pregnant with Aidan. Apart from the physical aspects, we compared notes and shared the excitement. Then, of course, when the babies were born, we would compare notes as new parents." Myles also complimented Jill's attention to detail. On the morning of September 10, 2001, Jill presented Myles with a complete travel package, leaving no room for doubt as to Myles's itinerary for travel to Boston to see a customer on the 12th. According to Myles, "She was so positive. Well suited to her job in that she just wanted to give people the best service she could give them."[343]

Brian Branco, the accounting software consultant, also remembers Jill in a very special way: he proudly wears a tattoo on his right arm featuring Jill's name. In fact, it is a work of art portraying the American flag along with the names of three of his Baseline friends that died on 9/11—Jill, Bob Levine and Steve Weinberg.[344] At the official 9/11 commemoration ceremony at Ground Zero in 2005, Brian noticed a woman wearing a button of Jill's picture on it. So Brian introduced

himself—to Jeanne Maurer, Jill's mother.

According to Brian, Jeanne immediately noticed his ink work and said, "You have my daughter's name on your arm?"

Brian admits feeling very apprehensive at that moment as he didn't know how she would react. Brian simply replied, "Yes, I do."

"That's just beautiful!" said Jeanne.[345] Thus began a lifelong friendship.

As for Jill's son, Jake, I had the privilege of sitting down with him in the summer of 2019. He was 18 years old. He and I met over lunch in Florida while he was in the state for a summer job. Jake is everything that Jill would have imagined and hoped for. Jake is currently a student at the University of Michigan in Ann Arbor. It is not easy to gain admission into that highly regarded institution. Jake's admittance speaks highly of his upbringing, and is all the more impressive given that both his father and grandfather passed away during Jake's high school years. His dad, Steve, a member of "New York's Finest" (a NYPD officer), died from a heart attack. His grandfather, Joe, died due to complications from esophageal cancer. Jake cites the conditions Joe developed while working at the WTC, in post-9/11 recovery efforts as an FDNY officer, as the reason for his grandfather's passing in 2014[346].

Obviously, Jake did not have the typical American upbringing. Before he reached the age of one, he suffered the substantial loss of maternal love and support. According to Jake, he was "raised by a village," but primarily by Jill's parents and her sister, Linda. Jake credits his grandmother, Jeanne, as having the greatest influence on his life. Additionally, since he lost both his father and grandfather during his high school years, he "felt some comfort pouring into (his)

Our accounting software consultant, Brian Branco, proudly displays an artful tattoo on his right arm: the names of his three lost Baseline friends.

studies." He also found himself on a mission to learn more about his mom and the entire 9/11 incident. According to Jake, he has "immersed" himself in the 9/11 discussion. "It's a part of me, but I just kind of want to own it. I have to accept it, and it's hard."[347]

On September 11, 2019, in an open letter to the *New York Times*, Jake talked of his relationship with his grandparents, and of the profound impact the loss of his grandfather had on him. Jake shared that Joe's death was "the first time I struggled emotionally with what had happened. . . . Missing my grandpa made me finally realize how much I had missed with my mom."[348]

Jake found happiness again "thanks to a relationship, new friends, reconnecting with my mom's co-workers and friends, and setting out on my own life."[349] In his letter to the *Times*, Jake wrote about his gratitude to the people who helped him make the best out of a very difficult situation. Specifically, he thanked his family "who when faced with their darkest hour took on the challenge of raising a baby and ran with it; and, for my mom, who went to work to help make a better life for her son and never came home." Finally, he added that "I can't change what has happened to me. I can only respond to it, and I owe it to some people to make the best out of my situation."[350]

Thank you, Jake.

May we never forget Jill.

RUTH SHEILA LAPIN
April 16, 1948–September 11, 2001

RUTH LAPIN was a woman of many talents. She was not only an effective systems analyst, but her passions also included the Girls Scouts, comedy, and NFL football. As such, she was a scout leader, a stand-up comic, and a season ticketholder of the New York Giants.

Ruth had only recently joined Baseline when the events of 9/11 unfolded. While her tenure with the firm amounted to only a couple of months, she touched the lives of several people in that short period of time. According to Andrew Stellman, who hired Ruth, "she brought maturity to the Business Requirements team."[351] That team had only recently been created at Baseline. As our systems became more complex, we needed to place more processes and procedures around the various software systems. Andrew Stellman was the chief proponent for Baseline adopting a formal SDLC (software development life cycle) process. He brought Ruth on board because of her specific skills in this area. The SDLC initiative also touched our product development team in Philadelphia. Barry Levine, who ran project management for us in that software office, interfaced with Ruth frequently. According to Barry, "Ruth was collaborative, easy to work with and very intelligent."[352] Ruth's daughter, Heather Daly, shared that "she loved it [at Baseline]. She was so happy to be on top of the world. She had worked very hard to get there, and she was happy and very excited."[353]

Ruth lived life to the fullest extent possible. At the age of 53, she was taken way too early in life. She had many interests that held her passion. Ruth was an active Girl Scout troop leader. In a tribute written soon after Ruth's death, her son Doug Schroeder wrote: "One of her favorite ways of contributing to the community was being a Brownie and Girl Scout leader. Ruth felt that the way that she could make a big difference was by being a positive role model for children."[354] When Ruth's daughter, Heather, was in the 3rd grade, Ruth jumped headlong into scouting. She re-entered the scouting world again when her husband, David Chazin, had a grandchild of scouting age. Ruth became young Lea's scout leader as well. Despite Lea's eventual advancement beyond her scouting years, Ruth continued on with troop leadership even though there was no longer a family connection. Fellow troop leader Isabel McGincy added that Ruth "was very motivating to the girls. I can't say enough about the work she did for the kids."[355]

In a recent conversation, David Chazin shared how Ruth possessed an incredible service ethic. As an example, he cited the trunk of Ruth's car. "She had all kinds of first aid stuff and blankets. That was just in case she was somewhere, and there was somebody on the side of the road, freezing to death—she would have a blanket for them. She was that kind of person."[356]

Ruth was also a fun-loving soul. She possessed such a penchant for joking with people that she actually became a part-time stand-up comic. According to her husband, David, "the thing that Ruth liked the most was making people laugh or bringing joy into their life."[357] One of her career stops, prior to Baseline, was with the Shubert Theatre on Broadway. While she did systems work for them, she was involved one evening at the theater in a volunteer capacity to raise money for AIDS research. That night, she had the pleasure of watching a comedienne, Rosie O'Donnell, captivate the audience. Ruth instantly caught the comic bug. She soon enrolled in a workshop at the American Comedy Institute, and on February 1, 1997, Ruth Lapin had her first gig at Caroline's in New York City. In recounting the experience for the *Windsor-Hights Herald*, Ruth shared that "nervous is an understatement. But we learned to channel our nervous energy into a joyous exuberance." According to Ruth, "there was a full house and the audience started laughing right away. It was the most incredible experience of my life." She went on to become a regular at The Upper Crest in Freehold, New Jersey. She and her husband, David, produced the shows. They called them "Ruthi's New York City Comedy Revue."[358]

Ruth's daughter, Heather, had the pleasure of watching those comedy events up close and personal. She described her mother as having "a big personality and very fun." In a recent conversation, Heather shared that her mom was inclusive and very accepting of others and had a large, diverse group of friends. Heather added:

> She had more friends than you could even imagine. When she would have a gathering, you would have a group of people and you would think, *I would never imagine a universe where these different people would all be in one location.* That's just how she was.[359]

The loss of every innocent life is tragic. It becomes especially sad when circumstances arise that place people in harm's way. This fact holds true for every victim of 9/11. In Ruth's case, her love of NFL football played a part in her whereabouts on the morning of 9/11. In addition to her scouting leadership and her on-stage performances, Ruth found time for football. She was an avid Giants fan. "So much so, that if you were anywhere in Giants Stadium, no matter where you were, you would hear her," exclaimed her husband. On the evening of Monday, September 10, 2001, the Giants were on the road to play the Denver Broncos in the weekly edition of ABC's "Monday Night Football." David Chazin recently shared that it was the Giants' first game of the 2001 season. Rather than commute ninety minutes to her central New Jersey home, Ruth decided to join David at his hotel room in midtown Manhattan. As an IT consultant for IBM, David was on a client assignment at AXA Financial, and needed a hotel in close proximity to the client. The two season ticket holders had dinner together, watched their beloved Giants play their opening game, and then spent the night in David's hotel room. As mentioned in an earlier chapter, spending the night in Manhattan allowed Ruth, an early riser, to arrive at work on 9/11 much earlier than usual. It was, yet again, another unfortunate circumstance to befall an innocent victim. In a 2019 interview, David Chazin shared with me that he hasn't been to a Giants game since. "I'm no longer interested in whether they win or lose."[360]

David Chazin and Ruth Lapin met because of their mutual interest in Information Technology. At the time, Ruth was working for a New Jersey firm by the name of ACI. She had decided to leave the firm, but first needed to train her replacement. David was her replacement. According to David, it was a "knowledge transfer assignment." Subsequently, the two of them got to know each other and began dating. Each had adult children who were on their own, and they eventually married.

In addition to David, Ruth was survived by her own two children, Doug Schroeder of North Carolina, and Heather Daly of New Jersey. She was also survived by David's three children and his five grandchildren. According to Heather, Ruth loved David's grandchildren as her own and would say, "There are no steps in grandchildren." Sadly, Ruth never got to know the additional six grandchildren that would eventually be born to her own son and daughter, Doug and Heather. The first of those six grandchildren was born in 2003. However, Ruth's legacy lives on in the names of those grandchildren, as Ruth is the first name of Heather's oldest child, and the middle name of Doug's oldest.

In a recent interview, David Chazin shared that on 9/11 Ruth was planning on retiring in the not-too-distant future. Her vision was to ultimately open up a Bed & Breakfast at the Jersey Shore and have fun serving others. "It was consistent with her whole personality," Chazin said.[361] "She delighted in touching a lot of lives in a very positive way."[362]

Thank you, David, Heather and Doug.

May we never forget Ruth.

ROBERT MICHAEL LEVINE
July 20, 1935–September 11, 2001

ROBERT "BOB" LEVINE was the chief financial officer of Baseline Financial Services. He was instrumental in the installation of many systems and procedures that easily and effectively tracked our growth. Bob had worked with Rob Patterson for more than eight years prior to the events of 9/11. He engineered the transition from an arcane, paper-based bookkeeping environment for a start-up, to a well-organized, semi-customized accounting system utilizing SBT software. He was the primary gatekeeper behind approving expenses, managing cash flow, challenging and managing budget forecasts, and ensuring that contracts were legible and complete. As such, he tended to present a "tough guy" exterior. Down deep, however, he was a very warm person, and several of his confidants knew it.

As the person responsible for overall revenue growth at Baseline, I naturally worked with Bob on an ongoing basis. It was a pleasure to work with him. He was serious about the numbers, but had a pragmatic side. In a company experiencing frenzied growth, he understood the necessary balance between unadulterated contract activity and paperwork perfection. He didn't let my sales team easily get away with sloppy contracts, nor would he let me easily keep my forecasts low. However, he also appreciated that sometimes sales people running at the speed of light, selling many contracts, might not dot every "i" or cross every "t". He and I worked closely together, often letting the cavalry charge ahead, while together acting like the infantry cleaning up all the details.

Inside the Accounting and Finance department itself, Bob Levine was revered. He set a fine example. He would be in his office promptly each morning by 7:30 AM, and often left punctually at 4:00 PM if everything was sailing smoothly. Lystra Archer, our Accounts Payable analyst, had high praise for Bob. "He brought out the best in me . . . made me step up my game." According to Lystra, regarding Travel & Entertainment approvals, Bob would make her look through every receipt, and make sure it exactly matched what a salesperson was expensing. "He paid attention to such little details. He had an eye for accounting." The outside consultant, Brian Branco, described Bob as "very firm, but understanding. Stubborn, but easy to work with." Brian was appreciative that Bob, as a finance leader, had a very good understanding of accounting software technology, and always "knew what problems were being worked on." Lystra also offered that Bob "wasn't just a boss. He was a leader. He led us, and we respected him a lot. When Bob was around, we'd straighten up. But I loved him, he was really nice."[363]

Others echoed similar sentiments. Our office manager, Helen Byrne, said "Bob put on the face of a tough guy, but he was really a teddy bear inside."[364] Lorena Munoz-Udik added that she "had a soft heart for Bob. He was that 'rough guy' who was always trying to be that tough guy. It was all bull. He was actually very nice and very sweet."[365] Florence Jones, our contracts administrator, interfaced with Bob so often they became good friends. According to Florence, Bob became a father figure in her life, because she had lost her father when she was fourteen. "Bob was like my surrogate Dad. He came along at the right time. He and I just clicked. I could talk to him about anything and everything. We just hit it off because he had a dry sense of humor, just like my dad."[366]

Bob had originally been set to retire on September 1, 2001.[367] However, his dedication to finishing the 2002 budget for Thomson Financial was of paramount importance to him. He also had some health issues that had slowed him down. On 9/11, he was just back from cancer surgery on his finger. He had also suffered a scare with a spot discovered on his lung. A subsequent biopsy thankfully came back negative, but colleagues found him a changed man. Prior to that health scare, Bob would often be found outside, or even in the stairwell at 61 Broadway on frigid days, sneaking a quick cigarette.

His smoking buddies were often Lorena, Jill Campbell and Alfredo Guzman. According to Lorena with a laugh in her voice, "I caught him a few times in the stairwell when we were on Broadway, and I'd tell him 'you're gonna get us in trouble!' Bob would often say 'I don't care. This is where I gotta go. It's too cold outside. I'm gonna smoke really quickly, and go back in.'"[368] Lorena wasn't shy about giving "the business" to a more senior executive. After his scare with the biopsy, Bob quickly decided to stop smoking. According to Lystra, Bob started wearing a "patch." That was approximately two months prior to 9/11. She also added:

> He was so happy that he had stopped smoking. He felt
> he had a new lease on life. He was a changed person.
> He became very talkative, and he would talk to me
> on a personal level. He was so happy this thing wasn't
> what he thought it was. And, all of a sudden, he wasn't
> so serious. Just a jovial person. And in a matter of a
> month, 9/11 happened.[369]

Bob was also happy that his retirement was fast approaching. At sixty-six years old, he had contributed handsomely to several companies throughout his career. He was looking forward to enjoying the things that made him smile. His passions included golf, world travel, and occasionally casino gambling. He had even introduced golf lessons to his wife, Roberta, so they could both enjoy it in retirement. According to Florence, Bob "was a fun and friendly person who adored his wife."[370]

Sadly, Bob Levine never had the chance to enjoy retirement. His career and his life were brutally cut short. He is missed by all of us. Lorena recently shared a thought about Bob:

> Hands down, he was one of the best guys that worked
> there. Everything was about Baseline for him. He loved
> working there. He was also a great husband, and talked
> fondly about his family. He was also a confidant for
> me . . . he was always someone you could talk to and
> get great advice. He was older and easy to talk to.[371]

Bob left behind his wife Roberta, his son Andrew, and a sister Carole. In memory of his father, for many years since 9/11, Andrew has held the Annual Robert Michael Levine Foundation Golf Tournament in the Las Vegas area. According to Andrew, the event is to keep his father's memory alive, to help with his own healing, and to raise money for local police and firefighter causes.[372]

Thank you, Andrew.

May we never forget Bob.

STEVEN JAY WEINBERG
December 7, 1959–September 11, 2001

STEVE WEINBERG was the epitome of the phrase "family man." He adored his wife of fifteen years, Laurie, and was very involved in the lives of his three children: Lindsay, Sam, and Jason. Living in Rockland County, New York, he volunteered in the local PTA, coached his kids' basketball teams, and took his turn in neighborhood car pools.[373] On September 11, 2001, he was already planning for Lindsay's bat mitzvah in October of 2002. According to Myles Donnelly, who reported to Steve at Baseline, "Steve would regale me on Mondays about his coaching of his kids. Little League stuff. He was such a family man. Many photographs of the kids in 'Rec' activities adorned his office. He was very involved in his home town."[374] Steve was also a very attentive son, staying in constant contact with his parents, Lenny and Marilyn Weinberg.

Steve made many friends at Baseline. As controller, he would often involve himself in the revenue forecasts, which meant I had plenty of contact with him. Our relationship was more than just numbers. We were both great baseball fans. His love of the Mets, and mine of the Yankees, made for many interesting and fun debates. He was also a big fan of the television show, "Survivor." Brian Branco recalls talking to him often about the episodes, and that Steve would watch with his whole family.

On the History Channel documentary, "Escape from the Towers," Steve's wife, Laurie, exclaimed: "We think of Steve all the time. We have pictures of Steve around. We were a happy family. We all knew that we were sad. But we smile and we laugh when we talk about him and the things he did or the things he said. He's only one of a few thousand we lost that day. But, I'll tell you, he was probably one of the nicest."[375] I couldn't agree more. Steve was an incredibly pleasant person. In a recent interview, Laurie added that Steve was "so darn likeable. Everywhere he went he made friends. Everybody who knew him, liked him. I never heard a bad word from anybody. Anybody." During his memorial service at the Nanuet Hebrew Center, he was eulogized as "a devoted husband and father whose favorite hobby was collecting friends."[376]

Steven attended Mepham High School in Bellmore, New York, where he played the clarinet in the marching band. He then earned his undergraduate degree from Syracuse University. His grasp of numbers and accounting regulations was evident daily. According to consultant Brian Branco, Steve "was a numbers guy. Very firm on everything needing to balance." As we were undertaking an accounting system upgrade at the time of 9/11, it was Steve who led the charge. He directed the work of Brian, who was with Leading Edge Consulting. Brian so respected Steve that he also included his name on his forearm's tattoo tribute. During the years after 9/11, Brian stayed in touch with Steve's mother, Marilyn Weinberg, and his brother, Paul. To this day, they often get together at the annual memorial ceremony at Ground Zero each September 11th.[377]

While at Baseline, Steve left an indelible mark upon two co-workers in particular. Coincidentally, they made up the bookend sides of the balance sheet: Accounts Payable and Accounts Receivable. They were Lystra Archer and Myles Donnelly. Having started as a temp in 1997, Lystra had progressed quickly under the tutelage of Bob Levine. In 2001, she was in charge of the firm's payables. Soon after Steve's arrival, Lystra and Steve discovered that they were both avid exercise junkies. They soon would take their lunch hour together going to the gym to run. Lystra did not report to Steve, and according to Lystra, they "never talked about work" during the lunchtime gym routine. Lystra also shared that Steve "was very much into his kids and family." She learned a lot about Steve's local school system, and also about Steve's love for cooking. She still recalls the specific barbecue sauce that Steve introduced to her. Steve's passing hit Lystra hard. "His death was the hardest for me due to our personal connection. He was a very lovable person." Lystra has yet to visit the memorial site at Ground Zero. She recently shared that "I have a lot of anxiety about it."[378]

Myles Donnelly, the immigrant from Northern Ireland, also talked quite admiringly about his respect for Steve. "Steve was a superb man." Myles's platitudes for our controller were based on Steve's encouragement of Myles and the entire Accounts Receivable team. Myles recently talked openly about the type of work that is involved in collecting money from clients who haven't paid on time. "It's not glamorous. But Steve presented us in a positive light. He encouraged us. Gave us a good name in Accounts Receivable." Myles has subsequently spent his career in receivables, and credits Steve's counsel as critical in how he manages others today. According to Myles:

> I've tried to take that attitude with me everywhere I've been since. I have a penchant for this type of work. When it's presented in a positive light, the contributions that the work actually gives to a company—and how a company operates—shine through. Steve Weinberg shined a light on the work we did.[379]

Myles also credits Steve with an incredible gesture of goodwill. Very early in his tenure at Baseline, and prior to showing Steve how effective he could be, Myles had quite a hurdle to jump. When he joined Baseline in February of 2000, he was in the States on a "fiancé visa" because he was engaged to a young lady from New York, and was in the process of applying for his green card. In the fall of that year, Myles's mother became gravely ill over in Northern Ireland, and he quickly flew home. His mom passed away while Myles was en route to the Emerald Isle, and after a few days of family time he attempted to fly back to New York. However, Myles ended up in a paperwork snafu with US Customs and INS. The reality was that, according to Myles, his green card had indeed been granted in September of 2000, but US systems didn't make that easily known to him or to the US border officials in Dublin in November. Myles was subsequently stuck in Northern Ireland for three months. During this time, Myles' first child was born. Fortunately, his wife travelled to Ireland to make sure they were together for the birth.

Steve Weinberg, from the moment Myles had called him with the unfortunate travel news, sprang into action. First, he quickly made Bob Levine and Rob Patterson aware of the situation. Next, according to Myles, Steve "came on the phone very early and said 'do not worry about a thing. Your job will be here when you get back.' And more than that, a paycheck continued to go into my bank account every two weeks. You can imagine, the amount of goodwill that came from that." Finally, Myles talked about how "Baseline put its attorney on the case, and it cleared up incredibly quickly. I suppose in terms of goodwill, and in terms of warm feelings, without Steve Weinberg that could not have happened." Myles summed up his experiences with Steve by simply saying "Steve was just phenomenal."[380]

As a businessman, Steve was focused and committed. As a family man he was very involved as a loving father and husband. In all facets of his life, Steve was selfless. According to Laurie, "he never talked about himself. He'd rather ask you a question about yourself." She also described Steve as having a "very calming influence," and added "he just had a way with the kids and with everybody. He never complained. I miss that person . . . having him around. It was so comfortable, and nice and pleasant. He was just a good soul. I hit the jackpot when I met him, and everybody says that!"[381]

Thank you, Laurie.

May we never forget Steve.

ACKNOWLEDGEMENTS

THE PUBLISHING OF this book would not have been possible without the continual and dedicated support, and contributions, from many people. The author extends his heartfelt thanks.

Jocelyn B. Abreu
Lystra Archer
Barbara Becker
Carl Boudakian
Brian Branco
Warren Breakstone
Helen Byrne
Jake Campbell
David Chazin
Simon Chen
Michael Chiappinelli
Seth Cohen
Henry D'Atri
Heather Daly
Aimee Day
Jyoti Dave Vyas
Bill DiPierre
Sharon Dipre

Myles Donnelly
Ray Dover
Michael Ehlers
Corbin Feenstra
Rachael Forest
Stephanie Greiner
Alfredo Guzman
Peter Haller
Mark Heiman
Matt Horne
Kathy Hume
Ken Hume
Renee Innis
August Jennewein
Florence Jones
Sangita Joshi
Kenneth Kadleck
Kellie Kenny

Evangeline Dukas King
John Lee
James Magalong
George Maniscalco
Tom Maurath
Ray McCombs
Danna McCormick
Marybeth McDonough
Ryan McDonough
Tony Mei
Lorena Munoz-Udik
Nicole A. Murray
Robert G. Patterson, Jr.
Ludo Pauliny
Ron Perez
Phil Reid
David Robison
Deirdre Rock
Bernadette Ross
Rob Rothman
Liz Santo Domingo
John Sharp
Goran Skoko
James Solomon, Jr.
John A. Squires
Kathleen Squires
John Tabako
Chris Tresse
Barbara Tripp
Allan Unger
Mark Van Faussien
Sam Wang
Nick Webb
Susan Webb
Mark Weiss
Ogden White

Emma Weinberg
Jonathan Weinberg
Laurie Weinberg
Nancy Wolf
Lisa Wroble
Igor Yampolsky
Kerriann Zier
Mary Tara Zier
Ronald E. Zier

DISCLAIMER FROM STANDARD & POOR'S

This disclaimer pertains to the Quick Report displayed on page 28.

The Quick Report from S&P Global Market Intelligence (SPGMI) on Apple Inc. dated April 14, 2021 is provided solely for the purpose of citing an example of a modern-day Tearsheet. Reproduction of any information, data or material, including ratings ("Content") in any form is prohibited except with the prior written permission of SPGMI. SPGMI, its affiliates and suppliers ("Content Providers") do not guarantee the accuracy, adequacy, completeness, timeliness or availability of any Content and are not responsible for any errors or omissions (negligent or otherwise), regardless of the cause, or for the results obtained from the use of such Content. In no event shall Content Providers be liable for any damages, costs, expenses, legal fees, or losses (including lost income or lost profit and opportunity costs) in connection with any use of the Content. A reference to a particular investment or security, a rating or any observation concerning an investment that is part of the Content is not a recommendation to buy, sell or hold such investment or security, does not address the suitability of an investment or security and should not be relied on as investment advice. Credit ratings are statements of opinions and are not statements of fact.

SOURCES

Archer, Lystra. Accounts Payable—Baseline. Personal Interview. October 7, 2019.

Associated Press—Staff writers. "A List of the 2,977 victims of the September 11, 2001, terror attacks." *The Toledo Blade*, September 11, 2011.

Babich Dumas, Rene. *Jake's Mom: Jill Maurer Campbell.* Lakeville, Mass.: Country Press, 2004.

Bloomberg Business News—Staff writers. "Primark to Buy VNU Unit in Financial Information." *The New York Times.* May 30, 1995.

Boudakian, Carl. Director (Marketing & Client Support)—Baseline. Personal Interview. August 2, 2019.

Bowie, Max. "Thomson Reuters, Blackstone Agree $20B Financial & Risk Unit Spin-Off." *Waterstechnology.com.* January 30, 2018. https://www.waterstechnology.com/organization-management/alliances-mergers-acquisitions/3482206/thomson-reuters-blackstone-agree-20-bn-financial-risk-unit-spin-off.

Bowne & Co, Inc. Form 10-K405 for Fiscal Year 1997 filed with the Securities & Exchange Commission. March 31, 1998. https://sec.report/Document/0000950123-98-003254/.

Branco, Brian. Consultant—Leading Edge Consulting. Personal Interviews. April 5-8, 2019.

Bryan-Low, Cassell, and Robin Sidel. "Exit Sign? Pattern of Exclusions, One-Time Charges Hurts Stocks." *The Wall Street Journal.* December 16, 2002.

Business Wire—Staff Writers. "PSI Services Acquires Caliper, Grows Talent Management Roster With Leaders in Assessing and Developing High Performance Sales Teams." *Businesswire.com.* December 3, 2019. https://www.businesswire.com/news/home/20191203006000/en/.

Byrne, Helen. Office Manager—Baseline. Personal Interview. September 6, 2019.

Caliper Corporation. "The Caliper Profile." https://calipercorp.com/caliper-profile.

Campbell, Jake. Son—Jill Campbell. Personal Interview. June 13, 2019.

Campbell, Jake. "Growing With Grief in the Shadow of Sept. 11." *The New York Times.* September 11, 2019.

Cauchon, Dennis. "For Many on Sept. 11, Survival was No Accident." *USA Today.* December 20, 2001.

Cauchon, Dennis and Martha Moore. "Machinery saved people in WTC." *USA Today.* May 17, 2002.

Cauchon, Dennis and Martha Moore. "Desperation Forces a Horrific Decision." *USA Today.* September 3, 2002.

Chazin, David. Husband—Ruth Lapin. Personal Interview. November 15, 2019.

Chen, Simon. EVP Product & Technology—Baseline. "Personal account of 9/11." September 25, 2001.

Chen, Simon. EVP Product & Technology—Baseline. Email correspondence. July 6, 2018.

Chen, Simon. EVP Product & Technology—Baseline. Personal Interview. August 13, 2018.

Chen, Simon. EVP Product & Technology—Baseline. Email Correspondence. July 14, 2020.

CNBC—Staff writers. "The List: CNBC First 25 - #20 Michael Bloomberg." *CNBC*. April 29, 2014. https://www.cnbc.com/2014/04/29/25-michael-bloomberg.html.

CNN.com—Staff writers. "Cheney recalls taking charge from bunker." *CNN.com*. September 11, 2002. http://edition.cnn.com/2002/ALLPOLITICS/09/11/ar911.king.cheney.

CNNfn—Staff writers. "Thomson to Buy Primark." *CNNfn*. June 5, 2000. https://money.cnn.com/2000/06/05/deals/primark/.

D'Atri, Henry. Sales Manager—Baseline. Personal Interview. May 1, 2020.

Daly, Heather. Daughter—Ruth Lapin. Personal Interview. June 4, 2020.

Dave Vyas, Jyoti. Quality Assurance Software Engineer—Baseline. Personal Interview. June 17, 2019.

Dekkers, Rudi. *Guilty by Association*. Minneapolis: BRIOpress. 2011.

DiPierre, Bill. Software Engineer—Baseline. Email Correspondence. June 25, 2020.

Donnelly, Myles. Accounts Receivable—Baseline. Personal Interview. October 3, 2019.

Dwyer, Jim. "Staircases in Twin Towers Are Faulted." *The New York Times*. April 6, 2005.

Ehlers, Michael. Executive Recruiter. Personal Interview. March 16, 2020.

FactSet. Form 10-K. Fiscal Year 1996.

FactSet. Annual Report. Fiscal Year 2020.

Graney, Ed. "From charity, hopefully, comes healing." *Las Vegas Review-Journal.* September 9, 2009.

Graff, Garrett. *The Only Plane in the Sky.* New York: Avid Reader Press, 2019.

Graff, Garrett. "On 9/11, Luck Meant Everything." *The Atlantic.* September 10, 2019.

Greiner, Stephanie. Client Services—Vestek. Personal Interview. June 9, 2020.

Groysberg, Boris, and Jeremiah Lee, and Jesse Price, and J. Yo-Jud Cheng. "The Leader's Guide to Corporate Culture." *Harvard Business Review.* January-February 2018 issue. https://hbr.org/2018/01/the-leaders-guide-to-corporate-culture.

The Guardian—Staff writers. "The year dot.com turned into dot.bomb." *The Guardian.* December 29, 2000.

The Guardian—Staff writers. "Thomson buys Primark to challenge information leaders." *The Guardian.* December 6, 2000.

Guzman, Alfredo. Manager (Pricing Team)—Baseline. Personal Interview. July 22, 2019.

Haller, Peter. Manager (System Quality and Distribution)—Baseline. Personal Interview. March 30, 2020.

History.com. "This Day in History—Plane Crashes into Empire State Building." November 13, 2009. https://www.history.com/this-day-in-history/plane-crashes-into-empire-state-building.

The History Channel. "Escape from the Towers." September 2018. (Documentary produced by Arrow Communications, London, UK.)

Holt, Vanessa S. "Funny Business." *The Windsor-Hights Herald*. May 9, 1997.

Jones, Florence. Contracts Administrator—Baseline. Personal Interview. July 11, 2019.

Kenny, Kellie. Account Manager—Baseline. Personal Interview. June 22, 2020.

King Hall, Diane. "After Losing 658 Employees on 9/11, Cantor Fitzgerald Maintains Commitment to Help Victims' Families." *Spectrum News NY1*. September 10, 2016.

Kinney, Pat. "Japanese Residents of Fort Lee, Victims of 9/11 Attacks." *The Patch*. September 10, 2011. https://patch.com/new-jersey/fortlee/japanese-residents-of-fort-lee-victims-of-911-attacks.

Koch, William. "Teamwork, Technology, and Talent: The T³ Approach." *The Corporate Board*. January/February 1994.

Kolker, Robert. "Stairwell A." *New York Magazine*. August 27, 2011.

Leal, Ralph. Portfolio Manager—Marine Midland Bank. CompuServe client visit. May 1991.

Lee, John. Senior Managing Director—PGB Trust & Investments. Personal Interview. August 16, 2018.

Levine, Barry. Project Manager—Baseline. Email correspondence. October 11, 2019.

Lipton, Eric. "Study Suggests Design Flaws Didn't Doom Towers." *The New York Times*. October 20, 2004.

Lucchetti, Aaron. "A Battered Firm's Long Road Back." *The Wall Street Journal*. September 6, 2011.

McCombs, Ray. Account Manager—Baseline. Personal Interview. April 14, 2017.

McCormick, Danna. Sales Executive—Baseline. Personal Interview. April 2, 2020.

McKay, Peter. "Carr Futures, Devastated on 9/11, Is Assailed by Families of Victims." *The Wall Street Journal.* September 16, 2002.

McKinnon, Jim. "The phone line from Flight 93 was still open when a GTE operator heard Todd Beamer say: 'Are you guys ready? Let's roll.'" *Pittsburgh Post-Gazette.* September 16, 2001.

Macrotrends.com. FactSet Market Cap. https://www.macrotrends.net/stocks/charts/FDS/FactSet-research-systems/market-cap.

Magalong, James. Data Analyst—Baseline. Personal Interview. May 31, 2020.

Maniscalco, George. Account Manager—Baseline. Personal Interview. April 8, 2020.

Marsh & McLennan Companies. "Memorial Tribute." https://memorial.mmc.com.

Maurath, Tom. SVP & Portfolio Manager—Goelzer Investment Management. Email Correspondences. August through November 2018.

Maxey, Daisey. "Beyond 9/11: Alger Thrives, Remembers." *The Wall Street Journal.* September 8, 2015.

Moore, Martha and Dennis Cauchon. "Life and Death on the 78th Floor." *USA Today (via The Bolton News—U.K.).* September 11, 2002.

Munoz-Udik, Lorena. Administrator—Baseline. Personal Interview. July 2, 2019.

Museum of Modern Art. "Steamboat Willie." *MoMA Learning.* https://www.moma.org/learn/moma_learning/walt-disney-ub-iwerks-steamboat-willie-1928/.

Neely, Michelle Clark. "Banks and Investment Funds: No Longer Mutually Exclusive." *Federal Reserve Bank of St. Loui.* October 1, 1993. https://www.stlouisfed.org/publications/regional-economist/october-1993/banks-and-investment-funds-no-longer-mutually-exclusive.

Obituary. "Caliper Corporation Announces Passing of Founder and Chief Executive Officer Dr. Herbert Greenberg." *PR Newswire.* January 20, 2016. https://www.prnewswire.com/news-releases/caliper-corporation-announces-passing-of-founder-and-chief-executive-officer-dr-herbert-greenberg-300207067.html.

Obituary. "Francis Xavier Deming." *The Boston Globe.* September 27, 2001. http://www.legacy.com/sept11/story.aspx?personid=100271

Obituary. "Richard Koontz, 56, a Printing Executive." *The New York Times.* November 23, 1996.

Obituary. "Robert Patterson." *The New York Times.* July 15, 2018. https://www.legacy.com/obituaries/nytimes/obituary.aspx?n=robert-patterson&pid=189594966.

Obituary. "Ruth Sheila Lapin." *Legacy.com.* https://www.legacy.com/obituaries/name/ruth-lapin-obituary?pid=161304.

Obituary. "Steven Weinberg—Guestbook comment." *Legacy.com.* March 8, 2002. https://www.legacy.com/guestbooks/lincolncourier/steven-weinberg-condolences/100295.

Oxbow Carbon LLC. "CEO profile." https://www.oxbow.com/About_Us_Governance_William_I._Koch,_Chief_Executive_Officer_and_Chairman_of_the_Board.html.

Patterson, Rob. "Time Waits for No Man." *Baseline Connections.* Summer 2002.

Perez, Ron. VP Product Management—Baseline, Personal Interview. April 23, 2018.

Perez, Ron. VP Product Management—Baseline. Lunch meeting and follow-up. October 17-18, 2018.

Perez, Ron. VP Product Management—Baseline. Personal Interview. August 31, 2020.

Pollack, Andrew. "Venture Capital Loses its Vigor." *The New York Times.* October 8, 1989.

Port Authority Police Department. "Memorial." https://www.panynj. gov/police/en/september-11—2001—fallen-papd.html.

Referenceforbusiness.com. "CompuServe Interactive Services, Inc.—Company Profile." https://www.referenceforbusiness.com/ history2/55/CompuServe-Interactive-Services-Inc.html.

Reid Norman, Jean. "Man recalls father's words before second tower was struck." *Las Vegas Sun.* September 11, 2009.

Rock, Deirdre. Manager (Business Descriptions)—Baseline. Email Correspondence. April 18, 2020.

Ross, Bernadette. Manager (Earnings Team)—Baseline. Personal Interview. April 22, 2020.

Ross, Phillip E. "Primark Plans Spinoff of its Michigan Utility." *The New York Times.* January 14, 1988.

Rothman, Rob. Manager (Quality Assurance)—Baseline. Personal Interview. September 17, 2020.

Santayana, George. *The Life of Reason.* 1905. (The Project Gutenberg E-book, 2005). https://www.gutenberg.org/files/15000/15000- h/15000-h.htm.

Schmerken, Ivy. "BREAKING NEWS: Weinstein, ILX Founder, to Leave Thomson." *WallStreet & Technology.* June 18, 2002. https:// www.wallstreetandtech.com/careers/breaking-news-weinstein-ilx- founderto-leave-thomson-/d/d-id/1255279.html.

Schroeder, Doug. Son—Ruth Lapin. Tribute on Legacy.com. https:// www.legacy.com/guestbooks/fredericknewspost/ruth-sheila-lapin- condolences/161304.

Sharp, John. Director, Software Development—Baseline. Personal Interview. May 20, 2018.

Shook, Ellyn and Julie Sweet. "Creating a Culture that Drives Innovation." Accenture. 2019. https://www.accenture.com/us-en/about/inclusion-diversity/gender-equality-innovation-research.

Skoko, Goran. EVP Global Wealth Management—FactSet. Email correspondences. June 20, 2020 and July 14, 2020.

Soucheray, Stephanie. "US hits record COVID vaccine distribution pace." Center for Infectious Disease Research and Policy—University of Minnesota. April 12, 2021. https://www.cidrap.umn.edu/news-perspective/2021/04/us-hits-record-covid-vaccine-distribution-pace.

Stellman, Andrew. Manager (SDLC)—Baseline. Linked-in Messaging. March 18, 2020.

Stout, David. "Original Plan for 9/11 Attacks Involved 10 Planes, Panel Said." *The New York Times.* June 16, 2004.

Swanson, Peder L., Lieutenant Colonel—U.S. Army. "Talent Management—Sharpening the Focus." April 2013. https://apps.dtic.mil/dtic/tr/fulltext/u2/a592554.pdf.

Swanson, Stevenson. "For AON Corp. it has been a struggle to move on." *The Chicago Tribune.*" March 11, 2002.

Tabako, John. Network Manager—Baseline. Personal Interview. May 2, 2020.

Tresse, Chris. West Coast Sales Manager—Baseline. Personal Interview. March 31, 2020.

Tripp, Barbara. Director, Data Integrity—Baseline. Personal Interview. May 23, 2018.

Tweney, Dylan. "Once King of Enterprise Software, Lotus Notes is dragging IBM Down." *Venturebeat.* January 22, 2013. https:// venturebeat.com/2013/01/22/lotus-notes-history.

Unger, Allan. Product Design Specialist—Baseline. Personal Interview. August 12, 2019.

Van Faussien, Mark. Senior Managing Director—Azimuth Capital Management. Personal Interview. August 20, 2020.

Visitpearlharbor.org. "Frequently Asked Questions." https:// visitpearlharbor.org/faqs-questions-pearl-harbor.

Wang, Sam. Founder, Runnymede Capital. Personal Interview. August 14, 2018.

Watson, Nashua. "Sweet Purity... Companies that Abstain from Earnings Write-offs Outperform those that Partake." Fortune Magazine. September 16, 2002.

Webb, Nick. VP of Sales—Baseline. Personal Interview. April 24, 2018.

Webb, Nick. VP Sales—Baseline. Email correspondence. November 28, 2020.

Webb, Susan. Wife—Nick Webb. Email Correspondence. May 1, 2020.

Weinberg, Jonathan. VP Technology—Baseline. "What did it feel like to be inside the World Trade Center at the time of the 9/11 attacks?" *Quora.com.* March 20, 2011.

Weinberg, Jonathan. VP Technology—Baseline. Personal Interview. March 14, 2018.
Weinberg, Laurie. Wife—Steve Weinberg. Personal Interview. August 6, 2020.

Weiss, Mark. CIO –Virtonos Capital, Linked-in Tribute to Rob Patterson, October 27, 2017.

White, Ogden. Sales Executive—Baseline. Personal Interview. April 13, 2020.

Whitford, David. "Sandler O'Neill's journey from Ground Zero." *Fortune Magazine.* September 1, 2011.

World Health Organization. "WHO—Coronavirus (Covid-19) Dashboard," March 26, 2021. https://covid19.who.int.

Yampolsky, Igor. Data Analyst—Baseline. Personal Interview. September 15, 2020.

Yates, Eames, and Shana Lebowitz. "The way Walt Disney inspired his team to make 'Snow White' reveals his creative genius—and insane perfectionism." *BusinessInsider.* Sept 20, 2015. https://www.businessinsider.com/how-walt-disney-inspired-snow-white-2015-9.

Yun, William Y. Statement to the National Commission on Terrorist Attacks Upon the United States, 5th Public Hearing. November 19, 2003. https://govinfo.library.unt.edu/911/hearings/hearing5/witness_yun.htm.

Zuckoff, Mitchell. *Fall and Rise–The Story of 9/11.* London: HarperCollins. 2019.

END NOTES

CHAPTER 1: THE INFAMOUS MORNING

1   History.com, November 13, 2009, "This Day in History—Plane Crashes into Empire State Building," https://www.history.com/this-day-in-history/plane-crashes-into-empire-state-building.

2   Garrett Graff, *The Only Plane in the Sky* (New York: Avid Reader Press, 2019), 32-34.

3   Rudi Dekkers, *Guilty by Association* (Minneapolis: BRIOpress, 2011), 100.

4   Graff, 19.

5   Dekkers, 100.

6   Graff, 19.

7   Ibid, 63.

CHAPTER 2: GOOD FORTUNE OR JUST DUMB LUCK

8   Jim McKinnon, "The phone line from Flight 93 was still open when a GTE operator heard Todd Beamer say: 'Are you guys ready? Let's roll,'" *Pittsburgh Post-Gazette*, September 16, 2001.

9 David Stout, "Original Plan for 9/11 Attacks Involved 10 Planes, Panel Said," *The New York Times*, June 16, 2004.

10 Garrett Graff, *The Only Plane in the Sky* (New York: Avid Reader Press, 2019), 105.

11 CNN.com, "Cheney recalls taking charge from bunker," September 11, 2002, http://edition.cnn.com/2002/ALLPOLITICS/09/11/ar911.king.cheney.

12 Graff, *Sky*, 85.

13 Mitchell Zuckoff, *Fall and Rise–The Story of 9/11* (London: HarperCollins, 2019), 180.

14 Graff, 94.

15 Zuckoff, 185.

16 Ibid.

17 Visitpearlharbor.org, "Frequently Asked Questions," https://visitpearlharbor.org/faqs-questions-pearl-harbor.

18 Zuckoff, *Rise and Fall*, 428.

19 Graff, xix.

20 Rudi Dekkers, *Guilty by Association* (Minneapolis: BRIOpress, 2011), 103-105, 117-118, 155.

21 Ibid, 152.

CHAPTER 3: THE ASCENT OF BASELINE

22 George Maniscalco, Account Manager—Baseline, Personal Interview, April 8, 2020.

23 Ibid.

24 Obituary, "Robert Patterson," *The New York Times* (online article powered by Legacy), July 15, 2018, https://www.legacy.com/obituaries/nytimes/obituary.aspx?n=robert-patterson&pid=189594966.

25   Sam Wang, Founder Runnymede Capital, Personal Interview, August 14, 2018.

26   Andrew Pollack, "Venture Capital Loses its Vigor," *The New York Times* (Section 3, Page 1), October 8, 1989.

27   John Sharp, Director Software Development—Baseline, Personal Interview, May 20, 2018.

28   Barbara Tripp, Director of Data Integrity—Baseline, Personal Interview, May 23, 2018.

29   Simon Chen, EVP Product & Technology—Baseline, Email Correspondence, July 14, 2020.

30   Michelle Clark Neely, "Banks and Investment Funds: No Longer Mutually Exclusive," *Federal Reserve Bank of St. Louis*, October 1, 1993, https://www.stlouisfed.org/publications/regional-economist/october-1993/banks-and-investment-funds-no-longer-mutually-exclusive.

31   John Lee, Senior Managing Director—PGB Trust & Investments, Personal Interview, August 16, 2018.

32   Ibid.

33   Chen, Email, July 14, 2020.

34   Lee, Interview, August 16, 2018.

35   Tom Maurath, SVP & Portfolio Manager—Goelzer Investment Management, Email Correspondences, August through November 2018.

36   Ivy Schmerken, "BREAKING NEWS: Weinstein, ILX Founder, to Leave Thomson," *WallStreet & Technology*, June 18, 2002, https://www.wallstreetandtech.com/careers/breaking-news-weinstein-ilx-founderto-leave-thomson-/d/d-id/1255279.html.

CHAPTER 4: A SPECIAL CULTURE

37 Referenceforbusiness.com. "CompuServe Interactive Services, Inc.—Company Profile," https://www.referenceforbusiness.com/history2/55/CompuServe-Interactive-Services-Inc.html.

38 Ralph Leal, Portfolio Manager—Marine Midland Bank, CompuServe client visit, May 1991.

39 Boris Groysberg, Jeremiah Lee, Jesse Price, and J. Yo-Jud Cheng, "The Leader's Guide to Corporate Culture," *Harvard Business Review*, January-February 2018 issue, https://hbr.org/2018/01/the-leaders-guide-to-corporate-culture.

40 Ibid.

41 Ibid.

42 Allan Unger, Product Design Specialist—Baseline, Personal Interview, August 12, 2019.

43 Bernadette Ross, Manager (Earnings Team)—Baseline, Personal Interview, April 22, 2020.

44 Nick Webb, VP of Sales—Baseline, Personal Interview, April 24, 2018.

45 Alfredo Guzman, Manager (Pricing Team)—Baseline, Personal Interview, July 22, 2019.

46 Lorena Munoz-Udik, Administrator—Baseline, Personal Interview, July 2, 2019.

47 Ellyn Shook and Julie Sweet, "Creating a Culture that Drives Innovation," Accenture, 2019, https://www.accenture.com/us-en/about/inclusion-diversity/gender-equality-innovation-research.

48 Brian Branco, Consultant—Leading Edge Consulting, Personal Interviews, April 5-8, 2019.

49 Lystra Archer, Accounts Payable—Baseline, Personal Interview, October 7, 2019.

50 Jyoti Dave Vyas, Quality Assurance Software Engineer—Baseline, Personal Interview, June 17, 2019.

51 Ibid.

52 Ray McCombs, Account Manager—Baseline, Personal Interview, April 14, 2017.

53 Ross, interview.

54 Peter Haller, Manager (System Quality and Distribution)—Baseline, Personal Interview, March 30, 2020.

55 Ross, interview.

56 Mike Ehlers, Executive Recruiter, Personal Interview, March 16, 2020.

57 Groysberg et al, "The Leader's Guide to Corporate Culture."

CHAPTER 5: A DIFFICULT FLASHBACK

58 Dennis Cauchon, "For Many on Sept. 11, Survival was No Accident," *USA Today*, December 20, 2001.

59 Ibid.

CHAPTER 6: A VISION WITH EARS

60 The Museum of Modern Art, "Steamboat Willie," *MoMA Learning*, https://www.moma.org/learn/moma_learning/walt-disney-ub-iwerks-steamboat-willie-1928/.

61 Simon Chen, EVP Product & Technology—Baseline, Email Correspondence, July 21, 2020.

62 Bill DiPierre, Software Engineer—Baseline, Email Correspondence, June 25, 2020.

63 Eames Yates and Shana Lebowitz, "The way Walt Disney inspired his team to make 'Snow White' reveals his creative genius—and

insane perfectionism." *BusinessInsider*, Sept 20, 2015, https://www.businessinsider.com/how-walt-disney-inspired-snow-white-2015-9.

64 Chris Tresse, West Coast Sales Manager—Baseline, Personal Interview, March 31, 2020.

65 William I. Koch, "Teamwork, Technology, and Talent: The T³ Approach," *The Corporate Board*, January/February 1994.

66 Oxbow Carbon LLC, "CEO profile," https://www.oxbow.com/About_Us_Governance_William_I._Koch,_Chief_Executive_Officer_and_Chairman_of_the_Board.html.

67 Koch, "Teamwork, Technology and Talent."

68 Ibid.

69 Ibid.

70 Ibid.

71 Lieutenant Colonel Peder L. Swanson—U.S. Army, "Talent Management—Sharpening the Focus," April 2013, https://apps.dtic.mil/dtic/tr/fulltext/u2/a592554.pdf.

CHAPTER 7: MANAGING GROWTH

72 Danna McCormick, Sales Executive—Baseline, Personal Interview, April 2, 2020.

73 Chris Tresse, West Coast Sales Manager—Baseline, Personal Interview, March 31, 2020.

74 Caliper Corporation, "The Caliper Profile," https://calipercorp.com/caliper-profile.

75 Obituary, "Caliper Corporation Announces Passing of Founder and Chief Executive Officer Dr. Herbert Greenberg," *PR Newswire*, January 20, 2016, https://www.prnewswire.com/news-releases/caliper-corporation-announces-passing-of-founder-and-chief-executive-officer-dr-herbert-greenberg-300207067.html.

76 Staff Writers, "PSI Services Acquires Caliper, Grows Talent Management Roster With Leaders in Assessing and Developing High Performance Sales Teams," *Businesswire.com*, December 3, 2019, https://www.businesswire.com/news/home/20191203006000/en/.

77 Ibid.

78 Dylan Tweney, "Once King of Enterprise Software, Lotus Notes is dragging IBM Down," *Venturebeat*, January 22, 2013, https://venturebeat.com/2013/01/22/lotus-notes-history.

79 Simon Chen, EVP Product & Technology—Baseline, Personal Interview, August 13, 2018.

80 Ogden White, Sales Executive—Baseline, Personal Interview, April 13, 2020.

81 Ron Perez, VP Product Management—Baseline, Personal Interview, August 31, 2020.

82 McCormick, interview.

CHAPTER 8: GROUND ZERO

83 Ron Perez, VP Product Management—Baseline, Personal Interview, April 23, 2018.

84 Garrett Graff, *The Only Plane in the Sky* (New York: Avid Reader Press, 2019), 19, 32, 34.

85 Dennis Cauchon, "For Many on Sept 11, Survival was No Accident," *USA Today*, December 20, 2001.

86 Nick Webb, VP Sales—Baseline, Personal Interview, April 24, 2018.

87 Perez, interview, 2018.

88 Alfredo Guzman, Manager (Pricing Team)—Baseline, Personal Interview, July 22, 2019.

89 Ibid.

90 The History Channel, "Escape from the Towers," September 2018. (Documentary produced by Arrow Communications, London, UK.)

91 Henry D'Atri, Sales Manager—Baseline, Personal Interview, May 1, 2020.

92 Ibid.

93 Ibid.

94 John Tabako, Network Manager—Baseline, Personal Interview, May 2, 2020.

95 History Channel, "Escape from the Towers."

96 Perez, interview, 2018.

97 D'Atri, interview.

98 Graff, 112.

99 Myles Donnelly, Accounts Receivable—Baseline, Personal Interview, October 3, 2019.

100 Brian Branco, Consultant—Leading Edge Consulting, Personal Interviews, April 5-8, 2019.

101 Ibid.

102 Ibid.

103 Jonathan Weinberg, VP Technology—Baseline, "What did it feel like to be inside the World Trade Center at the time of the 9/11 attacks?" *Quora.com*, March 20, 2011.

104 Simon Chen, EVP Product & Technology—Baseline, "Personal account of 9/11," September 25, 2001.

105 Florence Jones, Contracts Administrator—Baseline, Personal Interview, July 11, 2019.

106 Ibid.

107 Ibid.

108 Ibid.

109 Lorena Munoz-Udik, Administrator—Baseline, Personal Interview, July 2, 2019.

110 Jones, interview.

111 Jonathan Weinberg, "What did it feel like..."

112 Jonathan Weinberg, VP Technology—Baseline, Personal Interview, March 14, 2018.

113 Simon Chen, "Personal account of 9/11."

114 Guzman, interview.

115 James Magalong, Data Analyst—Baseline, Personal Interview, May 31, 2020.

116 Graff, 115.

117 Dennis Cauchon and Martha Moore, "Desperation Forces a Horrific Decision," *USA Today*, September 3, 2002.

118 Jonathan Weinberg, "What did it feel like..."

119 History Channel, "Escape from the Towers."

120 Graff, 63.

121 Webb, interview.

122 Bernadette Ross, Manager (Earnings Team)—Baseline, Personal Interview, April 22, 2020.

123 Kellie Kenny, Account Manager—Baseline, Personal Interview, June 22, 2020.

124 Ibid.

125 Ibid.

126 Perez, interview, 2018.

127 D'Atri, interview.

128 Mitchell Zuckoff, *Fall and Rise–The Story of 9/11* (London: HarperCollins, 2019), 256.

129 Ibid, 275-276,

130 Jones, interview.

131 Jonathan Weinberg, "What did it feel like . . ."

132 Eric Lipton, "Study Suggests Design Flaws Didn't Doom Towers," *The New York Times*, October 20, 2004.

133 Guzman, interview.

134 Allan Unger, Product Design Specialist—Baseline, Personal Interview, August 12, 2019.

135 Jyoti Dave Vyas, Quality Assurance Software Engineer—Baseline, Personal Interview, June 17, 2019.

136 Munoz-Udik, interview.

137 History Channel, "Escape from the Towers."

138 Ibid.

139 Ibid.

140 Laurie Weinberg, Wife—Steve Weinberg, Personal Interview, August 6, 2020.

141 Jean Reid Norman, "Man recalls father's words before second tower was struck," *Las Vegas Sun*, September 11, 2009.

142 Ed Graney, "From charity, hopefully, comes healing," *Las Vegas Review-Journal*, September 9, 2009.

143 Norman, "Man recalls father's words..."

144 David Chazin, Husband—Ruth Lapin, Personal Interview, November 15, 2019.

145 Heather Daly, Daughter—Ruth Lapin, Personal Interview, June 4, 2020.

146 Chazin, interview.

147 Jonathan Weinberg, "What did it feel like..."

CHAPTER 9: THE GREAT DESCENT

148 The History Channel, "Escape from the Towers," September 2018. (Documentary produced by Arrow Communications, London, UK.)

149 Florence Jones, Contracts Administrator—Baseline, Personal Interview, July 11, 2019.

150 Ibid.

151 Jyoti Dave Vyas, Quality Assurance Software Engineer—Baseline, Personal Interview, June 17, 2019.

152 Rob Rothman, Manager (quality Assurance)—Baseline, Personal Interview, September 17, 2020.

153 Jones, interview.

154 Alfredo Guzman, Manager (Pricing Team)—Baseline, Personal Interview, July 22, 2019.

155 History Channel, "Escape from the Towers."

156 Ibid.

157 Carl Boudakian, Director (Marketing & Client Support)—Baseline, Personal Interview, August 2, 2019.

158 Guzman, interview.

159 History Channel, "Escape from the Towers."

160 Ibid.

161 Boudakian, interview.

162 Jones, interview.

163 History Channel, "Escape from the Towers."

164 Ibid.

165 Ibid.

166 Guzman, interview.

167 Ibid.

168 Rothman, interview.

169 Jonathan Weinberg, VP Technology—Baseline, "What did it feel like to be inside the World Trade Center at the time of the 9/11 attacks?," *Quora.com*, March 20, 2011.

170 Rothman, interview.

171 Allan Unger, Product Design Specialist—Baseline, Personal Interview, August 12, 2019.

172 Martha Moore and Dennis Cauchon, "Life and Death on the 78th Floor," *USA Today (via The Bolton News—U.K.)*, September 11, 2002.

173 Ibid.

174 Unger, interview.

175 James Magalong, Data Analyst—Baseline, Personal Interview, May 31, 2020.

176 Unger, interview.

177 Moore and Cauchon, "Life and Death."

178 Ibid.

179 History Channel, "Escape from the Towers."

180 Simon Chen, EVP Product & Technology—Baseline, "Personal account of 9/11," September 25, 2001.

181 History Channel, "Escape from the Towers."

182 Guzman, interview.

183 Simon Chen, "Personal account of 9/11."

184 Jones, interview.

185   Jim Dwyer, "Staircases in Twin Towers Are Faulted," *The New York Times*, April 6, 2005.

186   Dennis Cauchon and Martha Moore, "Machinery saved people in WTC," *USA Today*, May 17, 2002.

187   Ibid.

188   Dwyer, "Staircases..."

189   Mitchell Zuckoff, *Fall and Rise–The Story of 9/11* (London: HarperCollins, 2019), 223-224.

190   Unger, interview.

191   Jones, interview.

192   Ron Perez, VP Product Management—Baseline, Personal Interview, April 23, 2018.

193   Garrett Graff, *The Only Plane in the Sky* (New York: Avid Reader Press, 2019), 68.

194   Ibid, 70.

195   Ibid.

196   Perez, interview, 2018.

197   Igor Yampolsky, Data Analyst—Baseline, Personal Interview, September 15, 2020.

198   Jyoti Dave Vyas, interview.

199   Andrew Stellman, Manager (SDLC)—Baseline, Linked-in Messaging, March 18, 2020.

200   Jyoti Dave Vyas, interview.

201   Jones, interview.

202   Guzman, interview.

203   Perez, interview, 2018.

204 Simon Chen, "Personal account of 9/11."

205 Rothman, interview.

206 Ibid.

207 Ibid.

208 Ibid.

209 Nick Webb, VP Sales—Baseline, Personal Interview, April 24, 2018.

210 Jyoti Dave Vyas, interview.

211 History Channel, "Escape from the Towers."

212 Ibid.

213 Susan Webb, Wife—Nick Webb, Email Correspondence, May 1, 2020.

214 History Channel, "Escape from the Towers."

215 Ibid.

CHAPTER 10: THE NEXT 24 HOURS

216 Obituary, "Francis Xavier Deming," *The Boston Globe*, September, 27, 2001, http://www.legacy.com/sept11/story.aspx?personid=100271

217 Florence Jones, Contracts Administrator—Baseline, Personal Interview, July 11, 2019.

218 Barbara Tripp, Director (Data Integrity)—Baseline, Personal Interview, May 23, 2018.

219 Deirdre Rock, Manager (Business Descriptions)—Baseline, Email Correspondence, April 18, 2020.

220 Brian Branco, Consultant—Leading Edge Consulting, Personal Interviews, April 5-8, 2019.

238 John Tabako, Network Manager—Baseline, Personal Interview, May 2, 2020.

239 Jonathan Weinberg, interview.

240 Jyoti Dave Vyas, interview.

241 Jonathan Weinberg, VP Technology—Baseline, "What did it feel like to be inside the World Trade Center at the time of the 9/11 attacks?," *Quora.com*, March 20, 2011.

242 Guzman, interview.

243 Haller, interview.

CHAPTER 11: NAVIGATING TRANSITIONS

244 Obituary, "Richard Koontz, 56, a Printing Executive," *The New York Times*, November 23, 1996.

245 Phillip E. Ross, "Primark Plans Spinoff of its Michigan Utility," *The New York Times*, January 14, 1988.

246 Bowne & Co, Inc., Form 10-K405 for Fiscal Year 1997 filed with the Securities & Exchange Commission, March 31, 1998, https://sec.report/Document/0000950123-98-003254/.

247 Bloomberg Business News, "Primark to Buy VNU Unit in Financial Information," *The New York Times*, May 30, 1995.

248 Stephanie Greiner, Client Services—Vestek, Personal Interview, June 9, 2020.

249 Chris Tresse, West Coast Sales Manager—Baseline, Personal Interview, March 31, 2020.

250 Ibid.

251 Mark Van Faussien, Senior Managing Director—Azimuth Capital Management, Personal Interview, August 20, 2020.

252 Ron Perez, VP Product Management—Baseline, Personal Interview, August 31, 2020.

253 Staff writers, "The year dot.com turned into dot.bomb," *The Guardian*, December 29, 2000.

254 Staff writers, "Thomson buys Primark to challenge information leaders," *The Guardian*, December 6, 2000.

CHAPTER 12: RECONSTRUCTION

255 Simon Chen, EVP Product & Technology—Baseline, Email correspondence, July 6, 2018.

256 Alfredo Guzman, Manager (Pricing Team)—Baseline, Personal Interview, July 22, 2019.

257 Barbara Tripp, Director (Data Integrity)—Baseline, Personal Interview, May 23, 2018.

258 John Christoffersen (AP), "Families Attempt to Cope," *The Advocate*, October 1, 2001.

259 Susan Webb, Wife—Nick Webb, Email Correspondence, May 1, 2020.

260 Kellie Kenny, Account Manager—Baseline, Personal Interview, June 22, 2020.

261 Ibid.

262 Brian Branco, Consultant—Leading Edge Consulting, Personal Interviews, April 5-8, 2019.

263 Ibid.

264 John Sharp, Director Software Development—Baseline, Personal Interview, May 20, 2018.

265 Tripp, interview.

266 John Tabako, Network Manager—Baseline, Personal Interview, May 2, 2020.

267 Ron Perez, VP Product Management—Baseline, Personal Interview, April 23, 2018.

268 Peter Haller, Manager (System Quality and Distribution)—Baseline, Personal Interview, March 30, 2020.

CHAPTER 13: REBOUNDING WITH FERVOR

269 Nashua Watson, "Sweet Purity . . . Companies that Abstain from Earnings Write-offs Outperform those that Partake," Fortune Magazine, September 16, 2002.

270 Cassell Bryan-Low and Robin Sidel, "Exit Sign? Pattern of Exclusions, One-Time Charges Hurts Stocks," *The Wall Street Journal*, December 16, 2002.

271 John Lee, Senior Managing Director—PGB Trust & Investments, Personal Interview, August 16, 2018.

272 Ibid.

273 Ron Perez, VP Product Management—Baseline, Personal Interview, August 31, 2020.

274 Lee, interview.

275 Ogden White, Sales Executive—Baseline, Personal Interview, April 13, 2020.

276 Ibid.

277 Mark Van Faussien, Senior Managing Director—Azimuth Capital Management, Personal Interview, August 20, 2020.

CHAPTER 14: THE ULTIMATE IRONY

278 Staff writers, "The List: CNBC First 25 - #20 Michael Bloomberg," CNBC, April 29, 2014, https://www.cnbc.com/2014/04/29/25-michael-bloomberg.html.

279 Goran Skoko, EVP Global Wealth Management—FactSet, Email correspondences, June 20, 2020 and July 14, 2020.

280 Ron Perez, VP Product Management—Baseline, Lunch meeting and follow-up, October 17-18, 2018.

281 Ibid.

282 Staff writers, "Thomson to Buy Primark," *CNNfn*, June 5, 2000, https://money.cnn.com/2000/06/05/deals/primark/.

283 Ron Perez, VP Product Management—Baseline, Personal Interview, August 31, 2020.

284 Ibid.

285 Ibid.

286 Nick Webb, VP Sales—Baseline, Email correspondence, November 28, 2020.

287 Ibid.

288 Max Bowie, "Thomson Reuters, Blackstone Agree $20B Financial & Risk Unit Spin-Off," *Waterstechnology.com*, January 30, 2018, https://www.waterstechnology.com/organization-management/ alliances-mergers-acquisitions/3482206/thomson-reuters-black- stone-agree-20-bn-financial-risk-unit-spin-off.

289 FactSet, Form 10-K, Fiscal Year 1996.

290 FactSet, Annual Report, Fiscal Year 2020.

291 Macrotrends.com, FactSet Market Cap, https://www.mac- rotrends.net/stocks/charts/FDS/FactSet-research-systems/ market-cap.

292 Skoko, Email correspondences.

293 Ibid.

294 Ibid.

295 Ibid.

296 John Lee, Senior Managing Director—PGB Trust & Investments, Personal Interview, August 16, 2018.

297 Tom Maurath, Senior VP and Portfolio Manager—Goelzer Investment Management, Email Correspondences, August through November 2018.

298 Ibid.

299 Ibid.

300 Mark Van Faussien, Senior Managing Director—Azimuth Capital Management, Personal Interview, August 20, 2020.

301 Mark Weiss, CIO—Virtonos Capital, Linked-in Tribute to Rob Patterson, October 27, 2017.

302 George Maniscalco, Account Manager—Baseline, Personal Interview, April 8, 2020.

303 Laurie Weinberg, Wife—Steve Weinberg, Personal Interview, August 6, 2020.

304 Ibid.

CHAPTER 15: REFLECTIONS

305 Garrett Graff, *The Only Plane in the Sky* (New York: Avid Reader Press, 2019), 44.

306 Diane King Hall, "After Losing 658 Employees on 9/11, Cantor Fitzgerald Maintains Commitment to Help Victims' Families," *Spectrum News NY1*, September 10, 2016.

307 March & McLennan Companies, "Memorial Tribute," https://memorial.mmc.com.

308 Garrett Graff, "On 9/11, Luck Meant Everything," *The Atlantic*, September 10, 2019.

309 Peter McKay, "Carr Futures, Devastated on 9/11, Is Assailed by Families of Victims," *The Wall Street Journal*, September 16, 2002.

310 Port Authority Police Department, "Memorial," https://www.panynj.gov/police/en/september-11--2001--fallen-papd.html.

311 Daisey Maxey, "Beyond 9/11: Alger Thrives, Remembers," The Wall Street Journal, September 8, 2015.

312 Graff, *The Only Plane in the Sky*, 123-124.

313 Stevenson Swanson, "For AON Corp. it has been a struggle to move on," *The Chicago Tribune*," March 11, 2002.

314 William Y. Yun (statement from), National Commission on Terrorist Attacks Upon the United States, 5th Public Hearing, November 19, 2003, https://govinfo.library.unt.edu/911/hearings/hearing5/witness_yun.htm.

315 Aaron Lucchetti, "A Battered Firm's Long Road Back," *The Wall Street Journal*, September 6, 2011.

316 David Whitford, "Sandler O'Neill's journey from Ground Zero," *Fortune Magazine*, September 1, 2011.

317 Robert Kolker, "Stairwell A," *New York Magazine*, August 27, 2011.

318 AP Staff Writers, "A List of the 2,977 victims of the September 11, 2001, terror attacks," *The Toledo Blade*, September 11, 2011.

319 Pat Kinney, "Japanese Residents of Fort Lee, Victims of 9/11 Attacks," *The Patch*, September 10, 2011, https://patch.com/new-jersey/fortlee/japanese-residents-of-fort-lee-victims-of-911-attacks.

320 Mitchell Zuckoff, *Fall and Rise–The Story of 9/11* (London: HarperCollins, 2019), 450.

321 Florence Jones, Contracts Administrator—Baseline, Personal Interview, July 11, 2019.

322 Graff, *The Only Plane in the Sky*, xix.

323 Zuckoff, *Fall and Rise*, 459.

324 Graff, *The Only Plane in the Sky*, 418.

325 Jyoti Dave Vyas, Quality Assurance Software Engineer—Baseline, Personal Interview, June 17, 2019.

326 Lorena Munoz-Udik, Administrator—Baseline, Personal Interview, July 2, 2019.

327 Graff, *The Only Plane in the Sky*, xxii.

328 George Santayana, *The Life of Reason*, 1905, (The Project Gutenberg E-book, 2005), https://www.gutenberg.org/files/15000/15000-h/15000-h.htm.

329 Zuckoff, *Fall and Rise*, 431.

330 World Health Organization, "WHO—Coronavirus (Covid-19) Dashboard," April 28, 2021, https://covid19.who.int.

331 Stephanie Soucheray, "US hits record Covid vaccine distribution pace," Center for Infectious Disease Research and Policy—University of Minnesota, April 12, 2021, https://www.cidrap.umn.edu/news-perspective/2021/04/us-hits-record-covid-vaccine-distribution-pace.

332 Kellie Kenny, Account Manager—Baseline, Personal Interview, June 22, 2020.

333 Ibid.

334 Rob Patterson, "Time Waits for No Man," *Baseline Connections*, Summer 2002.

TRIBUTES—FOUR WONDERFUL SOULS

Jill Maurer Campbell

335 Rene Babich Dumas, *Jake's Mom: Jill Maurer Campbell* (Lakeville, Mass.: Country Press, 2004), 27.

336 Ibid, 14.

337 Ibid, 26.

338 Ibid.

339 Ibid, 23-24.

340 Ibid.

341 Ibid, 7.

342 Lorena Munoz-Udik, Administrator—Baseline, Personal Interview, July 2, 2019.

343 Myles Donnelly, Accounts Receivable—Baseline, Personal Interview, October 3, 2019.

344 Brian Branco, Consultant—Leading Edge Consulting, Personal Interviews, April 5-8, 2019.

345 Ibid.

346 Jake Campbell, Student—University of Michigan, Personal Interview, June 13, 2019.

347 Ibid.

348 Jacob Campbell, "Growing With Grief in the Shadow of Sept. 11," *The New York Times*, September 11, 2019.

349 Ibid.

350 Ibid.

Ruth Sheila Lapin

351 Andrew Stellman, Manager (SDLC)—Baseline, Linked-in Messaging, March 18, 2020.

352 Barry Levine, Project Manager—Baseline, Email correspondence, October 11, 2019.

353 Heather Daly, Daughter—Ruth Lapin, Personal Interview, June 4, 2020.

354 Doug Schroeder, Son—Ruth Lapin, Tribute on Legacy.com, https://www.legacy.com/guestbooks/fredericknewspost/ruth-sheila-lapin-condolences/161304.

355 Obituary, "Ruth Sheila Lapin," *Legacy.com*, https://www.legacy.com/obituaries/name/ruth-lapin-obituary?pid=161304.

356 David Chazin, Husband—Ruth Lapin, Personal Interview, November 15, 2019.

357 Obituary, "Ruth Sheila Lapin."

358 Vanessa Sarada Holt, "Funny Business," *The Windsor-Hights Herald*, May 9, 1997, 11A.

359 Daly, interview.

360 Chazin, interview.

361 Ibid.

362 Obituary, "Ruth Sheila Lapin."

Robert Michael Levine

363 Lystra Archer, Accounts Payable—Baseline, Personal Interview, October 7, 2019.

364 Helen Byrne, Office Manager—Baseline, Personal Interview, September 6, 2019.

365 Lorena Munoz-Udik, Administrator—Baseline, Personal Interview, July 2, 2019.

366 Florence Jones, Contracts Administrator—Baseline, Personal Interview, July 11, 2019.

367 Ibid.

368 Munoz-Udik, interview.

369 Archer, interview.

370 Jones, interview.

371 Munoz-Udik, interview.

372 Jean Reid Norman, "Man recalls father's words before second tower was struck," *Las Vegas Sun*, September 11, 2009.

Steven Weinberg

373 Obituary, "Steven Weinberg—Guestbook comment," Legacy.com, March 8, 2002, https://www.legacy.com/guestbooks/lincolncourier/steven-weinberg-condolences/100295.

374 Myles Donnelly, Accounts Receivable—Baseline, Personal Interview, October 3, 2019.

375 The History Channel, "Escape from the Towers," September 2018. (Documentary produced by Arrow Communications, London, UK.)

376 Obituary, "Steven Weinberg".

377 Brian Branco, Consultant—Leading Edge Consulting, Personal Interviews, April 5-8, 2019.

378 Lystra Archer, Accounts Payable—Baseline, Personal Interview, October 7, 2019.

379 Donnelly, interview.

380 Ibid.

381 Laurie Weinberg, Wife—Steve Weinberg, Personal Interview, August 6, 2020.

CPSIA information can be obtained
at www.ICGtesting.com
Printed in the USA
BVHW081201090921
616447BV00006B/47